Operating Under High-Risk Conditions in Temporary Organizations

AF739691

Organizations increasingly use temporary designs. Many temporary organizations are assembled by "mixing and matching" building blocks from static, bureaucratic and parent organizations into a temporary configuration. At the same time, such "mixed and matched" temporary organizations often operate under difficult and dangerous circumstances. During operations, these temporary organizations can experience numerous internal problems: ranging from friendly fire in a military context to budget and time issues in construction projects and problematic coordination in a crisis management context.

This book develops insight into the relationship between a "mixing and matching" temporary design strategy and operational problems. To so do, military and crisis management contexts are systematically studied from a sociotechnical design perspective that emphasizes self-organization to develop organizational controllability.

Operating Under High-Risk Conditions in Temporary Organizations demonstrates that a "mixing and matching" design strategy can be related to system failure. Furthermore, it is shown that a process of self-design emerged in which operators attempted to create ad-hoc networks for meaningful, safe and controllable operations. The analyses result in a model that shows mechanisms between characteristics of organizational design and controllability of operations. Not only does this model have relevance to the military and crisis management contexts, relevance is also demonstrated for a broader family of temporary organizations and application of sociotechnical network design theory.

Matthijs Moorkamp is Assistant Professor in Organizational Design and Development at the Institute for Management Research, Radboud University Nijmegen, The Netherlands. He was previously affiliated with the Netherlands Defense Academy, Delft University of Technology and the University of Twente.

Routledge Advances in Management and Business Studies

Managing Social Purpose Driven Organizations
Looking at the Third Sector
Wee Beng Geok

Navigating Through Changing Times
Knowledge Work in Complex Environment
Edited by Anne Eskola

Transitions from Education to Work
Workforce Ready Challenges in the Asia Pacific
Edited by Roslyn Cameron, Subas Dhakal and John Burgess

Professions and Professional Service Firms
Private and Public Sector Enterprises in the Global Economy
Edited by Mike Saks and Daniel Muzio

Happiness, Wellbeing and Society
What Matters for Singaporeans
Siok Kuan Tambyah and Soo Jiuan Tan

Women in Business Families
From Past to Present
Jarna Heinonen and Kirsi Vainio-Korhonen

Transformative Management Education
The Role of the Humanities and Social Sciences
Ulrike Landfester and Jörg Metelmann

Operating Under High-Risk Conditions in Temporary Organizations
A Sociotechnical Systems Perspective
Matthijs Moorkamp

For more information about this series, please visit www.routledge.com/series/SE0305

Operating Under High-Risk Conditions in Temporary Organizations

A Sociotechnical Systems Perspective

Matthijs Moorkamp

Routledge
Taylor & Francis Group
NEW YORK AND LONDON

First published 2019
by Routledge
605 Third Avenue, New York, NY 10017

and by Routledge
2 Park Square, Milton Park, Abingdon, Oxon, OX14 4RN

First issued in paperback 2020

Routledge is an imprint of the Taylor & Francis Group, an informa business

© 2019 Taylor & Francis

The right of Matthijs Moorkamp to be identified as author of this work has been asserted by him in accordance with sections 77 and 78 of the Copyright, Designs and Patents Act 1988.

All rights reserved. No part of this book may be reprinted or reproduced or utilised in any form or by any electronic, mechanical, or other means, now known or hereafter invented, including photocopying and recording, or in any information storage or retrieval system, without permission in writing from the publishers.

Trademark notice: Product or corporate names may be trademarks or registered trademarks, and are used only for identification and explanation without intent to infringe.

Library of Congress Cataloging-in-Publication Data
A catalog record for this book has been requested

ISBN 13: 978-0-367-73262-2 (pbk)
ISBN 13: 978-0-8153-9502-7 (hbk)

Illustrations created by mavs design

Typeset in Sabon
by Apex CoVantage, LLC

Contents

Abbreviations

ALO	Air Liaison Officer
ASBt	Aerial Systems Battery
BG	Battle Group
CAOC	Combined Air Operations Center
CAT	Combined Arms Team
COC	Council of Consultation
DOPS	Directorate of Operations, Dutch Ministry of Defense
GCC	Ground Control Center
GDT	Ground Data Terminal
GLO	Ground Liaison Officer
FAC	Forward Air Controller
FRAM	Functional Resonance Analysis Method
FSO	Fire Support Officer
HOTO	Hand-Over-Take-Over
HRO	Highly Reliable Organizing
HRT	High Reliability Theory
ICAO	International Civil Aviation Organization
ICCB	Interdepartmental Crisis Control Team
IED	Improvised Explosive Device
IOR	Integral Organizational Renewal
ISAF	International Security Assistance Force, Afghanistan
ISTAR	Intelligence, Surveillance, Target Acquisition and Reconnaissance
JISTARC	Joint Intelligence, Surveillance, Target Acquisition and Reconnaissance Command
LANS	UAV Launching platform
LSO	Liaison Officer
LTFO	Dutch National Team of Forensic Investigations
MCCB	Ministerial Crisis Control Team
MLA	Dutch Military Aviation Authority
MOTTW	Military Operations Other Than War
MP	Military Police
NAT	Normal Accidents Theory

NATO	North Atlantic Treaty Organization
NCC	Dutch National Crisis Center
NCO	Network Centric Operations
NCTV	Dutch National Coordination on Counterterrorism and Security
NKC	Dutch National Crisis Communication Team
OPS	Operations
ORM	Operational Risk Management
PRT	Provincial Reconstruction Team
QRF	Quick Reaction Force
RAC	Report and Analysis Center
RC	Regional Command
ROZ	Restricted Operations Zone
SA	Situational Awareness
SFIR	International Stabilization Force, Iraq
SFOR	Stability Force, for Former Yugoslavia
SGBO	Staff of Large and Special Missions, Dutch Police
STSD	Sociotechnical Systems Design
STSL	Lowlands' Sociotechnical Design Theory
SUA	Smallest Unit of Action
TAC-P	Tactical Air Control Party
TACSAT	Tactical Satellite radio
TAME	Task Force Air Management Element
TFU	Task Force Uruzgan
TIC	Troops In Contact
TK	Tarin Kowt
UAV	Unmanned Aerial Vehicle
UNPROFOR	United Nations Protection Force, for Former Yugoslavia
VHF	Very High Frequency

Preface

Quite frequently organization design is regarded as something "static" and "top-down". The words "organization design" and "organizational structure" often seems to evoke all kinds of negative feelings about classic bureaucratic approaches that result in too many rules, too many procedures and hierarchical management strategies. In safety science, it is therefore sometimes even advocated to disregard "design" or "structure" as too many rules and procedures are often detrimental to safety in organizations. Although in practice, organization design interventions and proposals for new structures are indeed often implemented in archaic and bureaucratic ways, theorizing on organization design has developed significantly.

Sociotechnical design thinking, which was founded by Fred Emery and Eric Trist at the Tavistock Institute, and further developed in The Netherlands by Ulbo de Sitter, Herman Kuipers, Pierre van Amelsvoort and many others, acknowledges the dynamics and fluidity of organizational life. Also, the sociotechnical way of thinking about organization design acknowledges the intertwined relationship between organizational structures and human agency, also brought forward in a more sociological way in Giddens' concept "duality of structure", which seems to have gained substantial attention in organization science these days.

The sociotechnical approach can therefore be seen as especially suitable for studying influences of organizational design in organizations that operate under highly uncertain circumstances, like the particular temporary organizations at which this book is aimed. Hopefully, this book will not only contribute to theory in the field of high-risk operations, temporary organizing and sociotechnical thinking, but also to challenging long-held assumptions about organization design that were highlighted at the beginning of this preface.

The contents of this book are based on, and developed out of, my doctoral dissertation. Writing this book has therefore provided me with the unique, but also challenging, occasion to rethink and rewrite pieces of a previous work. Although this has led to improvement, changes turned out to be not fundamental.

I would like to take this opportunity to thank the people who have inspired, helped and loved me during the writing and rewriting process. First of all, Prof. Dr. Eric-Hans Kramer, who was the co-promotor of my doctoral dissertation. He has been (and still is) a great inspiration. His knowledge of organizational theory, philosophy, systems theory and psychology is eminent. Eric-Hans's way of supervising during my doctoral studies was invaluable. Also, I would like to thank Prof. Dr. Ben Ale, the promotor of my dissertation. I valued Ben's critical perspective to theory and practice in safety science. I also thank the members of the dissertation committee, the professors Jeroen van den Hoven, Pieter van Gelder, Pierre van Amelsvoort, René Torenvlied and Desiree Verweij. They approved my dissertation and ensured nice and lively discussions during the public defense at Delft University of Technology. At Radboud University, I thank Dr. Jan Achterbergh and Dr. Dirk Vriens because discussing with them sharpened my understanding of sociotechnical systems theory. Also, I am grateful to Prof. Dr. Kristina Lauche who provided me with the opportunity to work as an assistant professor at her department.

I would also like to thank David Varley and Professor Stewart Clegg, for providing me with the opportunity to publish at Routledge's Advances in Management and Business Studies series. At Routledge, I would also like to express my thanks to Brianna Ascher and Mary del Plato. They took great care of the publishing process. Of course, I thank my brother and sister, Frank and Liesbeth. In particular, I would like to express my gratitude to my darling Marie-Anne. Living with you (and our cats and chickens) is truly amazing. Thanks for all the love, warmth and support you gave me, and still give me every day.

Heelsum, August 2018

1 Introduction

It was like the Wild West out there . . .
We may have had countless near misses.
—Captain, Royal Netherlands Army

1.1 Introduction

The Army Captain quoted above was a commanding officer of a unit that operated with Unmanned Aerial Vehicles during a mission of the Dutch military in Afghanistan between 2006 and 2010. In this period, his unit was part of a military task force called Task Force Uruzgan. Task Force Uruzgan (TFU) was a large temporary organization, assembled out of about 49 different units from the Dutch Army, Air Force, Navy and Military Police. The quote reveals that his unit may have experienced countless near misses with other, friendly, flying units during operations in Afghanistan's Uruzgan province. Undoubtedly, Task Force Uruzgan was facing high-risk conditions. At the one hand, opposing forces were present in the environment in which TFU operated. On the other hand, as the quote seems to indicate, operations in this environment did not go without risky interactions between friendly units.

Operations of many temporary organizations are inseparably related to danger and risk. Next to military temporary organizations such as TFU, other temporary organizations such as crisis response organizations and mega-projects in the oil and gas industry, also have to deal with high-risk conditions on a daily basis. Although these organizations are mostly not confronted with hostile opponents that engage the temporary organization with weapons, conditions are often far from safe (see, for example, Comfort, 2007; Crichton, Lauche, & Flin, 2005). Dealing with such high-risk conditions in these temporary organizations is hence inherently associated with the challenge of developing safe operations. Not surprisingly, many studies that focus on high-risk organizational contexts are related to the topic of safety. Some examples of developments in this field are *Highly Reliable Organizing* (HRO; e.g., Weick & Sutcliffe, 2007) and *resilience* (e.g., Hollnagel, 2012). As such it can be argued that for dealing with high-risk conditions, the safety concept is of relevance. Concepts and premises on high reliability organizing and resilience, however, are often not developed in relation to temporary organizations. Main principles of high reliability theory, for example, are explicitly based on research in organizations such as air traffic control and aircraft carriers (see, for example, Rijpma, 1997; Rochlin, LaPorte & Roberts, 1987). While this in itself may not be a problem in transferring concepts and lessons from HRO or resilience literature to a high-risk temporary context, literature shows that characteristics unique to some temporary organizations may have a particularly relevant influence on dealing with high-risk conditions and the ability to develop safe operations.

According to De Waard and Kramer (2008), a key characteristic of many Western military task forces is that they are designed by "mixing and matching" different units from the Army, Air Force, Navy and Military Police into a temporary task force. They also point out that, in this way, these four military parent organizations serve as a "platform" from which, depending on the type and nature of mission, different "building blocks" are selected and merged into so-called expeditionary task forces. In an extensive study carried out on a friendly fire incident in a task force of the United States' military, Snook (2000) showed that the way the task force was designed contributed substantially to a friendly fire incident in which two US Army Black-Hawk helicopters were shot down by two US Air Force F-15 fighter jets. Using Lawrence and Lorsch's concepts of differentiation and integration, Snook shows that differentiation between units in military organizations at home was associated with issues of integration between units in the task force. These issues of integration played an important role in the way the friendly fire incident occurred. Interestingly, studies also indicate that other temporary organizations that operate under high-risk conditions are assembled by "mixing and matching" design strategies that seem similar to that of the military. The aforementioned mega-projects in construction, the oil and gas industry and crisis response organizations also seem to come into existence by merging organizational parts from different private, semi-public and public organizations into a temporary constellation (e.g., Flyvbjerg, Bruzelius, & Rothengatter, 2003; Wolbers, 2016). As such, it seems worthwhile to investigate in more detail whether and how aspects of organization design influence the ability of these temporary organization to deal with high-risk conditions and develop safety of their operations.

Hence, this book aims to contribute to organizational literature on high-risk operations by unraveling the relationship between organization design and ways in which temporary organizations are able to develop safe operations while facing high-risk conditions. For the studies presented in this book, military task forces are taken as an empirical starting point. Starting in a temporary military context offers insight into operations of particular "mixed and matched" temporary organizations working under extreme high-risk conditions. Literature seems to point out that valuable findings may be retrieved from extreme contexts that are also relevant for other organizational contexts (Chen, 2015; Hällgren, Rouleau, & De Rond, 2018). Hence, studying military task forces may provide valuable insight for the operations of other temporary organizations. However, although military task forces are an important context for the studies presented in this book, generalizing claims are also verified in the context of the crisis response organization that was initiated after Malaysia Airlines flight MH17 was downed above the eastern part of Ukraine on the 17th of July 2014.

This chapter continues in the following way. Firstly, the specific temporary organizational form at which this book aims is introduced in more detail. Also, a more precise definition is given of the phrase "high-risk conditions". Secondly, the stance that this book takes on the safety concept is detailed. In the third paragraph of this chapter it is highlighted why the studies presented in this book may have added value to scientific literature on temporary organizations and literature on safety during high-risk operations. In section 1.4, the goal and research strategy of the studies presented in this book are explicated. In section 1.5, the steps that are followed in the different studies are described. In section 1.6, a research model is presented that guides the studies in this book. Lastly, in section 1.7, the outline of this book is sketched.

1.2 Temporary Organization Design and Dealing With High-Risk Conditions

As military task forces were taken as an empirical starting point for this book, the next section will firstly elaborate in more detail on some specific design characteristics these organizations seem to have. After that, these characteristics will be related to literature on temporary organizations to get first insight into design characteristics of the type of temporary organizations this book is aimed at. Subsequently, a more precise description is given on what is meant by a "high-risk conditions". Lastly, the particular stance on the safety concept that is taken in this book is brought forward.

1.2.1 Task Forces and Temporary Design: Introducing the "Expeditionary Organization"

Military operations of most Western countries changed substantially after the cold war came to an end. Post–Cold War military tasks and roles became much more diverse compared to "traditional" tasks that focused on defense of national (and allied) territory. Nowadays, most Western military organizations conduct varying missions such as peace keeping, peace enforcing and reconstruction (or state building) activities (e.g., Edmunds, 2006). These types of missions are often referred to as Military Operations Other Than War (MOOTW; Taw & Peters, 1995). To carry out the wide range of MOOTW-missions, many Western military organizations are confronted with an organizational design challenge (e.g., Bonin & Crisco, 2004; Kramer & De Waard, 2007; Bloch, 2000). De Waard and Kramer (2010, p. 72) state on this challenge: "Many military organizations try to develop the capacity to generate different organizational configurations, while at the same time they try to retain the advantages of relatively fixed structures and functionalities". The "mixing and matching" way military task forces are assembled can be seen as a way to deal with this challenge. To give more detail on what "mixing and matching" as an organization design strategy entails, De Waard and Kramer (2008, p. 539) argue that the Dutch military uses "parent organizations" (Army, Navy, Air Force and Military Police) as a "tool box" in which the different units are used as "building blocks" for building temporary task forces. From an American perspective, Snook (2000, p. 33) highlights a similar design strategy and points out that: "Task Forces are designed by taking basic unit building blocks and assembling them along hierarchical lines consistent with the demands of the mission and time-honored military traditions of command and control". Although, De Waard and Kramer (2008) argue that the American way of designing military task forces is similar to the way Dutch and most Western military task forces are assembled, Snook's definition adds detail to what is understood by military task force design. Next to describing the "mixing and matching" assembly strategy, Snook adds that military task forces are assembled "consistent with the demands of the mission and *time-honored military traditions of command and control*" (italics added). Snook hence also gives a first insight into how, from an American perspective, design *in* military task forces is shaped. Apparently, traditional command and control mechanisms are used to shape interactions within the task force. Combined, the works of De Waard and Kramer and Snook, hence, give a first insight into what organization design entails for military task forces.

As was highlighted previously, a "mixing and matching" design strategy seems to be used more broadly to assemble temporary organizations operating under high-risk conditions. To elaborate on this point, a model developed by Modig (2007) is adapted[1] that is able to distinguish between different types, or forms, of temporary organizations. This model, as visualized below, is based on the works of Galbraith (1994) and describes temporary organizations based on their relationship with static (or stable) permanent organizations.

At the left end of the model, permanent organizations are stable and elements of these organizations are used as building blocks to assemble temporary organizations. At the right end of the model, "pure" temporary organizations are located. This means that elements of these temporary

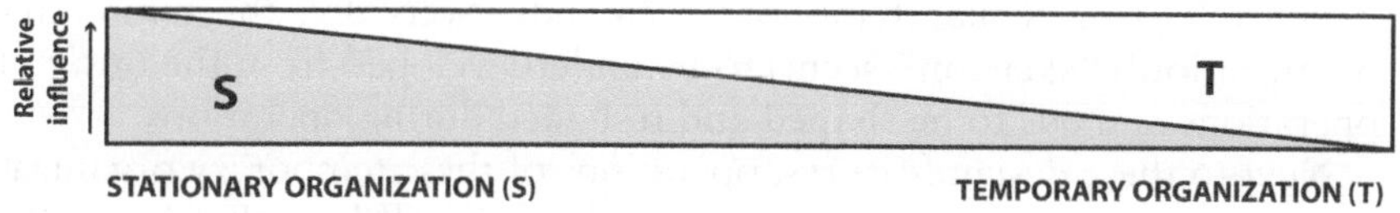

Figure 1.1 A model on temporary organizations
(Source: Modig (2007))

organizations do not originate from stable parent organizations. Instead these organizations are assembled of independent professionals that are hired for a particular project only. The design strategy that resembles the strategy of the military is located at the left end of Modig's model because at this end of the model, stable parent organizations are used as a platform for selecting building blocks from which temporary organizations are built. As already mentioned briefly earlier, some examples of this particular organizational design strategy outside the military context seem to be present in (mega) project organizations in construction, oil and gas extraction projects and crisis response organizations.

Next to a mixing and matching assembly strategy, literature provides indications that some temporary organizations that operate under high-risk conditions are characterized by a design that is underdeveloped from the onset of operations. Their organizational "skeleton" (cf. Weick, 2004) has to be developed along the way. In his well-known work "Organizations in action" Thompson highlighted that large crisis response organizations can be characterized as "synthetic organizations". With his concept of the synthetic organization, Thompson pointed out that these organizations need to "simultaneously establish its structure and carry on operations" (1967, p. 53). These remarks seem to be in line with the recent findings of Johannessen (2017), who emphasizes that within crisis organizations internal structures are broken down and transformed to cope with the inherent dynamics of the crisis environment. Similar design properties are found in the military context. In their study on Task Force Uruzgan, Kramer et al. (2012) found that soldiers needed to invest major effort in finding out with whom to cooperate. As a result, operators were constantly shaping and re-shaping configurations of units to find suitable organizational configurations to conduct missions (Kramer et al., ibid.). Such findings were not unique for TFU. Previous research has found similar design issues and accompanying bottom-up design processes within Dutch UNPROFOR[2] and SFOR[3] missions (see Vogelaar et al., 1996; Kramer, 2007).

In sum, and at first glance, the type of temporary organization at which this book is focused is characterized by two organization design features. Firstly, parent organizations are used as a platform to select building blocks from, these building blocks are subsequently "mixed and matched" to particular temporary demands. Secondly, the temporary organization's "skeleton" seems to be underdeveloped from the onset of operations and has to be shaped and reshaped during operations.

Next to these design features, operations of these temporary organizations often seem to be taking place on a location off-base that is specific to the temporary task at hand. Of course, this is the case for military task forces, that are subsequently called "expeditionary forces" in literature (e.g., Watson, 2005). Mega-projects in oil, gas and construction and crisis management organizations operate on specific, and sometimes remote, off-base location too. Hence, the term *expeditionary organization* is used to refer to the type of temporary organization this book is aimed at. This phrase is chosen because the word "expedition" seems to be able to grasp the temporary, off-base and inherently risky nature of the particular temporary organizational form emphasized in this section.

1.2.2 Defining High-Risk Conditions: the Relevance of the Dynamic Complexity and Enactment Concepts

After more detail has been presented on the type of temporary organizations this book focuses on, more detail has to be given on what is meant by the phrase "high-risk conditions". For this, the concept of "dynamic complexity" as developed by Senge (1992) and Kramer (2007) is used.

Senge (1992) developed the concept of dynamic complexity to highlight that for social systems, explaining behavior is less straightforward than simply transforming all unknowns into knowns. He states:

> The answer lies in the same reason that sophisticated tools of forecasting and business analysis, as well as elegant strategic plans, usually fail to produce dramatic breakthroughs in managing a business. They are all designed to handle the sort of complexity in which there are many variables: detail complexity. But there are two types of complexity. The second type is dynamic complexity, situations where cause and effect are subtle, and where the effects over time of interventions are not obvious. (. . .) When the same action has dramatically different effects in the short run and the long, there is dynamic complexity. When an action has one set of consequences locally and a very different set of consequences in another part of the system, there is dynamic complexity. When obvious interventions produce nonobvious consequences, there is dynamic complexity.
>
> (p. 71)

Kramer (2004, 2007) uses Senge's concept to characterize interaction between actions of organizations and reactions of elements in the organization's operating environment. According to Kramer (2004, p. 73), dynamic complexity refers to the result of: "interaction between purposeful behavior of an organization and an uncertain, ambiguous, equivocal but reactive environment". This means that organizational actions trigger reactions of elements in the environment that, for the organization, are hard to predict, hard to interpret and filled with double meaning.

For the military operating context, it seems to be quite straightforward why this context can be characterized as dynamically complex and how dynamic complexity relates to risk and danger. First of all, the presence of opposing forces in the operating environment that react intelligently to the actions of the task force, quite obviously results in interactions that are uncertain and equivocal. Also, as opposing forces and the task force interact with dangerous equipment and weapons, these interactions directly present military task forces with high-risk environmental conditions.

It can, however, be questioned whether "civil" expeditionary organizations, such as mega-projects in construction, are confronted with similar dynamically complex "high-risk conditions". After all, these temporary organizations are mostly not confronted with opposing forces that react with weapons to the actions of the temporary organization. Yet, it is argued for two reasons that "civil" expeditionary organizations are confronted with high-risk conditions too. Firstly, their operating environment is also characterized by dynamic complexity. For example, it is well known that many temporary organizations are confronted with fierce financial and time pressure within what can be called "hyper competitive" contexts (see for example: Flyvbjerg et al., 2003). So, although "civil" expeditionary organizations are, mostly, not operating in an environment that is as hostile and dangerous as the operating environment military task forces face, they certainly encounter some degree of uncertainty, ambiguity and reactiveness. Secondly, because these temporary organization too are facing dynamically complex conditions, they are challenged with the "necessity to act" (cf. Kramer, 2007). This means that in dynamically complex contexts, expeditionary organizations cannot wait behind closed fences to figure out what needs to be done, instead they need to "swing into action" (cf. Thompson, 1967, p. 53). They have to act in order to discover "what is going on". Weick (1979, p. 147) refers to this phenomenon as *enactment*.[4] A similar point is stressed by Lundin and Söderholm (1995) that emphasize the importance of action for temporary organizations. Hence, along previous findings in temporary military task forces and Thompson's concept "synthetic organization", expeditionary organizations seem to have to "swing into action" (cf. Thompson, 1967) and enact their environment while the organizational skeleton is underdeveloped and needs extensive shaping and reshaping. In this process, critical interdependencies between elements of the organization may still have to be worked out. Therefore, the necessity to act *may* make interacting within expeditionary organizations inherently risky.

The closely related dynamic complexity[5] and enactment concepts, along with Thompson's notions on the "synthetic organization", are hence able to nuance what is meant in this book by the phrase "high-risk conditions". At the one hand, in some cases, such as in the military context, dynamic complexity resulting from interaction between the organization and environmental elements can be seen as a main source for high-risk events. On the other hand, the necessity to act, combined with the apparent underdeveloped nature of expeditionary organizations, may make interactions within the organization inherently risky. The next section will discuss the particular stance on safety that is central to the studies in this book.

1.2.2 The Safety Concept and Dealing With High-Risk Conditions

The concept of safety has a central place in this book as it was argued above that *dealing with* high-risk conditions is inherently related to the challenge of developing safe operations. Due to the more detailed definition of the phrase "high risk conditions" outlined previously, a specific stance on the safety concept has to be taken that suits the elaborations presented in the previous section.

In contrast to safety literature that defines safety as the *absence* of hazard and risk (cf. Ale, 2009), literature that acknowledges uncertainty and complexity and its consequences for the safety concept is growing. A major cornerstone of this relatively novel avenue in safety science is that attaining "absolute safety" is impossible due to the fundamental uncertainties present in many contemporary organizational contexts. Some examples can be found in the work of Grote (2012), Hollnagel (2012), Dekker (2005) and Weick and Sutcliffe (2007). Following this perspective on the safety concept, it is highlighted that safety while faced with fundamental environmental uncertainty cannot be attained by simply following strict rules and procedures (see also Dekker, 2005). Instead, safety is developed by means of *self-organization* and adaptation of employees conducting "normal work" (cf. Dekker, 2005) at the operational level in an organization. Such a perspective on the safety concept acknowledges safety as an "emergent system property" (see Dekker, Ciliers, & Hofmeyr, 2011; Leveson, Dulac, Marais, & Caroll, 2009). This means that due to complex interactions between system elements and the system and its environment, system behavior cannot one-on-one be reduced to individual actions of its components. Instead, for understanding system behavior and system safety, the interplay between individual actions, system properties and environmental conditions has to be taken into account.[6]

Combining this stance on the nature of the safety concept with the two design features of expeditionary organization design that were already introduced above, points the investigations in this book into a particular direction. It points to exploring *how the two design features introduced above influence self-organization and the emergence of safety in expeditionary organizations.*

In the next section, a preliminary theoretical reflection will be presented that aims to find out whether contemporary theorizing is able to address this. Although the aim of this book is to contribute to organizational literature on safety during high-risk operations, the preliminary theoretical reflection section also highlights contemporary developments on theorizing in the field of temporary organizations. This is done to position the contents of this book in this particular theoretical avenue, which also opens up the possibility to contribute to this theoretical avenue.[7] It should be noted that the later section is not to be understood as an exhaustive theory review, this book will direct more attention to an extensive theoretical reflection in Chapter 2. Nevertheless, by means of the preliminary reflection presented later, potential theoretical issues can be highlighted.

1.3 Preliminary Theoretical Reflection

In this section, first a preliminary reflection will be carried out on recent developments in literature on temporary organizations. After that, some key aspects of theorizing on safety in high-risk contexts will be reflected upon.

1.3.1 Literature on Temporary Organizations

Since Lundin and Söderholm's (1995) remarks that theorizing on temporary organizations was underdeveloped, much has changed. Developments in the field of project management (e.g., Turner & Müller, 2003) and organization science (e.g., Bakker, 2010; Bakker, DeFillipi, Schwab, & Sydow, 2016), show substantial progress in theorizing on temporary organizational forms. Notwithstanding these developments, literature on temporary organizations that relates aspects of organization design to outcomes in temporary organizations is scarce (e.g., Miterev, Turner, & Mancini, 2017). Some studies that do address organization design in relation to outcomes of temporary and project organizations often use contingency theory as a perspective to build on (see also Aubry & Lavoie-Tremblay, 2018; Kenis, Janowicz, & Cambré, 2009). As Scott and Davis (2015) emphasize, a main premise of contingency theory is that a "fit" between structural design characteristics of the organization and elements of the organizational environment should be present to achieve success. Also, citing the works of Lawrence and Lorch, Scott and Davis state that dependent on the specific contingencies that different parts of an organization face, different structural configurations may be appropriate for different parts of an organization. Theorizing on so-called hybrid organizational structures stresses a similar point (see Mintzberg, 1980). Although contingency theory, and its variant configuration theory, are still rather prevalent organizational design approach (see, for example, Burton, Obel, & Håkansson, 2015), there seem to be two issues in applying this perspective to expeditionary organizations as defined in this book. These issues are both of a more abstract and of a more specific nature.

Firstly, general critiques to the contingency and configuration approach have been formulated by Mohr (1971), Schreyögg (1980) and Donaldson (2006). Schreyögg for example, highlights that an assumption underlying contingency theory is that organizations have "no influence on their contextual situation" (Schreyögg, 1980, p. 310). Organizations "simply" need to adapt to environmental contingencies in order to have success. This assumption underlying a contingency perspective on organization design seems to be contrasting sharply with the notions of Weick on enactment and sensemaking in dynamic contexts. Weick's concept "enactment", which is central to sensemaking theory, not only entails that organizations gradually build a "workable level of certainty" while enacting an uncertain, equivocal and reactive environment, it also entails that repertoires for action retained within the organization, such as structures, rules and procedures, influence the process of enactment in a specific way. It influences what is selected or "bracketed" in the environment. In this sense, organizations also "create" their operating environment. In the studies presented in this book, it will turn out that this is a crucial aspect of understanding behavior of expeditionary organizations in their environment and the way design characteristics influence such organizational behavior. Secondly, and of a more specific nature, theoretical developments on temporary organization design seem to be mainly focused on project organizations (e.g., Miterev et al., 2017; Aubry & Lavoie-Tremblay, 2017). A major difference between project organizations and expeditionary organizations, as defined in this book, is that project organization are *intra*-organizational constellations whereas expeditionary organizations are *inter*-organizational constellations. The two design features of expeditionary organizations as introduced earlier, hence can be interpreted as main features of particular inter-organizational temporary organizations, that may not be present (or manifest themselves differently) in intra-firm project organizations. Hence, based on the two previous arguments, it is questionable whether theorizing on intra-organizational project organizations from the perspective of contingency theory is applicable to the context of expeditionary organizations.

1.3.2 Literature on Safety During High-Risk Operations

As already briefly mentioned, recent developments on highly reliable organizations (HROs) and resilience acknowledge that the inherent dynamics of dealing with an uncertain and inherently risky environment have consequences for the safety concept. This book, however, questions whether advances in the field of HROs and resilience are a suitable starting point for studying the relation between organization design, self-organization and the emergence of safety in expeditionary organizations. The first doubt originates from the explicit choice in resilience (engineering) theory to favor process over structure.[8] Hollnagel (2012), as one of the key academics in the field of resilience engineering, argues that "when things do not go according to plan", structure in organizations becomes irrelevant. Quite obviously, in (military) expeditionary organizations, things very often do not go as planned. However, instead of becoming irrelevant, Snook's study shows that characteristics of organizational structure, such as differentiation and integration, become highly relevant under challenging circumstances. A second doubt originates from the specific organizational contexts that served as an empirical basis for the development of high reliability theory. As was also highlighted at the beginning of this chapter, developments in the field of highly reliability organizing mainly originate from organizations that are not temporary. As such, the two specific design features of expeditionary organizations may not have been present in the organizational context on which high reliability theory is built. Not surprisingly, the design-related influences on high reliability that are addressed often relate to characteristics of non-temporary organizations. Examples of such design-related influences are fixed rules and procedures and tight coupling between organizational elements (see Rijpma, 1997; Sagan, 1993). So, although high reliability theory and resilience engineering theory seem to have a conceptualization of safety that suits expeditionary high-risk operations, this preliminary reflection points out that these approaches seem to be unsuitable as a starting point for a study that aims to develop insight into the relationship between organization design, self-organization and the emergence of safety in expeditionary organizations.

As a result of this first and preliminary reflection on theorizing in the fields of temporary organizations and safety during high-risk operations, developing theory that fosters *understanding* the influence organizational design on self-organization and the emergence of safety within expeditionary organizations seems a fruitful contribution to literature. Therefore, the next section defines the goal of this book.

1.4 Research Goal and Research Strategy

Based on the preceding sections, the following goal for this book is formulated:

Developing theory on the influence of organization design on self-organization and the emergence of safety in expeditionary organizations, by:

1. **Studying this relationship in specific expeditionary organizations and**
2. **Generalizing these findings to expeditionary organizations in general.**

To attain this goal, the next section explicates what characteristics such a theory should have in order to address the issues highlighted in the previous section.

1.4.1 The Nature of the Theory to Be Developed

The main purpose of the theory to be developed in this book is *understanding* the relationship between organizational design, self-organization and the emergence of safety in expeditionary organizations. This, at the one hand, demands that the theory possesses certain characteristics. On the other hand, it limits the contents of the theory in a particular way.

Firstly, the theory that is developed in this book should be applicable to a family of temporary organizations. The previous sections not only placed emphasis on military task forces but also highlighted the broader relevance of the expeditionary organizational form. This implies that the studies presented in this book aim to develop a particular type of knowledge. To pinpoint the type of knowledge that is developed in this book, the works of Van Strien (1986, 1997) are used. Van Strien defined three distinct levels of (epistemological) knowledge generalization, which he quite straightforwardly named levels A, B and C. Level A knowledge consists of abstract, ontological, assumptions within a particular research discipline. Level B knowledge represents problem-oriented knowledge, suitable for a particular empirical field. Level C knowledge represents context-specific knowledge for specific empirical situations. A theory on the influence of organization design on self-organization and the emergence of safety in expeditionary organizations is located at Van Strien's level B, that of problem-oriented knowledge. Such a theory is oriented towards a specific problem that a family of organizations seems to have, but at the same time aims to be more general than context-specific knowledge. Although the type of theory this book is aimed at is located at Van Strien's level B, this does not mean that the other levels of knowledge generalization are irrelevant for the studies in this book. On the contrary, knowledge at levels A and C are addressed extensively in this book. For example, the more abstract ontological points on enactment and dynamic complexity outlined in preceding sections of this chapter can be defined as level A knowledge. Furthermore, context-specific arguments that relate to specific expeditionary organizations such as Task Force Uruzgan, outlined in the introduction section of this chapter, are located at Van Strien's level C.

Secondly, Morse (1997, p. 174) points out that a theory that fosters deep understanding of a particular phenomenon should possess both *explanatory* and *predictive* characteristics. With regard to explanatory characteristics, this means that within the theory developed in this book, particular mechanisms, or relationships between concepts, have to be unraveled. For the problem this book is aimed, this implies that specific characteristics of organizational design have to be related to particular safety outcomes in expeditionary organizations. With regard to its predictive characteristics, the theory developed in this book has to provide mechanisms between concepts that can be observed in all expeditionary contexts.

Regarding the limits of the theory to be developed, it should be emphasized that the theory developed in this book does not aim to be a prescriptive organizational redesign or safety management theory. This means that it is not attempted to create a theory on redesigning expeditionary organizations to deal with high-risk conditions in a better way. Yet, it can be argued that before any redesign theory can be constructed, diagnostic knowledge has to be developed. In this sense, the work presented in this book can be interpreted as a necessary and inevitable step that has to be taken before any prescriptive redesign or safety management theory can be constructed.

1.4.2 Research Strategy: Using the "Geographical Map" and "Compass" Metaphor

As was highlighted previously, this book aims to develop a theory at Van Strien's level B. To do so, a particular research strategy is chosen that adopts research approaches suggested by Christis (1998, p. 25) and Kuipers, Van Amelsvoort, and Kramer (2010).

Christis (ibid.) uses the analogy of a geographical map to highlight that including all possible theoretical perspectives would lead to a study that is overly complex. As a metaphor, he states that geographical map can never reflect the area that it aims to map in full detail. Otherwise the map would become too big, complex and impractical to use. Therefore, during a map-making process, choices are made what to include in the map and what to leave out in order to make it useful for everyday navigation. By using this metaphor, this book will develop a "map" on the relationship between organizational design, self-organization and the emergence of safety in expeditionary organizations. By using such a principle of selectivity, complexity is reduced because it seems unrealistic to develop a theory on *all* aspects that influence safety in expeditionary organizations. It was highlighted in the preceding sections that for the particular topic this book is interested in, no ready-made "map" seems to be available because existing theory does not seem to take essential characteristics of expeditionary organizations into account. Although such a map does not seem to be available, it is argued that some aspects of theory in organization science can be used to construct a map on the relation between expeditionary organizational design and safety in high-risk contexts. Within organization science, and the so-called Integral Organizational Renewal

(IOR) approach in particular, the influence of an organization's structural design on self-organization of employees, the ability of an organization to deal with environmental uncertainty and subsequent outcomes at the organizational level is well defined (e.g., De Sitter, 1994; Kuipers et al., 2010; Van Eijnatten & Van der Zwaan, 1998). IOR, sometimes referred to as the Lowlands' Sociotechnical Design Theory (STSL; Van Amelsvoort, 2016),[9] is originating from a wider tradition in organization science, that of Socio-Technical Systems Design (STSD), which has its roots in works by Emery and Trist (see, for example, Trist & Bamforth, 1951; Emery & Thorsrud, 1964). IOR's premises are, however, not applied deductively in the different studies in this book. Instead, IOR is used as a "conceptual compass" (cf. Kuipers et al., 2010, p. 281) that is applied reflexively to develop a map on the relation between expeditionary organizational design, self-organization and the emergence of safety in expeditionary organizations. Such a strategy is chosen because IOR can be regarded as a theory that provides analytical concepts and design premises that can *guide* design-related questions in organizations, it does not provide an all-fitting conceptual framework for design-related scientific work in organizations (see also Kuipers, 1998). As such, IOR concepts are used *heuristically* (cf. Richardson & Kramer, 2006) in the different studies of this book.[10]

1.5 Research Steps

In this section, the different steps that are followed in this book are explicated.[11] In the first step, the main premises on expeditionary organizations and dealing with high-risk conditions, that were described in section 1.2, are used to review existing theory. This is done because the preliminary reflection described in this chapter only presented some indications for a theoretical gap in literature. To determine a theoretical gap in more detail, three frequently used theories on safety during high-risk operations are reviewed: resilience engineering theory (e.g., Hollnagel, 2012), Normal Accidents Theory (Perrow, 1999) and High Reliability Theory (e.g., Weick & Sutcliffe, 2007). In the second research step, and by using IOR heuristically, it is *explored* what aspects of organizational design influenced self-organization and the emergence of safety in a particular expeditionary organization. As military task forces were taken as an empirical starting point for the studies in this book, the exploration is carried out in a military expeditionary organization. More in particular the exploration focuses on the operations of the UAV unit of which the Army Captain, who was quoted at the beginning of this chapter, was a commanding officer. His UAV unit is the Royal Netherlands Army's 107th Aerial Systems battery (107 ASBt). The 107 ASBt conducted three expeditionary missions within Task Force Uruzgan between August 2006 and May 2009. During their deployment, 107 ASBt was the only unit within the Dutch Army that operated with Unmanned Aerial Vehicles.

In step three, the main goal is to detail the relation between organizational design, self-organization and the emergence of safety for expeditionary organizations in general. This is a crucial step in developing a theory at van Strien's level B of knowledge generalization. To do so, a second case study is conducted within Task Force Uruzgan. This case study firstly aims to generalize the results of the exploratory study carried out in step one, to the organizational level of TFU. After that, by means of analytical generalization (cf. Yin, 2003, pp. 32–33),[12] hypotheses are formulated for expeditionary organizations in general.

In step four, it is attempted to verify the hypotheses developed in the previous step by means of studying two other expeditionary cases: a case on the Dutch military contribution to SFIR[13] in Iraq and a case on the Dutch national crisis response organization that was initiated after the crash with flight MH17. In this way, it can be investigated whether analytically developed hypotheses can indeed be generalized to expeditionary organizations in general. This is a necessary step in developing theory at Van Strien's level B that has applicability to the family of expeditionary organizations this book aimed on. Subsequently in step five, the level B theory on the influence of expeditionary organizational design on self-organization and the emergence of safety is constructed. In this step, a conceptual model is developed that explicates explanatory and predictive mechanisms between the central concepts of this book.

1.6 Research Model and Central Research Questions

This section will present the research model that is used to attain the research goal that was detailed in section 1.4. The model is built out of the steps presented in the previous section and subsequently enables to derive central research questions. Each of these research questions will be addressed and answered in separate chapters as is visualized in Figure 1.2. The research model presented in this section is developed by using a procedure proposed by Verschuren and Doorewaard (2007). Their method is chosen because it offers a systematic procedure for developing research questions that are all aimed at attaining an overarching research goal. In this method, a distinction is made between the particular conceptual perspective used (in Dutch: "optiek") and the object of study. In the previous section, different perspectives and objects of study were highlighted. For example, it was highlighted in the first research step that "characteristics of expeditionary organizations and safety in high-risk context" (the perspective, or "optiek") will be used to study three frequently used theories (the object). Confronting these two (visualized by two headed

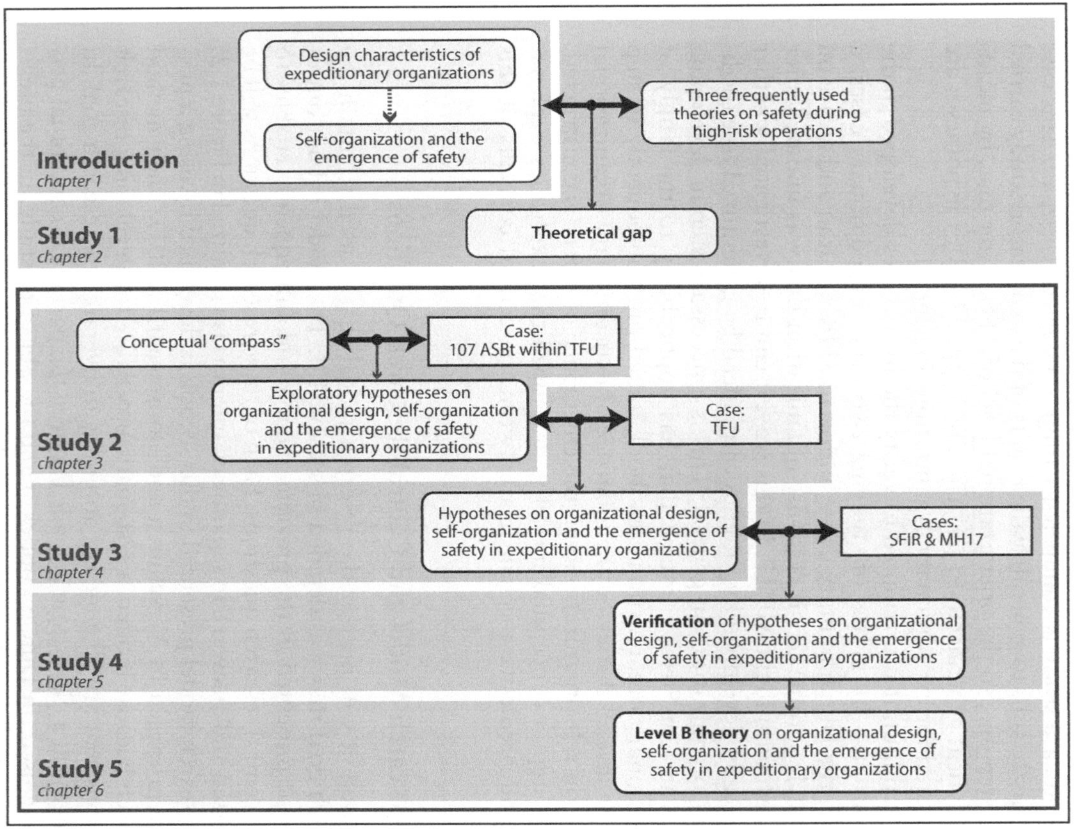

Figure 1.2 Research model of this book

ASBt = Aerial Systems battery; TFU = Task Force Uruzgan; SFIR = international Stabilization Force in Iraq; and MH17 = Malaysia Airlines Flight MH17

arrows in the model), opens up the possibility to formulate a research question. As such, based on Figure 1.2, the following research questions can be formulated:

1. What gap in literature on safety during high-risk operations can be identified?
2. What aspects of organizational design influenced self-organization of 107 Aerial Systems battery and the emergence of safety during their operations within Task Force Uruzgan?
3. What hypotheses on the relation between organization design, self-organization and the emergence of safety in expeditionary organizations can be formulated?
4. Can hypotheses on the relation between organizational design, self-organization and the emergence of safety in expeditionary organizations be verified by studying other expeditionary organizations?
5. What theory on the relation between organizational design, self-organization and the emergence of safety in expeditionary organizations can be constructed?

In the next section, it is pointed out in which chapter each of the research questions will be addressed.

1.7 Structure of This Book

This book consists of seven chapters. This first chapter focused on introducing the main subject, research premises, research goal and central research questions. In the second chapter the first study is presented that is aimed at a theoretical review in which three frequently used theories in the domain of safety during high-risk operations will be analyzed to detail a theoretical gap. The third chapter will focus on the exploration carried out on the operations of 107 Aerial Systems battery within Task Force Uruzgan. The fourth chapter will present a second case study within Task Force Uruzgan. After that, the fifth chapter aims to verify findings by means of confronting the results of Chapter 4 with two other expeditionary cases. The sixth chapter will construct the content of the level B theory at which this book is aimed. Finally, the seventh chapter provides a discussion to reflect on the contributions and limitations of the research carried out in this book.

Notes

1. The original model by Modig also addresses aspects as learning, diversity, economies of scale and uncertainty as elements of the dependency that temporary organizations have on parent organizations. Her point here is that, for example in relation to uncertainty, temporary organizations that rely on static parent organizations face less uncertainty than "pure" temporary organizations that do not rely on static parent organizations. The military tem-

porary context, however, seems to contest Modig's argument. Hence, these aspects are left out in the representation in Figure 1.1 as the more general nature of her model seems more relevant to stress the arguments in this section.

2. UNPROFOR: United Nations Protection Force, for Former Yugoslavia
3. SFOR: Stability Force, for Former Yugoslavia
4. See also Weick (1988) for a paper on the relevance of the enactment perspective in crisis situations.
5. It should be noted that the term "dynamic complexity" is used to refer to characteristics of the operating environment at the level of the temporary organization. Of course, parent organizations can be, and often are, confronted with dynamic complexity. It may even be argued that the strategy to "mix and match" temporary organizations in the first place can be seen as a way for parent organizations to cope with such uncertainty at the level of the parent organization(s). This issue is, however, not addressed in the first four chapters. It will be acknowledged though later on in this book, in the Chapters 5 and 6.
6. For the studies in this book, this argument is important because the methodologies used in the chapters to come explicitly distinguish between operators' self-organizing strategies for dealing with high-risk conditions on a daily basis, and the safety concept at the level of the organizational system.
7. Potential contributions to literature on temporary organizations will be highlighted in Chapter 7.
8. It has to be noted that the perspective chosen later on in this chapter does not reverse this statement in the sense that organizational structure as a concept is chosen in favor of process. The studies in this book aim to be sensitive to the "duality" between process and structure (cf. Giddens, 1984) in organizations, as its importance for organizational studies is frequently advocated in organizational literature (see, for example, Feldman & Orlikowski, 2011).
9. In this book, the pros and cons of the different traditions within STSD are not discussed in detail. The interested reader is referred to Van Eijnatten (1993) or Kuipers et al. (2010).
10. More detail on this particular methodological choice is given in Chapter 3.
11. As these different steps require different methodologies, this section lacks detailed methodological descriptions. Instead, the different studies outlined in the chapters of this book have their own methodological section.
12. In contrast to most quantitative social research that aims to generalize results by means of statistical generalization, qualitative social research can (partly) rely on analytical generalization instead of statistical generalization for achieving external validity. Analytic generalization is done by means of argument building, which means that it needs to be elaborated why and to what extent findings are relevant for other ("mixed and matched" temporary) organizational contexts. To attain external validity however, also replication has to be employed (Yin, 2003). This is done in the fourth research step.
13. International Stabilization Force

References

Ale, B. J. M. (2009). *An introduction to risk*. New York: Routledge.

Aubry, M., & Lavoie-Tremblay, M. (2017). Rethinking organizational design for managing multiple projects. *International Journal of Project Management*, *36*(1), 12–26.

Bakker, R. M. (2010). Taking stock of temporary organizational forms: A systematic review and research agenda. *International Journal of Management Reviews*, *12*(4), 466–486.

Bakker, R. M., DeFillippi, R. J., Schwab, A., & Sydow, J. (2016). Temporary organizing: Promises, processes, problems. *Organization Studies*, *37*(12), 1703–1719.

Bloch, G. A. (2000). French military reform: Lessons for America's army? *Parameters*, *30*(2), 33.

Bonin, J. A., & Crisco, T. E. J. (2004). The modular army. *Military Review*, *84*(2), 21.

Burton, R., Obel, B., & Håkonsson, D. (2015). *Organizational design: A step-by-step approach*. Cambridge: Cambridge University Press.

Chen, K. K. (2015). Using extreme cases to understand organizations. In K. D. Elsbach & R. M. Kramer (Eds.), *Handbook of qualitative organizational research: Innovative pathways and methods* (pp. 33–44). New York: Routledge.

Christis, J. (1998). *Arbeid, Organisatie en Stress. Een visie vanuit de sociotechnische arbeids-en organisatiekunde*. Amsterdam: Het Spinhuis.

Comfort, L. K. (2007). Crisis management in hindsight: Cognition, communication, coordination, and control. *Public Administration Review*, *67*, 189–197.

Crichton, M. T., Lauche, K., & Flin, R. (2005). Incident command skills in the management of an oil industry drilling incident: A case study. *Journal of Contingencies and Crisis Management*, *13*(3), 116–128.

Dekker, S. W. A. (2005). *Ten questions about human error*. New York: Lawrence Erlbaum.

Dekker, S. W. A., Cilliers, P., & Hofmeyr, J. H. (2011). The complexity of failure: Implications of complexity theory for safety investigations. *Safety Science*, *49*(6), 939–945.

Donaldson, L. (2006). The contingency theory of organizational design: Challenges and opportunities. In R. M. Burton, D. D. Hakonsson, B. Eriksen, & C. C. Snow (Eds.), *Organization design* (pp. 19–40). Boston, MA: Springer Verlag.

Edmunds, T. (2006). What are armed forces for? the changing nature of military roles in Europe. *International Affairs*, *82*(6), 1059–1075.

Emery, F., & Thursrud, E. (1964). *Industrial democracy*. London: Tavistock Publications.

Feldman, M. S., & Orlikowski, W. J. (2011). Theorizing practice and practicing theory. *Organization Science*, *22*(5), 1240–1253.

Flyvbjerg, B., Bruzelius, N., & Rothengatter, W. (2003). *Megaprojects and risk: An anatomy of ambition*. Cambridge: Cambridge University Press.

Galbraith, J. R. (1994). *Competing with flexible lateral organizations: European journal of engineering education* (Vol. 19). Reading, MA: Addison-Wesley Longman.

Giddens, A. (1984). *The constitution of society*. Berkeley, CA: University of California Press.

Grote, G. (2012). Safety management in different high-risk domains-all the same? *Safety Science*, *50*, 1983–1992.

Hällgren, M., Rouleau, L., & de Rond, M. (2018). A matter of life or death: How extreme context research matters for management and organization studies. *Academy of Management Annals*, *12*(1), 111–153.Hollnagel, E. (2012). *Fram: The functional resonance analysis method, modelling complex socio-technical systems*. Farnham: Ashgate Publishing.

Johannessen, S. (2017). *Strategies, leadership and complexity in crisis and emergency operations*. New York: Routledge.

Kenis, P., Janowicz, M., & Cambré, B. (2009). *Temporary organizations: Prevalence, logic and effectiveness*. Cheltenham: Edward Elgar Publishing.

Kramer, E. H. (2004). *Organizing doubt: Self-organization and army units in crisis operations* (Doctoral dissertation). Eindhoven: Eindhoven University of Technology.

Kramer, E. H. (2007). *Organizing doubt: Grounded theory, army units and dealing with dynamic complexity* (Vol. 22). Copenhagen: Copenhagen Business School Press.

Kramer, E. H., & de Waard, E. J. (2007). Componeneren met componenten. *Carre*, *1*, 38–44.

Kramer, E. H., de Waard, E. J., & de Graaff, M. C. (2012). Task force Uruzgan and experimentation with organization design. In R. Beeres, J. Van der Meulen, J. M. M. L. Soeters, & A. L. W. Vogelaar (Eds.), *Mission Uruzgan*. Amsterdam: Pallas, Amsterdam University Press.

Kuipers, H. (1998). The socio-technical designer as Wizard and Juggler. *Concepts and Transformation*, *3*(3), 229–254.

Kuipers, H., van Amelsvoort, P., & Kramer, E. H. (2010). *Het Nieuwe Organiseren: alternatieven voor de bureaucratie*. The Hague: Acco.

Leveson, N., Dulac, N., Marais, K., & Carroll, J. (2009). Moving beyond normal accidents and high reliability organizations: A systems approach to safety in complex systems. *Organization Studies*, *30*(2–3), 227.

Lundin, R. A., & Söderholm, A. (1995). A theory of the temporary organization. *Scandinavian Journal of Management*, *11*(4), 437–455.

Mintzberg, H. (1980). Structure in 5's: A synthesis of the research on organization design. *Management Science*, *26*(3), 322–341.

Miterev, M., Mancini, M., & Turner, R. (2017). Towards a design for the project-based organization. *International Journal of Project Management*, *35*(3), 479–491.

Modig, N. (2007). A continuum of organizations formed to carry out projects: Temporary and stationary organization forms. *International Journal of Project Management*, *25*(8), 807–814.

Mohr, L. (1971). Organizational technology and organizational structure. *Administrative Science Quarterly*, *16*(4), 444–459.

Morse, J. M. (1997). Considering theory derived from qualitative research. In J. M. Morse (Ed.), *Completing a qualitative project: Details and dialogue* (pp. 163–190). Thousand Oaks: Sage Publications, Inc.

Perrow, C. (1999). *Normal accidents: Living with high-risk technologies*. Princeton: Princeton University Press.

Richardson, R., & Kramer, E. H. (2006). Abduction as the type of inference that characterizes the development of a grounded theory. *Qualitative Research*, *6*(4), 497.

Rijpma, J. A. (1997). Complexity, tight-coupling and reliability: Connecting normal accidents theory and high reliability theory. *Journal of Contingencies and Crisis Management*, *5*(1), 15–23.

Rochlin, G., LaPorte, T. R., & Roberts, K. H. (1987). The self-designing high-reliability organization: Aircraft carrier flight operations at sea. *Naval War College Review*, *40*(4), 76–90.

Sagan, S. D. (1993). *The limits of safety*. Princeton: Princeton University Press.

Schreyögg, G. (1980). Contingency and choice in organization theory. *Organization Science*, *1*(4), 305–326.
Scott, W., & Davis, G. (2015). *Organizations and organizing: Rational, natural and open systems perspectives*. New York: Routledge.
Senge, P. (1992). *The fifth discipline*. London: Century Business.
Sitter, L. U. de. (1994). *Synergetisch produceren: Human Resources Mobilisation in de produktie een inleiding in structuurbouw*. Assen: Uitgeverij Van Gorcum.
Snook, S. A. (2000). *Friendly fire: The accidental shootdown of U.S. Blackhawks over northern Iraq*. Princeton: Princeton University Press.
Taw, J. M., & Peters, J. E. (1995). Operations other than war: Implications for the us army. *Small Wars & Insurgencies*, *6*(3), 375–409.
Thompson, J. D. (1967). *Organizations in action*. New York: McGraw-Hill.
Trist, E. L., & Bamforth, K. W. (1951). Some social and psychological consequences of the Longxwall method of coal-getting: An examination of the psychological situation and defences of a work group in relation to the social structure and technological content of the work system. *Human Relations*, *4*(1), 3–38.
Turner, J. R., & Müller, R. (2003). On the nature of the project as a temporary organization. *International Journal of Project Management*, *21*(1), 1–8.
van Amelsvoort, P. (2016). Human talent mobilization: Improving both quality of working life and productivity by organizational design in the lowlands. In B. J. Mohr & P. van Amelsvoort (Eds.), *Co-creating humane and innovative organizations* (pp. 73–98). Portland, ME: Global STS-D Network.
van Eijnatten, F. M. (1993). *The paradigm that changed the workplace*. Assen: Van Gorcum.
van Eijnatten, F. M., & Van Der Zwaan, A. H. (1998). The Dutch IOR approach to organizational design: An alternative to business process re-engineering? *Human Relations*, *51*(3), 289–318.
van Strien, P. J. (1986). *Praktijk als wetenschap: methodologie van het sociaalwetenschappelijk handelen*. Assen: Uitgeverij Van Gorcum.
van Strien, P. J. (1997). Towards a methodology of psychological practice: The regulative cycle. *Theory & Psychology*, *7*(5), 683–700.
Verschuren, P. J. M., & Doorewaard, J. A. C. M. (2007). *Het ontwerpen van een onderzoek*. Den Haag: Lemma.
Vogelaar, A. L. W., Bosch, J., Kuipers, H., Metselaar, M., Nederhof, F., Witteveen, A., . . . Van der Vlist, R. (1996). *Leiderschap in crisisomstandigheden*. Breda: FMB.
Waard, E. J. de, & Kramer, E. H. (2008). Tailored task forces: Temporary organizations and modularity. *International Journal of Project Management*, *26*(5), 537–546.
Waard, E. J. de, & Kramer, E. H. (2010). Expeditionary operations and modular organization design. In J. Soeters, P. C. Van Fenema, & R. J. Beeres (Eds.), *Managing military organizations* (pp. 71–83). London: Routledge.
Watson, B. (2005). *Reshaping the expeditionary army to win decisively: The case for greater stabilization capacity in the modular force*. Carlisle Barracks, PA: Army War College, Strategic Studies Institute.
Weick, K. E. (1979). *The social psychology of organizing*. New York: McGraw-Hill.

Weick, K. E. (1988). Enacted sensemaking in crisis situations. *Journal of Management Studies*, *25*(4), 305–317.
Weick, K. E. (2004). Rethinking organizational design. In F. Collopy & R. J. Boland (Eds.), *Managing as designing* (Vol. 36, pp. 36–50). Stanford: Stanford Business Books.
Weick, K. E., & Sutcliffe, K. M. (2007). *Managing the unexpected*. San Francisco: Jossey-Bass.
Wolbers, J. J. (2016). *Drawing the line: Cross-boundary coordination processes in emergency management*. Amsterdam: Ridderprint.
Yin, R. K. (2003). *Case study research: Design and methods* (Vol. 5). Thousand Oaks, CA: Sage Publications, Inc.

2 A Review of Three Frequently Used Theories[1]

2.1 Introduction

In this chapter, the first study of this book is presented. This chapter is therefore guided by the first research question, which is this:

> **What gap in literature on safety during high-risk operations can be identified?**

The preliminary reflection in the previous chapter indicated that frequently used theories on safety during high-risk operations may have some crucial limitations. This seemed to hinder their suitability as an integral conceptual framework for empirical study of the relation between organization design, self-organization and the emergence of safety in expeditionary organizations. These indications may hence point to a gap in this particular avenue of theoretical work. However, quite obviously, in the previous chapter only indications of such a theoretical gap were highlighted. This chapter will therefore examine whether these indications indeed point to a particular theoretical gap. To do so, three frequently used theories are analyzed on their ability to get deeper insight into the relationship between organizational design, self-organization and the emergence of safety in expeditionary organizations. The three theories reviewed are resilience engineering theory (e.g., Hollnagel, 2012), Normal Accidents Theory (NAT; Perrow, 1999) and High Reliability Theory (HRT; e.g., Weick & Sutcliffe, 2007).

One could argue that an analysis on these theories can be done by directly confronting these theories with the key characteristics of expeditionary organizations described in section 1.2. However, Reiman and Rollenhagen (2011) argue that safety theory often suffers from assumptions that are used implicitly. As a consequence, establishing whether the three theories mentioned are able to get a deeper understanding of the relation between organizational design, self-organization and the emergence of safety in expeditionary organizations may become difficult. Therefore, an analytical framework is constructed that is able to

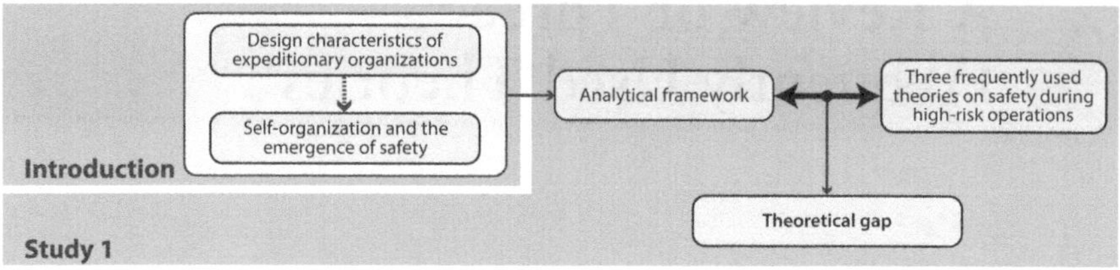

Figure 2.1 Research model of Study 1

explicate assumptions on ways in which these theories address the relation between organizational design and the ability of an organization to deal with dynamic circumstances. After these assumptions are explicated, it can be analyzed whether these theories are indeed unsuitable as an integral conceptual framework for the empirical studies this book aims to carry out.

Including an analytical framework into the research approach of this chapter, however, complicates the research model for the study presented in this chapter. Therefore, parts of the research model presented in Chapter 1 have to be changed. Based on the research model presented in Figure 1.2 in the previous chapter, the analytical steps followed in this chapter are guided by the following research model in Figure 2.1.

This chapter proceeds as follows. Firstly, the analytical framework is constructed. Secondly, the three previously mentioned theories are described. Thirdly, the analytical framework is confronted with these theories to explicate assumptions on organizational design and dealing with dynamic circumstances. Finally, conclusions are drawn on the ability of these three theories to address the relationship between organizational design, self-organization and the emergence of safety in expeditionary organizational contexts.

2.2 Analytical Framework

The analytical framework that is used to facilitate the analysis in this chapter is mainly built on a categorization of systems theory[2] made by Blom (1997). His categorization is used because he explicates three fundamentally different, rather normative, paradigms on how "systems" may deal with and control (i.e. reduce) environmental uncertainty. Both safety theory and organizational design theory seem to have their roots in systems theory (e.g., Grote, 2012; Kuipers et al., 2010). It can hence be argued that constructing an analytical framework based on systems theory may be able to link the two theoretical streams to each other and hence enable explicating assumptions on the way the three theories selected conceptualize on organization design, safety and their relationship. It should be noted that, in Van Strien's (1986) terms, systems theory is located at level A of knowledge generalization, the level of abstract ontological knowledge, whereas organizational design theories and safety theories are located at level B, the level of problem-oriented theory. This chapter therefore aims to link these levels of knowledge generalization. In the next section, Blom's rather abstract categorization is detailed.

2.2.1 *A Categorization of Systems Theory and Paradigms on Organizational Design and Dealing With Uncertainty*

Before Blom's categorization can be presented, first an understanding of what a "system" is needs to be explicated. According to Rapoport (in: Kramer, 2007, p. 63), crucial to understanding system is that a system is the following:

- something consisting of a set of elements
- among which relationships are specified so that
- deductions are possible from such relations to others or from the relations among the elements to the behavior or history of the system.

In his categorization of systems theory, Blom distinguishes between *classic*, *open* and *self-referential* paradigms in systems theory. By means of this categorization, Blom develops three fundamentally different perspectives on how characteristics of relationships between elements, the "inside" of a system, enable the system to deal with the environment, its "outside". It is emphasized that using systems theory does not imply that an organization "is" a system. Instead, systems theory is used because it is regarded useful to understand an organization as a system in order to get more insight into its behavior and challenges (cf. Kramer, 2004, p. 69).

Furthermore, Blom's paradigms are linked to organizational theory in order to develop three fundamentally different perspectives on the role that organizational design can play in dealing with environmental uncertainty. The link with organizational theory in the analytical framework is made because this shows what explicit assumptions on organizational design may look like in relation to dealing with environmental uncertainty. This subsequently opens up the road for detecting what conceptualizations the selected theories have on organization design, safety and their relationship. Subsequently, it can be established whether these theories are suitable for tapping into the relation between organizational design, self-organization and the emergence of safety in expeditionary organizations. These inferences are detailed in the analysis of this chapter.[3]

2.2.1.1 *Classic Systems Theory and Organizational Design*

A classic systems perspective acknowledges an environment, however, the relationship between the environment and the system is considered as static. This enables to define the relationships between elements entirely based on norms formulated inside the system by means of following a top-down "normative order" that defines what is relevant to the system and what is not. This implicates that the system is oriented towards internal stability, predictability and compliance to a prescribed "code" (Blom, 1997, p. 14). Consequently, the system is inflexible to any *change* in the operational environment. Dealing with environmental uncertainty in classic systems theory can be interpreted as making sure that the "normative order" within the system is maintained. This means that deviations due to environmental variation have to be removed so that the criteria for stable interaction between the elements within the system can be upheld. These premises of classic systems theory can be found in traditional bureaucratic organizational design theory, in which design is aimed controlling interactions by means of "top-down" procedures and creating maximum opportunity for internal predictability (Morgan, 2006, pp. 11–32). As such, often in such designs it is witnessed that "control" is achieved by designing organizations with a maximum division of labor and numerous control loops to keep behavior of the organization's primary process within "top down" defined criteria.

2.2.1.2 Open Systems Theory and Organizational Design

In contrast to the classic systems perspective, the open systems approach, developed by Von Bertalanffy and many others, defines a system as a set of elements that interact with each other *and* with the environment. In other words, the relationship between system and environment is theorized as dynamic and interactive. Within open systems theory the central focus is on maximum adaptation of the system to a *changing* environment. Blom and Haas (1996) point out that open systems theory assumes that sensing changes in an environment and making subsequent changes within the system is not problematic. This means that open systems theory assumes that change can be sensed and recorded successfully, so that the system can perform the necessary adaptations accordingly. Hence, the system is expected to change along with environmental cues. Consequently, dealing with environmental uncertainty in open systems theory can be interpreted as attaining "absolute" flexibility.

Open systems perspectives on organizational design and dealing with environmental uncertainty are characterized by concepts such as "contingency" and "best fit" (e.g., Schreyögg, 1980; Morgan, 2006, pp. 39–65). Donaldson (2006) points out that within the contingency approach, the set of relationships between organizational actors, that according to him can be called the organization's structure, should vary along with variation of "contingency factors". He (ibid., p. 51) points out that a premise of the contingency approach is that: "its sees structure that is optimal as varying according to certain factors (. . .). Thus, the optimal structure is contingent upon these factors". Such contingency factors are (cf. Donaldson, ibid.): strategy, size, task uncertainty and technology. Hence, Donaldson highlights that within such contingency approaches the "best way" of designing organizations depends on contingency factors.

According to Schreyögg (1980, p. 308), the "open system" contingency approach can be summarized by the following three principles:

1. There is only one "best answer" to deal with a specific contextual situation. This means that within given situations there is no choice among alternative structural arrangements.
2. The environment is considered as a given, which means that the organization has no possibility of influencing or controlling its environmental situation.
3. The organization has to achieve a certain level of economic performance in order to survive. The criteria against which its performance is assessed are defined externally, which means that level and criteria are out of control for the organization.

Morgan formulates critique to the "open systems" approach to organizational design. He states (2006, p. 74) that: "it can be misleading to suggest that organizations need to 'adapt' (. . .) this tends to make organizations and their members dependent on forces operating in an external world". It can therefore be argued that dealing with environmental uncertainty is somewhat more challenging than hypothesized by an open system perspective. Blom's (1997) third systems-theoretical perspective addresses this issue.

2.2.1.3 Self-Referential Systems Theory and Organizational Design

The self-referential systems perspective (see, for example, Luhmann, 1990; Maturana, 1980) advocates that the relationship between system and environment is not as straightforward as is assumed by "open" systems theory. Blom (1997) emphasizes that self-referential systems theory does not assume openness. Instead, it reintroduces the idea of a system's "closedness" (Kramer, 2004). This closedness within self-referential systems theory points to the realization of "circularity": the system's structure influences its adaptive capacities and survivable qualities. That is to say, the nature of the relationships between elements, that in an abstract sense can be called the structure of the system, largely influences whether the system can "reproduce" itself in such a way that survivability of the system in its environment is attained (see also Achterbergh & Vriens, 2010). In this sense, systems adapt *in reference* to themselves. Heylighen and Joslyn argue that the principle of circularity is one of the cornerstones of self-referential systems thinking because it points out that: "circularity, (. . .), can help us to understand fundamental phenomena, such as self-organization, goal-directedness, identity, and life, in a way that had escaped Newtonian science" (2001, p. 9). The circular relationship between the system's structure and its adaptive capacities is highlighted by the concept *emergence*. Emergence acknowledges how specific survivable patterns of relationships, or interactions, can emerge out of indeterminate relationships ("chaos") (e.g., Waldrop, 1992).

The concept of emergence and the principle of circularity highlight the intertwined relationship between self-organization and system structures within a self-referential systems perspective. Within organization science, contributions that can be interpreted as possessing self-referential characteristics, hence theorize on characteristics of the "inside" of an organization that influence self-organization of employees in such a way that it impacts adaptability and survivability of the organizational "system" against the background of a changing environment. As a consequence, a major difference between organizational design theories that can be interpreted as having "self-referential" properties and an "open systems" perspective on organizational design, is that "self-referential" contributions elaborate on ways in which the organizational skeleton, or "inside" of an organization influences self-organizing abilities of employees, given that it has to deal with an uncertain environment. For example, Morgan (2006, pp. 95–105) uses the metaphor of the holography to point to the notion that labor divided in a "holographic" (i.e. recursive) way facilitates the organization's survivability in a dynamic environment. Similar self-referential ideas can be found in socio-technical systems design (STSD) and IOR in particular. De Sitter (1994) for example, points out that grouping and coupling activities in a particular way facilitates self-organizing abilities of operators, which subsequently is thought to improve flexibility at the organizational level.

Summing up, from a self-referential systems perspective, dealing with environmental uncertainty can be interpreted as "bounded", or selective (cf. Blom & Haas, 1996), adaptation. A self-referential perspective on organizational design hence acknowledges that organizational design both enables and restricts the organization's options to adapt to environmental demands, due to the influences of design characteristics on self-organizing abilities of employees.

2.2.1.4 A Systems Theory Perspective on Organizational Design and Dealing With High-Risk Conditions in Expeditionary Organizations

A self-referential systems perspective and accompanying assumptions on the relation between organizational design, self-organization and emergence seems to suit the goal of this book best. That is to say, this book is interested in finding out in what way expeditionary organization design influences dealing with high-risk conditions, in which dealing with high-risk conditions was conceptualized by means of the concepts self-organization and the emergence of safety at the organizational level. As such, it can

Table 2.1 3 × 2 matrix on the relation between systems theory and organizational design

Level A systems theoretical premises		**Reducing environmental uncertainty by**	**Organizational design assumptions for dealing with environmental uncertainty**
	Classic	Creating and maintaining stability and predictability	Top-down design of control loops
	Open	"Absolute" adaptation	Aimed at maximum variation and adaptability
	Self-referential	Bounded or selective adaptation	Aspects of design influence "self-organization" and adaption at the organizational level

be argued that theories on safety during high-risk operations that enable getting a deeper understanding of this relationship, have to address the "circular" relationship between characteristics of organizational design and safety, in which safety should be conceptualized by means of self-organization and emergence. This emphasizes that such theories have to possess either an implicit or explicit self-referential systems perspective that is systematically translated into premises on organizational design, safety and their relationship. The questions subsequently addressed in the next sections therefore are these: 1) to what extent can (explicit or implicit) self-referential systems theory assumptions be found in the three frequently used theories, 2) to what extent are these assumptions systematically translated into conceptualizations of organization design, safety and the relationship between these concepts and 3) do the three frequently used theories enable understanding the relationship between organizational design, self-organization and the emergence of safety in expeditionary organizations?

To facilitate finding an answer on the three questions formulated, in the 3 × 2 matrix in Table 2.1, the relationships between systems-theoretical premises and assumptions on the role of an organization's design on the ability to adapt to environmental uncertainty are explicated.

2.3 Three Frequently Used Theories on Safety During High-Risk Operations

In this section, three frequently used theories on safety during high-risk operations are explicated: resilience engineering theory (e.g., Hollnagel et al., 2006; Hollnagel, 2012), Normal Accidents Theory (Perrow, 1999) and High Reliability Theory (e.g., Weick & Sutcliffe, 2007).

2.3.1 Resilience Engineering Theory

Resilience engineering theory aims to account for the problem that quite often work situations seem to be dynamic and that aiming for a stable "steady state" may not be the best way to attain safety in such dynamic situations. Although Jens Rasmussen (e.g., 1994, 1997) did not label his own work as "resilience engineering theory", it can be argued that he was one of the first theorists who addressed the influence of operational dynamics on safety as a reaction to the then dominant "human error" approach in safety science. Moreover, resilience engineering theory seems to be building on Rasmussen's theoretical premises, such as in the work of one of the main contributors to resilience engineering theory, Erik Hollnagel (e.g., 2012; Hollnagel & Goteman, 2004).

In his 1997 article, Rasmussen pointed to the effects of "dynamic" operational conditions on managing safety. He stated that:

> Control of activities and their safety by the classic prescriptive command-and-control approach deriving rules of conduct top-down may be effective in a stable society where instruction and work tools at all levels can be based on task analysis. In the present dynamic situation, this approach is inadequate and a fundamentally different view on system modeling is required.
>
> (p. 185)

In the same paper, Rasmussen proposes that: "safety in the direct interaction with the work environment must be based on an identification of the boundary of safe performance by analysis of the work system, and the criteria that drive the continuous adaptive modification of behavior" (1997, p. 206). In line with Rasmussen, Woods (in Hollnagel et al., 2006, p. 22) states: "Resilience then concerns the ability to recognize and adapt to handle unanticipated perturbations that call into question the model of competence, and demand a shift of processes, strategies and coordination". These quotes highlight that instead of reducing deviations in order to ensure stability, resilience engineering theory acknowledges that it might be impossible to remove all uncertainty in many organizational settings. Consequently, resilience engineering emphasizes that organizations should cope with this uncertainty and consequently focuses on how an organization might adapt safely.

A more recent development within resilience engineering is the concept "functional resonance" and the accompanying Functional Resonance Analysis Method (FRAM; e.g., Hollnagel, 2012; Hollnagel & Goteman, 2004). FRAM aims to understand and analyze the influence of organizational dynamics on safe performance and incorporates such an understanding into an organizational safety management method. For understanding "functional resonance" and FRAM, the underlying concepts "intractability" and "emergence" are central. According to Hollnagel, large socio-technical systems are (partly) intractable. This means that: "the conditions of work are underspecified, in principle as well as in practice. To the latter must be added the fact that resources materials, manpower, information and especially time usually are limited and sometimes insufficient" (Hollnagel, 2012, p. 24). So, while classic safety theories often aim for a detailed description of the production process of an organization in order to come up with solutions, the concept of intractability points to the issue that such efforts will always come up short. Therefore, according to Hollnagel, understanding the influence of dynamics on safety should start with looking at "emerging" relationships at the operational level that come into existence in doing everyday work (2012, p. 25). To get insight into these emerging relationships, he proposes to define an organizational system on the basis of "functions" instead of "structures". Hollnagel writes:

> Systems are usually defined with reference to their structure, that is, in terms of their parts and how they are connected or put together. (. . .) It is, however, entirely possible to define a system in a different way, namely in terms of how it functions rather than in terms of what the components are and how they are put together. From this perspective, a system is a set of coupled or mutually dependent functions.
>
> (p. 6)

According to Hollnagel, safety issues too may arise as a result of emergence because the performance of functions is subject to variability that originates from the: "approximate adjustments of people, individually and collectively and of organizations that are the basis of everyday functioning" (2012, p. 29). Consequently, in a system of interdependent functions "the functions may interact or combine so that a specific function is incorrectly performed or even missed" (Hollnagel & Goteman, 2004). This is referred to as "resonance". To identify potential sources for resonance and prevent safety consequences from emerging, Hollnagel (2012, p. 36) proposes to do the following:

1. Identify functions that are required for everyday work to succeed.
2. Characterize the variability of these functions.
3. Look at a specific state and determine how functions may become coupled.
4. Propose ways to manage the possible occurrences of performance variability.

To describe functions and visualize their interaction, Hollnagel proposes a hexagonal representation in which the performance of each function is specified in six characteristics (2012, p. 46). In addition to the inputs, outputs, controls and resources that are often motioned in safety management theory (see Hale, Heming, Carthey, & Kirwan, 1997), Hollnagel proposes to add the notion of "time" and "necessary preconditions" to the analysis of functions because any function is in some sense governed by time and almost all functions need "something that has to exist" before the function can be carried out (2012, p. 46). Hollnagel explicitly points to the notion that the hexagonal model is to be used to both visualize the functions themselves and the interaction between functions as people in the organization adapt to a particular situation.

Summing up, resilience engineering aims to account for the constantly changing nature of dynamic operational conditions. Attaining safe operations, from the perspective of resilience engineering, is not about removing deviations on the basis of pre-defined criteria. Instead resilience engineering theory intends to get insight into the organization's adaptation process to dynamic operational situations. FRAM aims to do so by highlighting the concepts of "intractability" and "emergence", defining the organization in terms of "functions" instead of "structures" and consequently identifying resonating functions in order to propose ways to manage performance variability of these functions.

2.3.2 Normal Accidents Theory

In the aftermath of a major incident at the nuclear power plant of Three Mile Island, Charles Perrow developed his Normal Accidents Theory (NAT; 1999). The major premise of NAT is that accidents in particular organizations are inevitable. Due to their design, such organizations will eventually experience a serious accident without any major technical failure or human error. Instead, small failures eventually add up to failure of the entire system.

Before detailing the specific characteristics of organizations that, according to NAT, have particularly high chances of experiencing a "normal accident", Perrow (1999, pp. 65–66) distinguishes different "system levels" within the organization: a part, a unit and a sub-system. Parts refer to single parts such as a particular valve. A unit refers to a "functional collection of parts" such as a steam generator. Subsequently, a sub-system refers to a cluster of units such as the cooling system of a nuclear power plant. The entire "system" (i.e. a nuclear power plant) is then comprised of several sub-systems. Consequently, he distinguishes between an incident and an accident. An incident refers to the failure of a part or unit, an accident to the failure of a sub-system or the disruption of the entire system. After that, he defines two types of accidents: component failure accidents and system accidents. Component failure accidents "involve one or more component failures (part, unit, sub-system) that are linked in an unanticipated sequence" (Perrow, 1999, p. 70). System accidents "involve the unanticipated interaction of multiple failures" (ibid.).

Central in Perrow's theory are the concepts *coupling* and *interaction*. Coupling refers to the degree of interdependence between elements.[4] When the operations of one element requires the output of another element as its input, these elements are tightly coupled. When these elements are loosely coupled, they do not rely on each other's in or output in order to function properly, as a result they can operate independently from each other. With regard to interaction, Perrow distinguishes linear and complex interaction. Linear interaction between organizational elements occurs when elements interact exactly as designed. Complex interaction occurs when unexpected interactions between elements take place. According to Perrow, a combination of tight coupling and complex interaction in any organization is a recipe for disaster. That is to say, such organizations are confronted with incompatible control demands. At the one hand, Perrow argues that tight coupling requires centralized control because local insight into the dependencies between the elements of the system is limited. Complex interaction, on the other hand, requires decentralized control because operators may have the best understanding of the specifics of the system's elements and can solve disturbances before interactions become complex at the central level. Because to Perrow the control problem in tightly coupled and complex interacting organizations is fundamentally unsolvable, these organizations run the inevitable risk of a system accident. He uses the phrase "normal accident" because, to Perrow, a system accident is a "normal" consequence of the way these particular organizations are designed.

2.3.3 High Reliability Theory

Extensive research into the daily operations of, amongst other organizations, aircraft carriers has resulted in the identification of strategies and processes that are believed to produce impressive safety records in high-risk organizations (Sagan, 1993, p. 15). High Reliability Theory (HRT), also referred to as High Reliability Organizing (HRO; e.g., LaPorte & Consolini, 1991; LaPorte & Rochlin, 1994; Roberts, 1993; Weick & Sutcliffe, 2007), can be interpreted as being developed as a "reaction" to NAT. High reliability theorists point to interactive processes between operators that are thought to be able to overcome the dangers of tight coupling and complex interaction pointed out by NAT. According to Sagan, high reliability theorists focus on hazardous organizations that have achieved nearly error-free operations through "intelligent organizational design and management" (1993, p. 14). Early HRT theorizing identified redundancy, decentralization and "conceptual slack" as such reliability enhancing strategies (cf. Rijpma, 1997).

Firstly, with regard to redundancy Rochlin, LaPorte, and Roberts (1987) pointed out that, on aircraft carriers, a particular kind of redundancy was present: decision/management redundancy,[5] which ensured that critical decisions are timely and correct. As much safety-critical information is spread constantly through the organization in order to "assure that any critical element that is out of place will be discovered or noticed by someone before it causes a problem" (Rochlin et al., 1987). Also, decision/management redundancy entails the creation of "shadow units" that, if necessary, can take over the tasks of other units immediately (Rochlin et al., ibid). A second strategy is decentralization of authority. Next to an organization that possesses redundancy, high reliability theorists stress the relevance of decentralization (Rijpma, 1997). Sagan (1993, p. 22) argues that operators must have considerable decision-making authority concerning safety issues. Rijpma points out that "this is done in order to solve problems as they emerge" (1997, p. 17). Decentralization is often associated with a "culture of reliability". As Rijpma points out such a culture:

> imbues members of the organization with clear operational goals, decision premises and assumptions. It gives them the competence and autonomy to respond to complex interactions, once these reach the surface, and correct them before tightly-coupled processes are set in motion which might lead to disaster.
>
> (ibid.)

Thirdly, Rijpma (1997) points to Schulman's notion of "conceptual slack". According to Schulman (1993): "Conceptual slack is a divergence in analytical perspectives among members of an organization over theories, models, or causal assumptions pertaining to its technology or production processes". Hence, by deliberately creating discussion and reflection conceptual slack is thought to create a certain "buffer" in the actions of operators in order to improve safety.

More recent theorizing in HRT can be interpreted as building on the work of Weick and Sutcliffe (2007). Weick and Sutcliffe highlight that dealing with the unexpected is influenced by existing "expectations" that create "blind spots" within the organization. Such expectations are based on existing "roles, routines and strategies" (Weick & Sutcliffe, 2007, p. 23). Expectations hinder dealing with the unexpected because they encourage searching for confirmation while filtering out evidence that does not confirm our expectations. Weick and Sutcliffe propose the concept of mindfulness to overcome these problems and deal with the unexpected successfully. They (2007, p. 18) define mindfulness as "a rich awareness of discriminatory detail" and continue with the following: "By that we mean that when people act, they are aware of context, of ways in which details differ, and of deviations from their expectations".

Weick and Sutcliffe subsequently argue that highly reliable organizations possess a "mindful infrastructure" in order to deal with the "unexpected". According to Weick and Sutcliffe, such a mindful infrastructure enables organizations to:

> organize themselves in such a way that they are better able to notice the unexpected and halt its development. If they have difficulty halting the development of the unexpected they focus on containing it. And if the unexpected breaks through the containment, they focus on resilience and swift restoration of system functioning.
>
> (ibid.)

Weick and Sutcliffe subsequently advocate five principles that enable organizations to develop a mindful infrastructure and deal with the unexpected successfully and safely. These five principles are divided into three principles of anticipation and two principles of containment (Weick & Sutcliffe, 2007, pp. 45–82). Anticipation, according to Weick and Sutcliffe, deals with the ability to sense small disparities and stop the development of undesired events. Containment, according to Weick and Sutcliffe, refers to abilities "to prevent unwanted outcomes after an unexpected event has occurred" (2007, p. 65). Their three principles of anticipation are preoccupation with failure, reluctance to simplify and sensitivity to operations. Their principles of containment are commitment to resilience and deference to expertise. Preoccupation with failure entails practices that are aimed to spot so-called weak signals. Even when operations are taking place within predetermined safety margins "missteps, missing resources, miscommunications or mistakes have to be found and put right before they can turn into a tragic flaw" (2007, p. 47). Reluctance to simplify refers to the ability to scrutinize existing expectations, labels and categories in order to prevent deviations to propagate through the organization unnoticed (2007, pp. 53–58). Sensitivity to operations "is about work itself, about seeing what we are actually doing regardless of what we were supposed to do based on intentions, designs and plans" (2007, p. 59). After an unexpected event has happened, Weick and Sutcliffe quote Wildavsky in defining "commitment to resilience" and state:

> The mode of resilience is based on the assumption that unexpected trouble is ubiquitous and unpredictable; and thus accurate advance information on how to get out of it is short in supply. To learn from error and to implement learning through fast negative feedback, which dampens oscillations are at the forefront of operating resiliently.
>
> (p. 69)

Resilience, according to Weick and Sutcliffe, has three components: "the ability to absorb strain and preserve functioning despite the presence of adversity", "An ability to recover or bounce back from untoward events" and "an ability to learn and grow from previous episodes" (2007, p. 71). The fifth principle, deference to expertise, refers to the ability to "migrate decisions both up and down" in order to ensure that early warning signs are noticed and acted upon (2007, p. 74). As Weick and Sutcliffe highlight, this poses challenges to hierarchy within the organization. Therefore, as they point out, a "mindful culture" loosens hierarchy in favor of expertise, which is mostly located at the operational level. They also stress, that "expertise" is a relational concept: "expertise is an assemblage of knowledge, experience, learning and institutions that is seldom embodied in a single individual".

2.4 Analysis

The analysis presented in this section will confront the three theories with the analytical framework in order to investigate and explicate how these theories conceptualize on organization design, safety and the relationship between these concepts. This is done to subsequently establish whether these theories can be used as an integral conceptual framework for studying the relationship between expeditionary organizational design, self-organization and the emergence of safety in expeditionary organizations. By doing so, this section will answer the three aforementioned questions:

1. To what extent can (explicit or implicit) self-referential systems theory assumptions be found in the three frequently used theories?
2. To what extent are these assumptions systematically translated into conceptualizations of organization design, safety and the relationship between these concepts?
3. Do the three frequently used theories enable understanding the relationship between organizational design, self-organization and the emergence of safety in expeditionary organizations?

2.4.1 Analyzing Resilience Engineering Theory

In contrast to keeping organizational behavior between predetermined boundaries and closing the organization to environmental change, Rasmussen (1997) pointed out that attaining safety in organizations with "dynamic" operations should not be based on traditional assumptions of "command and control". Instead, attaining safety, according to Rasmussen, should be based on: "an identification of the boundary of safe performance by analysis of the work system, and the criteria that drive the continuous adaptive modification of behavior". To cope with, or manage, such dynamics and "become resilient", Woods argued that the organization needs to "adapt to handle unanticipated perturbations that call into question the model of competence, and demand a shift of processes, strategies and coordination" (2006, p. 22). In this sense, it can be argued that the relationship between organization design and safety, which seems to be present in resilience engineering theory, is that organizations should "move along" with environmental demands. This can be interpreted as a straightforward assumption from an "open systems" perspective on the relation between organizational design and adaptation. That is to say, open systems theory emphasized that to adapt to a changing environment and cope with environmental uncertainty, the relationships between elements within the system have to vary along with environmental change.

Some "self-referential" traces of explicit attention for the influence of the "inside" of the organization on safety can be found too in the works of Woods and Hollnagel. That is to say, Woods points to the influence of "processes, strategies and coordination" on adaptability and safety. Also, Hollnagel's concept of functional resonance seems have a particular interpretation of the relationship between characteristics of the inside of an organization and safety. In terms of Hollnagel, interacting functions hinder each other in their outcome, they "resonate". FRAM consequently proposes ways to reduce "functional resonance" within the organization. In this sense, resilience engineering theory seems to address particular influences of the organizational "inside" to safety outcomes, in which several aspects of this "inside" of the organization are related to adaptability and the emergence of safety. However, applicability of these definitions to expeditionary organizations is questioned. That is to say, in the previous chapter it was pointed out that design in expeditionary organizations was characterized by underspecification of the organizational "skeleton", which seems to point to a different problem than the influence of existing rules and procedures and resonating "functions". So, although FRAM and resilience engineering addresses some influences of organizational design on safety, it seems to be unable to get a deeper understanding of this relationship in expeditionary organizations. By means of the arguments presented below, is argued that problems with the applicability of FRAM are mainly due to an inconsistent systems-theoretical foundation that guides Hollnagel's deliberate choice to turn away from "structure" in favor of "functions".

Firstly, Hollnagel justifies his choice for functions over structure by arguing that a focus on functions enables one to study what the system "does", instead of what it "is". In a 2004 case study on the application of FRAM to operations of a navigation instrument for flight operations, Hollnagel and Goteman write:

> structure, however, represents the normative organization of functions, when everything goes according to plan. Since it is unrealistic

> to assume that this will always be the case, it is preferable to use a representation that makes it possible to account for how events may develop in reality.
>
> (p. 4)

Later on, they point out that an assumption in this particular case study is that "the steady-state performance of the underlying air navigation infrastructure and operational structure is assumed to be acceptable as it is". It is argued that these quotes reveal two, somewhat related, things: 1) FRAM has rather implicit "classic" assumptions on the concept of organizational structure that results in 2) the inability of FRAM to relate design of organizational structures to safety outcomes.

To highlight the first point, a classic systems perspective emphasized structure as something "static", created and controlled by a "normative order" in order to maintain a "steady state" within the organization. In their 2004 case study, Hollnagel and Goteman explicitly point out that, in their interpretation, structure refers to the "normative organization of functions", which clearly points to the notion that for Hollnagel, structure is something fixed and prescribed. This seems to point to "classic" systems theory assumptions present in FRAM. So, where FRAM at the one hand seems to be using some aspects of self-referential systems theory, assumptions on the relation between organizational structures and safety has rather implicit classic foundations.

Secondly, and probably due to this inconsistent mix of explicit and implicit assumptions from systems theory, Hollnagel's argues that "when things do not go according to plan" organizational structures become irrelevant. This seems to be in contrast with the experiences of operating in an expeditionary organization, that were highlighted in Chapter 1. As was already briefly mentioned in Chapter 1, in military expeditionary organizations, things rarely go as planned. Instead of becoming less relevant, Snook showed that organizational structures seem to become *more* relevant for safety during expeditionary operations. Moreover, Hollnagel specifically turns to "functions" instead of "structure" because to his interpretation, interactions between functions have "emergent" properties. However, his theorizing seems to have no account for the central concept of "circularity" within self-referential systems theory. That is to say, it was argued that the central premise of self-referential thinking is that interactions between elements within the system are influenced by properties of system structures. Interactions between functions in FRAM, however, are not described in reference to any characteristics of system structure because Hollnagel deliberately chooses to strike "structure" from the equation. As such, Hollnagel fails to theorize on the influence of an organization's structural "inside" on emergence, survivability and, eventually, the emergence of safety. In addition, Hollnagel's concept of "emergence" does not seem to refer to the emergence of "order" out of "chaos", as it is defined within complexity science (e.g., Kelly, 1994; Waldrop, 1992). In Hollnagel's terms, the process of emergence can go either way, resulting in either improved adaptability of the system or in an accident. In terms of self-referential systems theory however, an accident cannot be defined as "emerging" because it does not refer to any survivable state of the system (cf. Kramer & Moorkamp, 2017). A safety issue, such as an accident or near miss, may therefore only be interpreted as a symptom of a system with characteristics of problematic survivability instead of an "emergent" system property.

Summing up, resilience engineering theory and FRAM addressed some aspects of the relation between organizational design and safety. However, it was pointed out that the aspects that were addressed did not match the characteristics of expeditionary organizations that were pointed out in Chapter 1. For FRAM, this could be related to an inconsistent application of concepts from systems theory. Due to these issues, resilience engineering and FRAM cannot be applied to get a deeper understanding of the relationship between organizational design, self-organization and safety in expeditionary organizations.

2.4.2 Analyzing Normal Accidents Theory

Although self-organization as a concept is not central to NAT, it seems to explicitly relate organizational structural design characteristics to safety outcomes at the organizational level. Perrow's concepts of "coupling" and "interaction" address characteristics of the way elements (parts, subunits and units) within the organization are connected to each other in a particular structural design. Furthermore, he addresses how a combination of tight coupling and complex interaction is a recipe for disaster. In this sense, Perrow's theory clearly relates aspects of organizational design to organizational outcomes. As such, his theory shows implicit traces of a self-referential systems foundation. That is to say, he addresses how particular characteristics of the organizational "inside" influence outcomes at the level of the organization. In this way Perrow seems to account for some aspects of the "circularity" concept, which was regarded as the cornerstone of self-referential systems thinking by Heylighen and Joslyn (2001).

However, it is argued that despite the explicit relation between organizational structure and safety and apparent traces from "self-referential" systems thinking, NAT is not worked out in such a way that enables it to provide suitable ingredients for getting a deeper understanding on the influence of organizational design on self-organization and the emergence of safety in expeditionary organizations. It is argued so for two reasons. Firstly, originating from the Three Mile Island nuclear power facility, NAT's concepts of coupling and interaction seem be tailored to describe characteristics of an already existing (i.e. non-temporary) organizational design. That is to say, his conceptualization of mainly point to parts, units and sub-systems that are relating to each other in a particular existing setup. Subsequently it can be argued that the concepts that Perrow developed to describe the relation between aspects of design and safety outcomes are only suitable for analyzing organizations in which relationships between parts, units and sub-systems are already specified. The result of previous research in expeditionary organizations however, indicated that within expeditionary organizations design is underdeveloped (see also Thompson, 1967, p. 53). Hence, it can be argued that NAT does not match this key characteristic of expeditionary organizations and, hence, NAT cannot be applied to get a deeper understanding of the relationship between organizational design and safety in expeditionary organizations.

Secondly, NAT seems to be unable to theorize on safety in dynamically complex contexts. For Perrow, complexity does not seem to relate to uncertainty, ambiguity and reactiveness of an organization's environment. Instead, it seems to point to "noise" that in combination with a tightly coupled and complex technological design results in crippling internal complexity within the organization. Internal complexity and dynamic complexity are, however, not the same thing. As such, NAT is regarded as unsuitable for getting an understanding of the relationship between organizational design, self-organization and the emergence of safety in expeditionary organizations.

2.4.3 Analyzing High Reliability Theory

Within HRT multiple aspects of organizational design are addressed in relation to adaptability, self-organization and safety. For example, Weick and Sutcliffe (2007) point out that anticipation strategies of operators are influenced by procedures that can create "blind spots" in their ability to cope with unexpected events. Also, Sagan (1993) pointed out that early developments of HRT were aimed at achieving nearly error free high-risk operations through "intelligent organizational design and management". In this sense, it can be interpreted that HRT seems to have traces of an explicit "self-referential" perspective on the relation between organization design and safety outcomes. However, despite such attention for the relationship between aspects of design and safety, it is argued that HRT does not enable getting a deeper understanding of the relationship between organizational design and safety in expeditionary organizations. By means of the three arguments presented here it is pointed out that this is mainly due to a rather arbitrary conceptualization of organization design present in HRT.

Firstly, Rochlin et al. (1987) pointed to "management redundancy", which they defined as fast and timely information sharing to improve coordination and communication. Rochlin et al., however, do not address the underlying organizational "skeleton" in their lessons for improving coordination and communication. Improving coordination and communication without addressing the underlying configuration of units, may consequently result in treating symptoms of an ill-designed organization. That is to say, Kramer (2007; Kramer et al., 2012) relates problems in cooperation and flexibility in military expeditionary organizations to underspecification of design in these organizations. Hence, improving coordination and communication in expeditionary organizations may be able to "repair" symptoms of underspecification that expeditionary organizations face during operations, but it does not address the underlying design problem that may cause these issues in the first place. Furthermore, Rochlin et al. propose the creation of "shadow units" that are able to relieve other units of tasks in order to ensure continuity of operations. Their definition of shadow units however may end up providing "redundancy in parts" instead of "redundancy in functions". That is to say, creating shadow units that can replace other units one-on-one, seems to refer to redundancy in parts. Regarding redundancy in parts, Streeter (1991, p. 169) points out that "systems designed on the principle of redundancy in parts are organized and can be reorganized but do not have the ability to *self-organize*" (italics added). This may limit the applicability of the "shadow unit" concept to expeditionary organizations, as self-organization was regarded as relevant for developing safety in expeditionary organizations.

Secondly, Rijpma (1997) pointed to local autonomy of workers and decentralization of authority as an important pillar of HRT. However, it is well known that local autonomy is largely influenced by the nature of the organizational structure, or the way labor is divided within an organization (see, for example, Mintzberg, 1980). Maximum division of labor, for example, results in workstations with little autonomy. Hence implementing Rijpma's advice without addressing the nature of the underlying organizational structure may result in advising to increase autonomy in organizations in which a lack of local autonomy is structurally hindered.

Thirdly, the concept of "mindful infrastructure" (Weick & Sutcliffe, 2007) in later HRT developments is addressed. Weick and Sutcliffe point out that in highly reliable organizations, people organize themselves in ways that improve the ability of the organization to operate safely during challenging high-risk operations. They point to three principles of anticipation and two principles of containment that, in their perspective, foster a self-organizing process and result in the creation of mindful infrastructures within the organization. The concept of mindful infrastructure, however, does not account for the influence of design on repertoires of activity and routines of operators. This may be due to Weick's (e.g., 1979) definition of "structures" which is quite different from the definition used in organizational design theory. Organization science however, points out that the way labor is divided is a main source of such activity repertoires and routines (see, for example, Kuipers et al., 2010). Hence, an organization's design can be interpreted as an important source for "blind spots" and which may subsequently influence the ability of workers to self-organize and develop mindful infrastructures.

As a result of this analysis it can be argued that, both early and later developments of HRT show clear traces of "self-referential" systems thinking because it relates some aspects of "the inside" of organizations, such as rules and procedures, to self-organization and safety at the level of the organization. However, HRT fails to systematically theorize on the relation between organization design, self-organization and safety during high-risk operations. This renders HRT unsuitable as a perspective that can be integrally used to get a deeper understanding of the relationship between organizational design, self-organization and the emergence of safety in expeditionary organizations.

2.5 Conclusion

This chapter has reviewed three frequently used theories on safety during high-risk operations. The analysis has shown that, although some aspects of organizational design were explicitly related to self-organization and safety outcomes, all three theories were unsuitable as an integral conceptual framework for research on the relationship between organizational design, self-organization and the emergence of safety in expeditionary organizations. Some of these issues were attributed to inconsistent and implicit application of concepts from systems theory, for example in the case of FRAM. Other issues, for example in HRT, seemed to be originating from inconsistent application of the organization design concept. It should be noted, however, that although the analysis in this chapter is quite critical to the three theories reviewed with regard to their applicability as an integral conceptual framework, elements of these theories may be of added value in explaining particular phenomena related to safety during high-risk operations. The studies presented in the following chapters therefore remain sensitive to such added value. Nevertheless, the next chapter will start with taking a first step in "filling" the gap in theorizing on safety during high-risk operations by using Integral Organizational Renewal theory, introduced in Chapter 1, as a conceptual "compass" in studying ways in which organizational design influenced self-organization and the emergence of safety for 107 ASBt's operations within Task Force Uruzgan.

Notes

1. Some parts of this chapter were published as Moorkamp, Kramer, Van Gulijk and Ale (2014).
2. In the remainder of this chapter, the term "systems theory" will be used to refer to General Systems Theory (cf. Boulding, 1956).

3. It should be noted that within both systems theory and organization science, major differences exist in for example, definitions on what "elements" are and what "structure" is. To some extent, this will be explicated in the later sections. However, the main goal of the section below is not to contribute to these discussions on the definitions of "structure" or "elements" but to present fundamental differences in major streams of theorizing within organization science on the relation between the "inside" of an organization, its design in abstract terms and its ability to deal with, or adapt to, environmental dynamics.
4. Deliberately the word "element" is used here because, along NAT, it may refer to a part, unit or sub-system.
5. Rochlin et al. (1987) also stressed the importance of technical and supply redundancy for high reliable operations. Only decision/management redundancy is highlighted earlier because technical and supply redundancy are not directly relating to aspects of organizational design.

References

Achterbergh, J., & Vriens, D. (2010). *Organizations: Social systems conducting experiments*. Berlin: Springer Verlag.

Blom, C. (1997). *Complexiteit en Contingentie*. Kampen: Kok Agora.

Blom, C., & Haas, B. (1996). De ondragelijke lichtheid van systemen. *Tijdschrift Voor Sociologie*, *17*(2), 187–204.

Boulding, K. E. (1956). General systems theory—The skeleton of science. *Management science*, *2*(3), 197–208.

Donaldson, L. (2006). The contingency theory of organizational design: Challenges and opportunities. In R. Burton, D. Håkonsson, B. Eriksen, & C. Snow (Eds.), *Organization design* (pp. 19–40). Boston, MA: Springer Verlag.

Grote, G. (2012). Safety management in different high-risk domains-all the same? *Safety Science*, *50*, 1983–1992.

Hale, A. R., Heming, B. H. J., Carthey, J., & Kirwan, B. (1997). Modelling of safety management systems. *Safety Science*, *26*(12), 121–140.

Heylighen, F., & Joslyn, C. (2001). Cybernetics and second order cybernetics. *Encyclopedia of Physical Science & Technology*, *4*, 155–170.

Hollnagel, E. (2012). *Fram: The functional resonance analysis method, modelling complex socio-technical systems*. Farnham: Ashgate Publishing.

Hollnagel, E., & Goteman, O. (2004, November 4–5). The functional resonance accident model. *Cognitive System Engineering in Process Control*, 155–161.

Hollnagel, E., Woods, D. D., & Leveson, N. (2006). *Resilience engineering: Concepts and precepts*. Boca Raton, FL: CRC Press.

Kelly, K. (1994). *Out of control: The new biology of machines, social systems, and the economic world*. New York: Perseus.

Kramer, E. H. (2004). *Organizing doubt: Self-organization and army units in crisis operations* (Doctoral dissertation). Eindhoven: Eindhoven University of Technology.

Kramer, E. H. (2007). *Organizing doubt: Grounded theory, army units and dealing with dynamic complexity* (Vol. 22). Copenhagen: Copenhagen Business School Press.

Kramer, E. H., & Moorkamp, M. (2017). Understanding organizational vulnerabilities in military taskforces. In R. Beeres, G. Bakx, E. De Waard, & S. Rietjens

(Eds.), *NL ARMS Netherlands annual review 2016* (pp. 21–40). The Hague: T.M.C. Asser Press.

Kramer, E. H., de Waard, E. J., & de Graaff, M. C. (2012). Task Force Uruzgan and experimentation with organization design. In R. Beeres, J. Van der Meulen, J. M. M. L. Soeters, & A. L. W. Vogelaar (Eds.), *Mission Uruzgan*. Amsterdam: Amsterdam University Press.

Kuipers, H., van Amelsvoort, P., & Kramer, E. H. (2010). *Het Nieuwe Organiseren: alternatieven voor de bureaucratie*. The Hague: Acco.

LaPorte, T. R., & Consolini, P. M. (1991). Working in practice but not in theory. *Journal of Public Administration Research and Theory*, *1*(1), 19–47.

LaPorte, T. R., & Rochlin, G. (1994). A rejoinder to Perrow. *Journal of Contingencies and Crisis Management*, *2*(4), 221–227.

Luhmann, N. (1990). *Essays on self-reference*. New York: Columbia University Press.

Maturana, H. R. (1980). *Autopoiesis and cognition: The realization of the living* (Vol. 42). Dordrecht: Springer Verlag.

Mintzberg, H. (1980). Structure in 5's: A synthesis of the research on organization design. *Management Science*, *26*(3), 322–341.

Moorkamp, M., Kramer, E. H. van Gulijk, C., & Ale, B. (2014). Safety management theory and the expeditionary organization: A critical theoretical reflection. *Safety Science*, *69*, 71–81.

Morgan, G. (2006). *Images of organization*. Thousand Oaks: Sage Publications, Inc.

Perrow, C. (1999). *Normal accidents: Living with high-risk technologies*. Princeton: Princeton University Press.

Rasmussen, J. (1994). Risk management, adaptation, and design for safety. In B. Brehmer & N. E. Sahlin (Eds.), *Future risks and risk management*. Dordrecht: Kluwer.

Rasmussen, J. (1997). Risk management in a dynamic society: A modelling problem. *Safety Science*, *27*(2–3), 183–213.

Reiman, T., & Rollenhagen, C. (2011). Human and organizational biases affecting the management of safety. *Reliability Engineering & Systems Safety*, *96*(10), 1263–1274.

Rijpma, J. A. (1997). Complexity, tight-coupling and reliability: Connecting normal accidents theory and high reliability theory. *Journal of Contingencies and Crisis Management*, *5*(1), 15–23.

Roberts, K. H. (1993). Introduction. In K. H. Roberts (Ed.), *New challenges to understanding organizations* (pp. 1–10). New York: Palgrave Macmillan.

Rochlin, G., LaPorte, T. R., & Roberts, K. H. (1987). The self-designing high-reliability organization: Aircraft carrier flight operations at sea. *Naval War College Review*, *40*(4), 76–90.

Sagan, S. D. (1993). *The limits of safety*. Princeton: Princeton University Press.

Schreyögg, G. (1980). Contingency and choice in organization theory. *Organization Science*, *1*(4), 305–326.

Schulman, P. (1993). The negotiated order of organizational reliability. *Administration & Society*, *25*(3), 353–372.

Sitter, L. U. de. (1994). *Synergetisch produceren: Human Resources Mobilisation in de produktie een inleiding in structuurbouw*. Assen: Uitgeverij Van Gorcum.

Streeter, C. L. (1991). Redundancy in social systems: Implications for warning and evacuation planning. *International Journal of Mass Emergencies and Disasters*, *9*(2), 167–182.

Thompson, J. D. (1967). *Organizations in action*. New York: McGraw-Hill.
van Strien, P. J. (1986). *Praktijk als wetenschap. Methodologie van het sociaal-wetenschappelijk handelen*. Assen: Uitgeverij Van Gorcum.
Waldrop, M. M. (1992). *Complexity: The emerging science at the edge of order and chaos*. New York: Simon & Schuster.
Weick, K. E. (1979). *The social psychology of organizing*. New York: McGraw-Hill.
Weick, K. E., & Sutcliffe, K. M. (2007). *Managing the unexpected*. San Francisco: Jossey-Bass.
Woods, D. D. (2006). Essential characteristics of resilience. In E. Hollnagel, D. D. Woods, & N. Leveson (Eds.), *Resilience engineering: Concepts and precepts*. Hampshire: Ashgate Publishing.

3 Temporary Organization Design and Its Implications for Operations With Unmanned Aerial Vehicles in Afghanistan[1]

3.1 Introduction

It turned out that the three frequently used theories described in Chapter 2 could not be used as an integral conceptual framework for getting a deeper understanding of the relationship between organizational design, self-organization and the emergence of safety in expeditionary organizations. Hence, this chapter takes the first step in attempting to "fill" this gap by means of an empirical exploration. This chapter aims at answering the second research question, which is this:

> **What aspects of organizational design influenced self-organization of 107 Aerial Systems battery and the emergence of safety during their operations within Task Force Uruzgan?**

As was also addressed briefly in Chapter 1, the first empirical study of this book is carried out on the expeditionary operations of the 107th Aerial Systems Battery (107 ASBt) of the Royal Netherlands Army. This unit performed multiple expeditionary missions within Task Force Uruzgan between 2006 and 2009. The main reason for choosing this unit as a starting point for the empirical investigations in this book is that both the unit itself and the task force were "mixed and matched" out of different units from the military parent organizations in the Netherlands. Hence, starting at this unit enables exploring the relation between organization design and self-organization and the emergence of safety at the level of the unit itself and at the level of the task force. Of course, choosing to explore from the perspective of this unit has consequences for validity of findings at the level of the task force. These issues and the way they are handled in this book are discussed later on in this chapter. Furthermore, it was also introduced in Chapter 1 that a "conceptual compass" based on the Integral Organizational Renewal (IOR) tradition in sociotechnical systems design theory guides the exploration. The goal of this chapter, as visualized in Figure 3.1, is therefore to study 107 ASBt's operations within TFU by means of this conceptual compass to explore the relation

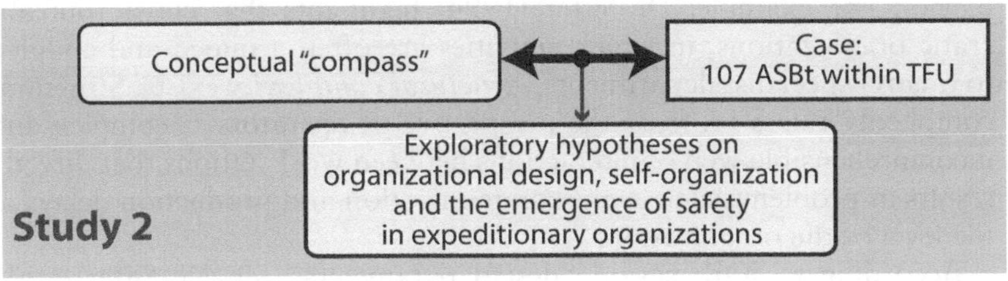

Figure 3.1 Research model of Study 2

ASBt = Aerial Systems battery; TFU = Task Force Uruzgan

between organization design, self-organization and the emergence of safety in expeditionary organizations. In order to do so, this chapter is divided into several sections. Firstly, the content of the conceptual compass is described in detail. Secondly, background information on 107 ASBt and Task Force Uruzgan is presented. Thirdly, the methodology that is used in this chapter is formulated. Fourthly, the results of this chapter are presented. Fifthly, the analysis is presented. Finally, this chapter concludes with a discussion.

3.2 Conceptual Compass: IOR's Main Premises

In this section the main premises of IOR are introduced, which are largely built on the works of De Sitter (e.g., De Sitter, 1994; De Sitter, Den Hertog, & Dankbaar, 1997). As a central starting point, De Sitter defines the organization as a social interaction network. He subsequently highlights that an organization's structural design, or *the way activities are grouped and coupled in relation to the flow of orders*,[2] influences the nature of social interactions in such a way that it both indirectly and directly impacts the ability of an organization to operate with as few disturbances as possible.

Firstly, the way activities are grouped and coupled influences the degree to which employees can solve problems at their own workplace, i.e. that they have "internal control capacity", or that they have to pass it on to other workplaces in the interaction network and use "external control capacity". Control capacity,[3] or autonomy of employees at the operational level in classic organizational science jargon (cf. Van Eijnatten & Van der Zwaan, 1998), is needed to respond to disturbances and environmental challenges and develop controllability, and it is hence largely influenced by choices on organizational structure. As such, by impacting control capacity, the organization's structural design has indirect influences on the way an organization can deal with disturbances. Secondly, the way activities are grouped and coupled impacts the social interaction network in such a way that it directly impacts the amount of disturbances. For example, De Sitter (1994) highlights that classic bureaucratic organizations, in which activities are often grouped and coupled to (many) specialist departments, *structural complexity* exists. Structural complexity refers to, from the perspective of operators, a complex and incomprehensible web of interactions between workstations that directly results in problems such as miscommunication and production delays at the level of the organization.

According to IOR, seven[4] "design parameters" (cf. De Sitter et al., 1997) can be used to relate the way activities are grouped and coupled to consequences for control capacity and structural complexity. The higher a particular organization "scores" on the parameters presented here, the more employees will be confronted with limited control capacity and crippling structural complexity that hinder their (self-organizing) efforts and is detrimental to organizational outcomes.

1. Functional concentration: the degree to which, in relation to the flow of orders, specialist activities grouped at specialist departments.
2. The degree to which performing activities (making, preparing and supporting) are divided and grouped at separate departments.
3. The degree to which performing activities are split into (even) smaller parts within departments.
4. The degree to which performing and controlling activities are separated and grouped at different departments.
5. Control specialization: the degree to which control activities are split per separate domain such as quality, safety, finance and Human Resources.
6. Control differentiation: the degree to which control activities are split into separate control levels (operational, tactic and strategic control).
7. Division of control activities: the degree to which measuring, evaluating and adjusting activities are split.

In defining organizational structure, IOR and De Sitter distinguish between the concepts[5] *production structure* and a *control structure*. Production structure refers to the way performance activities (i.e. preparing, supporting and making) are grouped and coupled in relation to the flow of orders of the organization's primary process. The first four parameters presented can be used for characterizing a production structure. Control structure refers to the way different control activities, such as measuring, evaluating and adjusting, are divided within an organization (i.e. design of control loops). The fifth, sixth and seventh parameter described can be used to characterize the control structure within an organization. De Sitter (1994) argues that the way performance activities are grouped and coupled accounts for the lion's share of the influence of organizational structure on the nature of the organizational interaction network and the accompanying consequences for employees and outcomes at the organizational level. Therefore, along the works of De Sitter, it depends largely on production structure characteristics whether individual efforts of employees will eventually result in an organization that is able to operate with as few disturbances as possible.

At first sight IOR seems to address key characteristics of organization design, self-organization and the emergence of outcomes at the organizational level. That is to say, it seems to relate a definition on organizational structure explicitly to aspects of self-organization and adaptation of employees at the operational level and outcomes at the level of the organization. This may lead one to conclude that IOR concepts can be applied one-on-one to get an understanding of the relationship between organizational design and safety in expeditionary organizations. However, and in line with Kuipers (1998), reflexive, heuristic use of IOR's concepts was advocated in Chapter 1. Furthermore, although IOR is often praised for its systematic and explicit translation of systems-theoretical assumptions into organization design concepts[6] (see, for example, Achterbergh & Vriens, 2010), it is not a theory about safety during high-risk operations, nor is it a theory tailored to expeditionary organizations. Firstly, IOR does not explicitly theorize on the relationship between organizational design, self-organization and safety outcomes at the organizational level. Instead, it theorizes on the relationship between organizational structure and the ability of an organization to operate with high quality of work, high quality of organization (i.e. flexibility and efficiency) and quality of working relations.[7] Secondly, De Sitter (1994) highlights explicitly that IOR is aimed at analysis and redesign of standard bureaucratic organizations that he refers to as "Mainstream-Holland Inc".[8] Although expeditionary organizations are "mixed and matched" from rigid, and probably often bureaucratic, parent organizations, expeditionary organization themselves are not rigid at all, as was also highlighted in Chapter 1. As such, IOR concepts cannot be used deductively for the studies presented in this book. This underlines the relevance of using IOR heuristically. A methodology that uses the concepts of IOR in a heuristic fashion is outlined in section 3.4.

3.3 Background Information

This section presents background information on both the unit of study in this chapter, the Dutch Army's 107th Aerial Systems Battery, and Task Force Uruzgan in which this unit operated.

3.3.1 107 Aerial Systems Battery

Within the Royal Netherlands Army, 107 ASBt is a unit of about 100 employees that operates with Unmanned Aerial Vehicles. From 1996 until 2010, they operated with Sagem's Sperwer-UAV. A Sperwer is a so-called Short Range Tactical UAV. This means that the UAV is able to gather tactical information with a maximum range of approximately 90 kilometers from its base station. For gathering such information, the Sperwer is equipped with a camera that can record both at daytime and at night. The camera can only record in black and white. The Sperwer-UAV does not have any weapons. Depending on local circumstances, it is able to operate at a maximum height of 15000 feet. The Sperwer-UAV is 3,5 meters in length and has a wingspan of 4,1 meters. It is propelled by a two-stroke petrol engine and is capable of carrying fuel for a four-hour flight. Next to the UAVs, a Sperwer "system" consists of a Ground Control Centre (GCC), a Ground Data Terminal (GDT) and a launching platform (LANS). During the operations of 107 ASBt in Uruzgan, a Report and Analysis Centre (RAC) was also part of the Sperwer "system".

In the sequence of getting a Sperwer-UAV in the air, the general activities required are depicted schematically in Figure 3.2 (see also: Moorkamp, Wybo, & Kramer, 2016). These activities refer to internal activities within the unit and are rather independent of the organizational configuration in which 107 ASBt is located. To be able to fly with an UAV, the UAV has to be maintained according to strict aviation rules. These rules determine how a particular maintenance job is carried out by the maintenance crew, from bolting a particular bolt onto the aircraft to using a specified type of glue. Next, the assembly crew prepares the aircraft for flight by filling the aircraft with fuel and carrying out pre-flight checks. After that, the aircraft is put on a launching device the size of a large truck, and the launching crew has—among other things—to make sure the aircraft is launched with a certain velocity. After that, the operating crew in the Ground Control Centre navigates the aircraft during its operations. When the assignment is complete, the UAV lands by using its parachute and airbags. The transport crew then moves to the recovery site to bring the UAV back to base. When returning from a particular assignment, post-flight checks determine whether the aircraft has to go to maintenance or only needs preparation for the next launch and flight.

Within the Dutch Army, 107 ASBt[9] has a particular place and role. The unit was formed in 1998 and had designated reconnaissance tasks

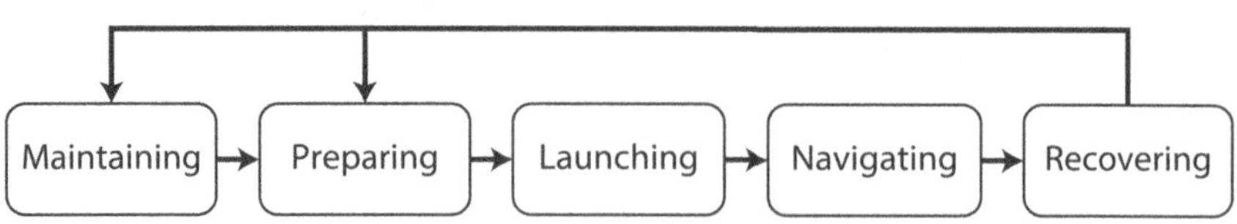

Figure 3.2 Activities 107 ASBt

for the Army's artillery. From 2006, 107 ASBt was part of the Army's Intelligence Surveillance Target Acquisition and Reconnaissance (ISTAR) battalion. The main task of 107 ASBt within the ISTAR battalion was to provide the battalion with "single source" intelligence information. This information was combined with information from other "sources" such as reconnaissance units and electronic warfare to meet the needs from brigade and/or army corps staff (Royal Netherlands Army, 2002, 2003). In 2006, 107 ASBt was organized by allocating Sperwer systems in three separate platoons (see Figure 3.3), which were supported by a logistics and maintenance platoon.

From 2008 on, a number of reorganizations have taken place within the Army, ISTAR and 107 ASBt. Within ISTAR, or Joint ISTAR Command (JISTARC) as it is called today, the concept of the "ISTAR-module" was introduced in 2007. This meant that ISTAR was expected to be able to provide two simultaneously operating expeditionary missions with an ISTAR module that comprised all main intelligence "sources", including UAVs. For 107 ASBt this meant that the unit needed to be able to deliver two operational UAV detachments (Royal Netherlands Army, 2007) for service in these "modules".

In 2008, reorganization within 107 ASBt transformed the unit from an organization structured by platoons into an organization structured in "green and blue" parts (see Figure 3.4). The "blue" parts of the unit are related to flying activities whereas the "green" parts are not related to flying activities of the unit. In Figure 3.4 the green parts are visualized in gray, the blue parts in black. The reorganization was based on directions from the Dutch military aviation authority (MLA; Royal Netherlands Army, 2007) and International Civil Aviation Organization guidelines (ICAO, 2006).

In the new organization "Flight OPS" refers to the crew that navigates the UAV in a Ground Control Centre and "Ground OPS" refers to the launching crew. With regard to maintenance, "Maintenance OS" refers to the crew that prepares the UAV for flight, recovers and transports the UAV. "Maintenance 145" refers to "regular" maintenance activities. 107 ASBt mostly trains at the artillery training grounds, located in 't Harde, The Netherlands and at the NATO training facilities in Bergen-Hohne in Germany. The airspace in which the unit trained was, and is, mostly closed for other aircraft.

From 2006 until 2010, 107 ASBt contributed three times to Task Force Uruzgan. For each mission, 107 ASBt needed to assemble detachments from their organization in the Netherlands. This meant that they had to select specific parts in the Dutch organization and assemble them into an "expeditionary" 107 organization (see Figure 3.5). The red-circled parts of 107 ASBt in Figure 3.3and 3.4 show the sub-units that were selected from the 107 "parent" organization before and after the reorganization.

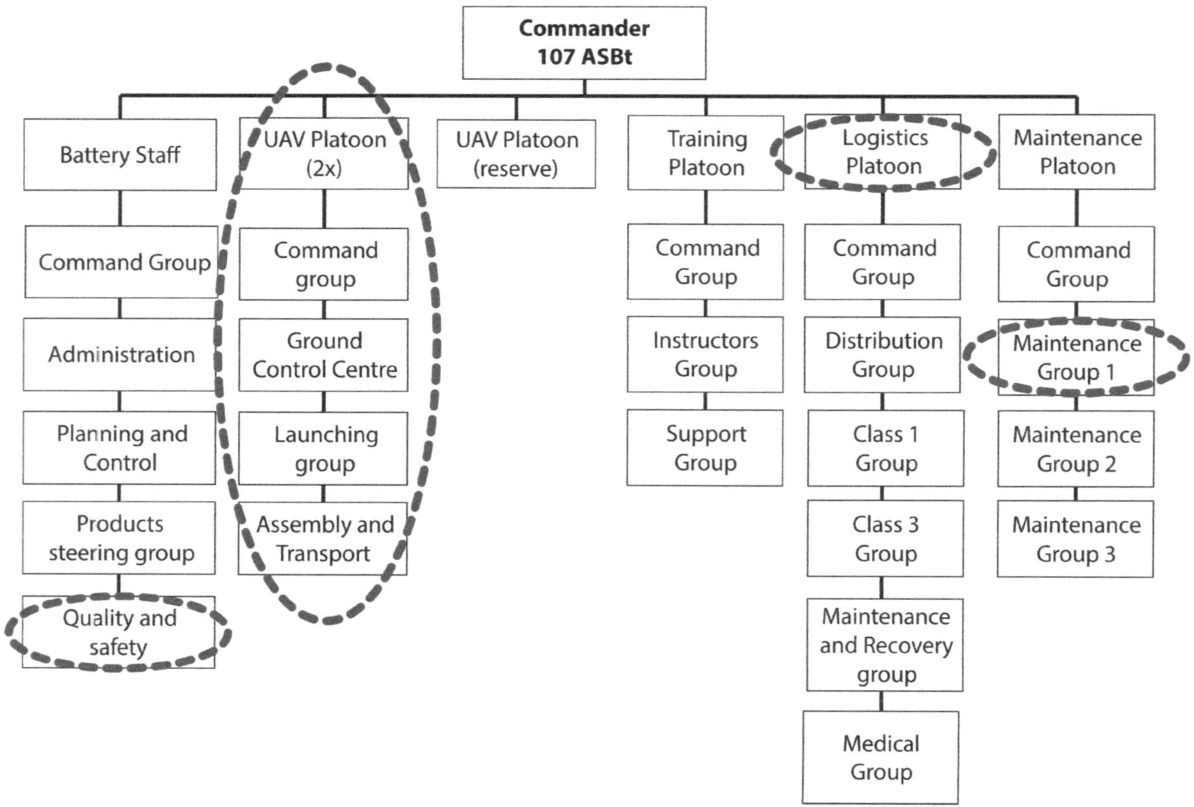

Figure 3.3 Layout 107 ASBt until 2008

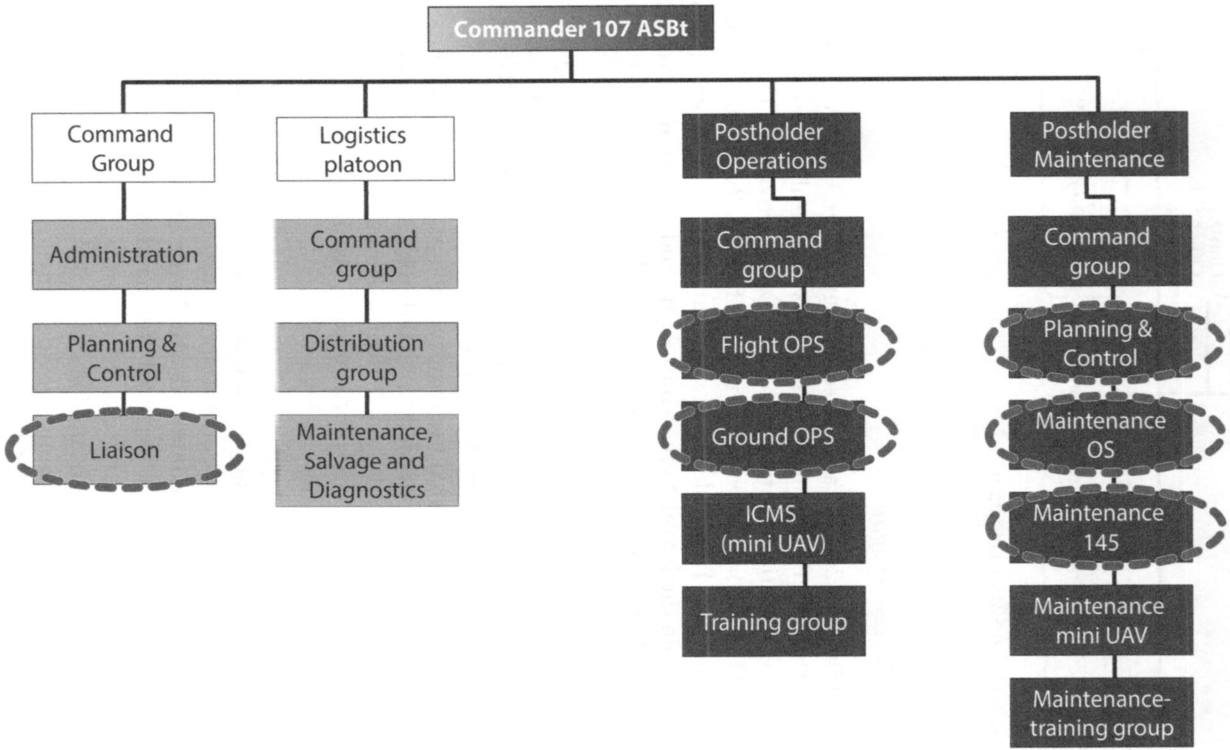

Figure 3.4 107 ASBt after reorganization in 2008

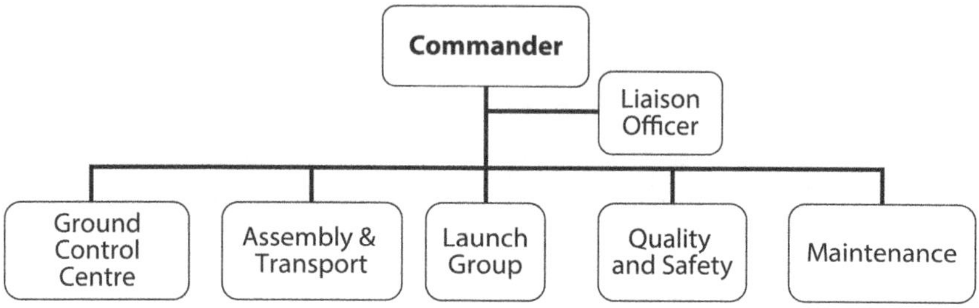

Figure 3.5 107 ASBt in Uruzgan

3.3.2 Task Force Uruzgan

Between 2006 and 2010, Task Force Uruzgan (TFU) was a temporary military expeditionary organization that was responsible for reconstruction and security duties in Afghanistan's Uruzgan province. TFU contributed to NATO's ISAF[10] forces and was part of ISAF's Regional Command South (RC-South). The Task Force was mainly built up from elements originating from the Royal Netherlands Army and consisted of two main parts: a Battle Group (BG) for security tasks and a Provincial Reconstruction Team (PRT) for reconstruction tasks. Units of TFU were located at two camps: "Camp Holland" in Tarin Kowt and "Camp Hadrian" in Deh-Rawood. Of these two camps, Camp Holland was the largest and housed the majority of the units and the Operations Room (TFU-OPS).

As previously described, the way in which the Army parent organization is designed did not match the requirements of the Uruzgan mission. This means that the Army needed to "handpick" several elements from the parent organization and "glue" them together to form TFU. The units that were selected from the Army and assembled into TFU-1 are shown between the dotted lines in Figure 3.6.

Also, several units from the Royal Netherlands Air Force were selected to operate in Uruzgan. Although some units were stationed at the same location as TFU's Army units, at Camp Holland, these units were not part of TFU's operational command. Air Force units were operationally commanded by NATO's "regional command south" (RC-South) in Kandahar. The units that were selected from the Air Force to conduct operations in Uruzgan are presented in Figure 3.7.[11] Within TFU, the Air Force's F16's and Apaches mainly provided intelligence and fire support for Army units on the ground. Chinook helicopters were mainly used for transport purposes.

The units that were selected from the different parent organizations were "mixed and matched" into Task Force Uruzgan. The layout of

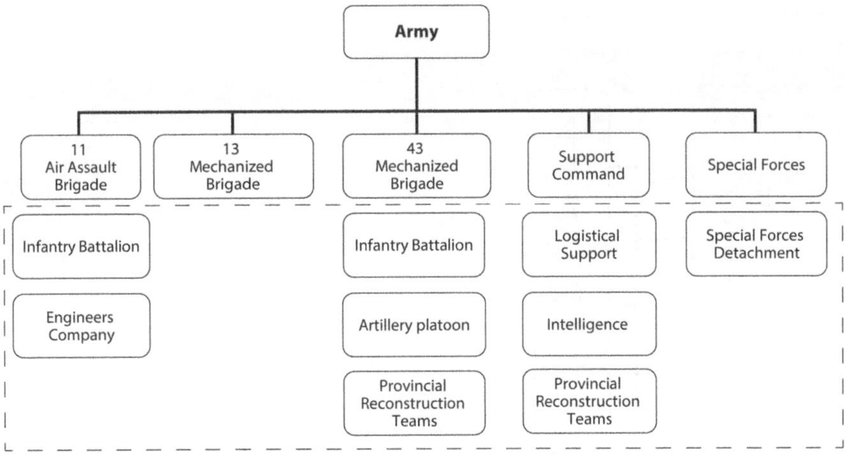

Figure 3.6 Army units in TFU-1

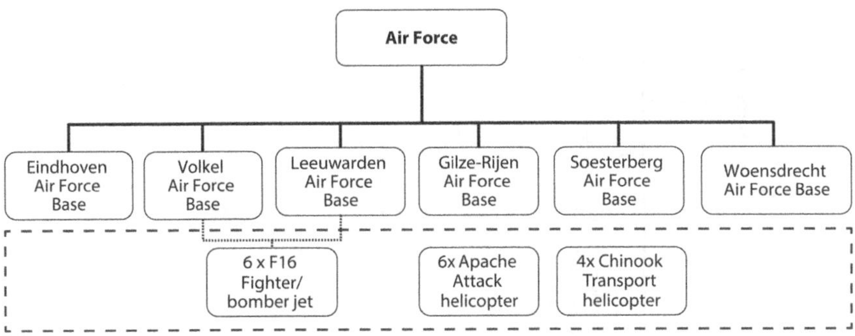

Figure 3.7 Air Force units in Uruzgan

TFU-1 is schematically presented later. Because 107 ASBt was assigned to the ISTAR detachment within TFU, this detachment is presented with more detail. Within TFU, the infantry battalions and the artillery platoon were grouped in the so-called Battle Group. Provincial reconstruction teams (PRTs) are units that do not exist as such within the Army parent organization. During the deployment of TFU, PRT tasks were conducted by several different units of the Army combined with specialists from the Army's reserve forces that are organized under to the Army's support command in the parent organization. The dotted lines in Figure 3.8 indicate that TFU staff had limited command and control over units from the Air Force, the Military Police and Special Forces.

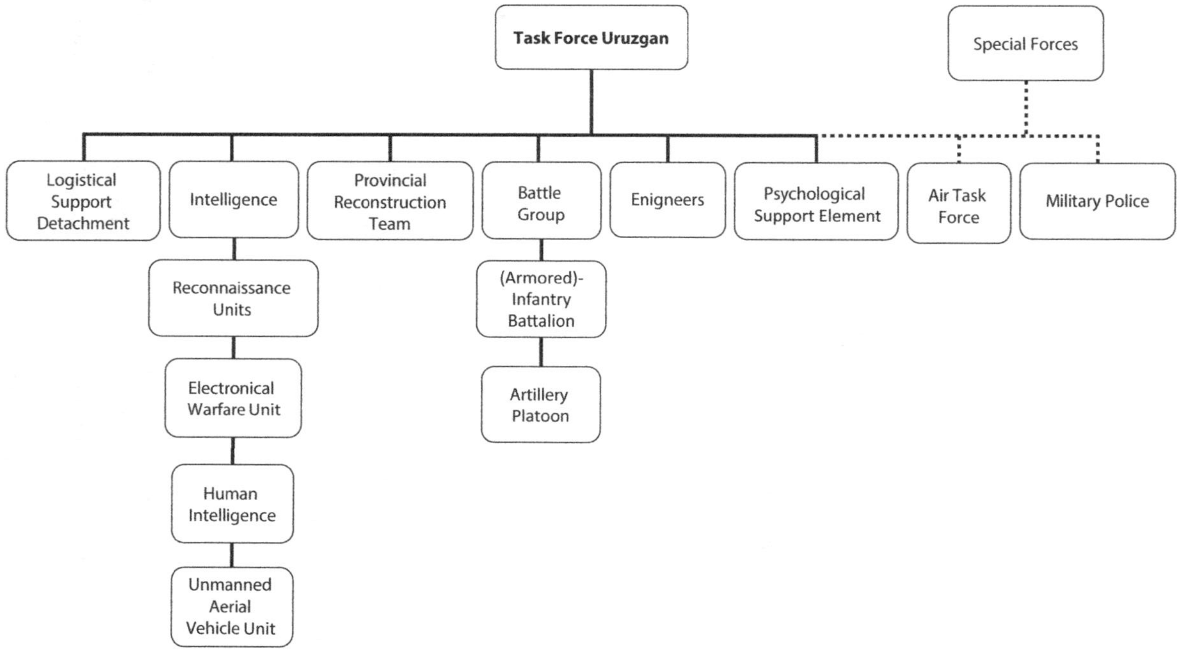

Figure 3.8 Organizational layout of TFU-1

3.4 Methodology

In this section, it is firstly described how the relationship between organizational design, self-organization and the emergence of safety is operationalized in order to be studied in a particular organizational context such as that of 107 ASBt within TFU. After that, the units that were studied and the way data was collected is explicated. Thirdly, the analytical approach that is used is described. Fourthly, issues of reliability and validity are addressed.

3.4.1 Operationalization by Means of a Particular "Normal Work" Approach

To explore the influence of organizational design on self-organization and the emergence of safety for 107 ASBt within TFU, these different concepts and their relationship have to be operationalized. That is to say, the relationship between these concepts cannot be studied empirically right away because they are located as Van Strien's level B of knowledge generalization. As such, a translation to level C has to be made in order to be able to study these concepts in the context of 107 ASBt's operations within TFU. To make this translation, it is argued that a particular understanding of everyday operations, or "normal work" (cf. Dekker, 2005) of 107 ASBt's operators, is necessary. Dekker's normal work approach, which is rather similar to Bourrier's (2002) plea for safety research on "normal operations" can be seen as a pro-active alternative for the traditional reactive research approaches in safety science. Traditionally, research on safety issues was done "after the event", after an accident had taken place. Bourrier (2002, p. 175) argues that this traditional approach has drawbacks, as it tends to focus on blaming and confirming causes that do not contradict organizational stories. According to Dekker (2005) and Bourrier (2002), a focus on normal work, or normal operations, has the ability to get insight into the dynamics of everyday organizational life that may offer a closer look into both the bright and the darker side of organizational behavior.

Taking this stance on accident and safety investigations, a normal work approach not only has the ability to turn from reactive to pro-active research, it also seems to 1) shift the analytical perspective to the operational level of the organization and 2) enable researchers and safety investigators to study local problem-solving activities of operators. Therefore, it is argued that a normal work approach is able to study the process of local self-organization. In which it should be noted that this process is interactive, experimentative and social by nature.[12]

Furthermore, Dekker points out that, while engaging in "normal work", operators find themselves on the crossroads between the dynamics of the environment and the organizational context in which they work (cf. Dekker, 2005). This means that, while self-organizing for safe operations, they constantly have to deal with aspects of the organizational context. Organizational structure, as defined by means of IOR concepts, can quite obviously be interpreted as a substantial part of this organizational context, as was also highlighted in Chapter 1. However, in order to get insight into the influences of this part of the organizational context on self-organization and the subsequent emergence of safety, a particular approach has to be taken because, as was also highlighted previously, due to the analytic character of IOR concepts one cannot directly observe how operators deal with aspects of organization structure[13] while engaging in "normal work".

Based on the content of the "conceptual compass" outlined earlier, it is argued that influences of organizational structure have to be analytically reconstructed from influences that the organizational interaction network has on self-organization. That is to say, in the section on the conceptual compass, IOR was used to point out that organizational structure influenced the ability of operators to deal with disturbances both *directly* and *indirectly* by its effects on the nature of the organizational interaction network. These effects manifest themselves in the amount of disturbances operators experience from the organizational interaction network itself (the degree of structural complexity) and the degree of control capacity that is needed to deal with environmental disturbances. This means that, with keeping the well-known *fallacy of the inverse*[14] in mind, inferences about structure can be made from investigating the influence of the organizational social interaction network on the amount of disturbances that operators experience from inside the organization and the ability of operators to deal with disturbances from the environment. It is argued, however, that such inferences however, can only be made by constantly combining empirical data with theoretical concepts. After all, and referring to the fallacy mentioned previously, not all influences from the organizational social interaction network may be interpreted as structural influences. As such, an analytical strategy is applied that Kramer (2007) refers to as "*analytical abduction*", in which existing theoretical concepts are constantly combined with case study data to construct analytical inferences.

Furthermore, this book is explicitly aimed at the relation between organization design and safety during expeditionary operations. Hence, the focus of empirical study is explicitly focused on safety issues and not on all possible disturbances and influences that can be related to organizational structure. As such, the way of reasoning as described above can be used to focus on the way organizational design influences the amount of safety issues and the way operators could solve these and whether self-organization, in the end, results in the emergence of safety at the organizational level. More specifically, by means of the previous elaboration, empirical study is enabled to focus on influences that the social interaction network has on the amount and type of safety problems operators experienced and the way they could solve safety issues originating from the environment. Using analytical abduction in the aforementioned way may then ensure that only those effects of the social interaction network are taken into account that relate to concepts of organizational design that were introduced in the "conceptual compass".

In sum, the elaboration implies that empirically studying the relationship between organizational design, self-organization and the emergence of safety focuses on the following: 1) local, interactive problem-solving strategies aimed at dealing with safety issues; 2) abductively studying influences from the social interaction network on safety issues and the way operators could solve these and 3) the degree in which safety subsequently emerges at the organizational level.

3.4.2 Research Strategy: Units Studied

As highlighted in the introduction of this chapter, 107 ASBt was chosen as a starting point for this study as it enabled exploring the relation between organization design, self-organization and the emergence of safety at two organizational levels: the level of 107 ASBt and the level of TFU. Hence, design of this study can be characterized as a single "embedded" case study design, which is visualized in Figure 3.9 (cf. Yin, 2003,

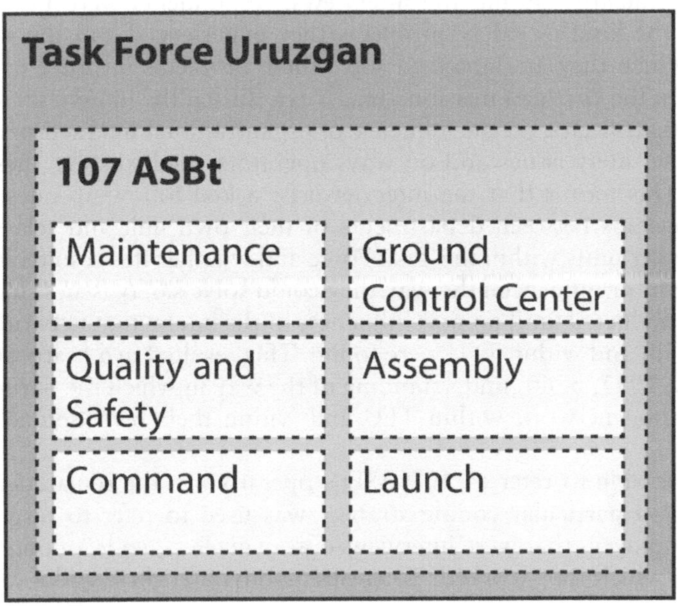

Figure 3.9 Case study design for Study 2

pp. 39–41), because a single case within TFU, with multiple embedded sub-units, is studied. As briefly mentioned in the Introduction, a single-case study approach has implications for validity of claims made, because findings at the level of TFU are reported from the perspective of one unit only. These issues with regard to validity are described in more detail in the last paragraph of this section.

3.4.3 Data Collection

To collect the type of data that is needed in this chapter, a qualitative study was conducted in which 13 in-depth interviews were conducted with employees of all sub-units of 107 ASBt who served one or multiple times in Uruzgan from 2006 until 2009. The main reason to conduct a qualitative study, instead of a quantitative study, is that according to Strauss and Corbin (1990), a qualitative case study methodology is especially suitable for studying phenomena that are highly contextualized. Expeditionary operations in a dynamically complex operating environment can, quite straightforwardly, be defined as such a highly contextualized phenomenon. Also, qualitative research has the ability to reconstruct interactions between individuals and the way these interactions shape the way individuals give meaning to a particular situation (e.g., Blumer, 1986), which is necessary for reconstructing the relation between organization design, self-organization and the emergence of safety, as highlighted in the operationalization described earlier.

Subsequently, during the interviews, respondents were firstly asked about the kind of safety problems they experienced and the strategies with which they attempted to solve these problems in order to operate safely in the Uruzgan mission area. Next, during the interviews information was collected on the influence of organizational interaction network on these safety issues and on ways operators tried to solve these problems. This meant that the interviewer(s) asked follow-up questions on relationships between departments of their own unit and relationships with other units within the Task Force and whether this resulted in safety problems or influenced the way they could solve safety issues. Interviews were conducted until no new influences of the interaction network within 107 ASBt and within TFU were found. This resulted in a "saturated" (cf. Wester, 1987, p. 60) understanding of the way in which the nature of the interaction network within TFU and within their own unit influenced safety.

To be able to refer to 107 ASBt's operators in the remainder of this chapter, a particular coding strategy was used to refer to respondents. The employees that were interviewed were given a "code" along the sub-unit in which they worked. To ensure anonymity, these codes cannot be linked to individual operators. The codes that were used are presented in Table 3.1.

Table 3.1 Interview codes

Sub-unit	*Code*
Ground Control Center	G
Maintenance	M
Assembly	A
Command	C
Launch	L
Quality and Safety	S

3.4.4 Data Analysis

For the analysis in this chapter, the qualitative methodology of Wester and Peters (2004) is followed. Their methodology is followed because the four steps proposed to construct a *grounded theory* provide a systematic guideline to combine experiences of individuals with theoretical constructs. This is needed in this chapter to analytically reconstruct the influence of organizational design on self-organization and the emergence safety, as was highlighted in the operationalization. In line with these remarks, and the specific "normal work" approach that is used, this chapter adopts the four phases proposed by Wester and Peters in a specific way, as detailed in the following steps.

Firstly, in the exploration phase, it is investigated what kind of safety problems 107 ASBt encountered and how they tried to solve these. Therefore, firstly, the safety issues 107 ASBt encountered were coded by means of "open coding" (cf. Boeije, 2005). Subsequently, "axial coding" was used to link problems with solutions in order to map self-organizing strategies. The phrase: "dealing with . . ." was used for grouping both problems and solutions in one category. The exploration phase resulted in a total of 45 different categories.[15]

In the specification phase, the 45 categories of the exploration phase were re-examined with regard to the influence of the organizational interaction network, both within TFU and within 107 ASBt. Subsequently, it was investigated whether aspects of the interaction network could be associated either with the safety problems 107 ASBt experienced and/or the way 107 ASBt's operators could solve problems in order to develop safety of their operations. After that, categories were grouped to form "central substantive concepts" (cf. Wester, 1987, pp. 56–58). As a result, four central substantive "dealing with . . ." categories were developed that all characterized the influence of the organizational network on both the safety problems 107 ASBt experienced and the solutions they found to solve safety issues.

Subsequently, in the reduction phase, the categories developed in the previous phase are analyzed to construct influences organizational design of both 107 ASBt and TFU on safety of 107 ASBt's operations within TFU. This part of the analysis is aimed at making analytical statements by means of analytical abduction in which the "conceptual compass" is used to interpret the data and construct analytical inferences by means of formulating propositions or hypotheses. This part of the analysis can be interpreted as the core of the grounded theory developed in this chapter. Finally, in the integration phase, conclusions are drawn on the influence of structural design characteristics on self-organization and the emergence of safety of 107 ASBt's operations within TFU.

3.4.5 Reliability and Validity

In this section, aspects are highlighted that relate to the scientific quality of the study presented in this chapter. Although the steps for data analysis are based on the works of Wester and Peters, this section relies on the works of Yin (2003), who elaborated extensively on characteristics of reliability and validity for case study research in general. His work is chosen because the characteristics of reliability and validity that he defines are largely similar[16] to those selected for the grounded theory approach by Wester and Peters (2004, p. 129), but defined in a more detailed manner as compared to the methodological guidelines of Wester and Peters.

According to Yin, the issue of reliability is focused on minimizing errors and bias in a study so that it is possible to conduct the same case study all over again (2003, p. 37). In order to establish reliability, Yin (2003, p. 38) advises documenting as many research steps as possible.[17] Therefore, in this study, all interviews were recorded digitally by means of a voice recorder and subsequently transcribed word for word. After that, a case study database was developed in which all categories and accompanying pieces of text from were stored.

With regard to validity, Yin points to three types of validity: construct, internal and external validity (2003, pp. 35). Construct validity, according to Yin, refers to the quality of measurements that are developed for studying relevant concepts. Yin points out that to meet the "test" of construct validity, a researcher must make sure to do the following: 1) "Select specific types of changes that are to be studied" and 2) "Demonstrate that the selected measurements of these changes do indeed reflect the specific types of change that has been selected". To attain construct validity, this chapter has to show that changes in safety of 107 ASBt's operations within TFU can be attributed to operators' self-organizing strategies that are influenced by characteristics of structural organizational design. In order to do so, a construct validity enhancing strategy that is proposed by Yin is employed in this study (see 2003, p. 34). In this study, a "chain of evidence is constructed". This means that one "must be able to move from one part of the case study to another, with clear cross-referencing to methodological procedures and to the resulting evidence" (Yin, 2003, p. 105). Consequently, constructing a chain of evidence applies to the interview transcripts, the case study database and the resulting case study report. With regard to such a case study report, the study that is reported in this chapter was part of an overarching research project on safety within Task Force Uruzgan (see Moorkamp & Kramer, 2014). Consequently, the chain of evidence can be traced in the case study report on that research project.

According to Yin, internal validity is relevant for research designs that aim to make causal inferences (2003, p. 36), which is the case in this chapter. This means that it has to be established that causal claims made, account for possible intervening variables. One strategy that can be followed in order to attain internal validity is "explanation building" (Yin, 2003, pp. 120–122), which Yin describes as an iterative process for explaining phenomena. It is described as an iterative process because "case study evidence is examined, theoretical positions are revised, and the evidence is examined once more from a new perspective". The methodology of Wester and Peters (2004) that is used in this chapter for analyzing the data can be defined as incorporating such an iterative process for explanation building. The different analytic phases described earlier are characterized by constantly going back and forth between data and the concepts that were developed to make sure that these concepts reflect the experiences of 107 ASBt adequately. Furthermore, in the analysis, possible intervening variables were sought explicitly. These are consequently reported in the integration phase of the study. Lastly, interviewees were all asked to review the interview transcript to ensure that the transcript is in concordance with interviewees' experiences and perceptions.

External validity, according to Yin (2003, p. 37), deals with the problem whether results are generalizable beyond the actual case studied. The nature of this chapter is explorative and it hence does not aim to result in generalizable claims. This means that external validity of the findings in this chapter is limited. It should be emphasized, however, that the results of this chapter play a significant role in the fourth chapter of this book in which it is attempted to verify parts of the findings of this chapter by studying experiences of other units within TFU. Methodological aspects of this generalization are therefore addressed in Chapter 4.

3.5 Results

The results section is divided into four parts that represent the four "substantive concepts" developed in this chapter. Consequently, the results are presented until the specification phase. This research stage made clear that for 107 ASBt, the organizational interaction network within both their own unit and TFU had such a large influence on the amount of safety problems and the way they could solve safety issues that operating safely within TFU seemed to be inherently compromised. In the following sections, these influences will be explicated.

3.5.1 Dealing With Assignments

In section 3.3, it was highlighted that 107 ASBt was used to training relatively isolated from other (military) units. Consequently, they were not accustomed to the types and number of assignments they had to conduct within TFU. As a result, 107 ASBt's self-organizing strategies were initially characterized by finding ways to discover what assignments they had to do and with whom they had to cooperate in order to contribute meaningfully and safely to TFU's operations. Due to the diversity of strategies associated with "dealing with assignments", this section is divided into four parts: dealing with new assignments, dealing with too many assignments, dealing with "re-tasks" and dealing with extension of the mission-period.

3.5.1.1 Dealing With New Assignments

From the start of the first mission in Uruzgan in 2006, 107 ASBt needed to learn how to operate with configurations of units within TFU. This meant that 107 ASBt had to discover what had to be done within ISTAR and TFU. Their activities at the beginning of their first mission in 2006 were therefore characterized by discovering how 107 ASBt could provide a safe and meaningful contribution to TFU's operations, as an employee of quality and safety explains (S-3):

> *The first questions* [from other units within TFU] *were: what can your unit do for me? So, the first things that had to be done were discovering possible partners, communicating a lot and thinking about the unit's PR.*

The 107 ASBt unit was not only unfamiliar with operating with other units within TFU, these units were also unfamiliar with operating with an UAV. Employees of 107 ASBt tried to improve these units' knowledge on the possibilities and limitations of operating with a Sperwer-UAV by giving "sales pitches" within TFU, as an employee of quality and safety explains (S-2):

> *One of the myths about UAVs was that we can track IEDs*[18] (. . .) *But we can't, so we had to organize sales pitches on what can be done, and what cannot be done.*

Due to such sales pitches, other units learned to use the Sperwer-UAV. During the first mission, the Sperwer was mostly used for mapping qualas (small villages), as another employee of quality and safety points out (S-3):

> *That was simply quala-watching: entrance, exits, mapping thickness of the walls. Fly a few circles around it and then to the next one.*

Despite the organization of sales pitches, learning to understand the possibilities and limitations of the Sperwer by other units within TFU was problematic. This resulted in assignments that could simply not be executed, as an operator from the Ground Control Centre explains (G-5):

> *People did not have the right understanding of the possibilities of the UAV, which frustrated us. We got assignments to look for a red car, while the Sperwer was only equipped with a black and white camera. Or we had to determine the depth of a river, which was simply impossible.*

These problems with regard to the possibilities and limitations of the Sperwer-UAV, also resulted in assignments that exceeded safety limitations of the UAV, as an employee of 107 ASBt's maintenance crew explicates (M-2):

> *We had to fly with heavy thunder. We explicitly told them that it was unsafe to fly with thunder both for the UAV and for the crew who had to elevate the UAV's radio tower. We could lose the airplane (. . .). The commander of TFU eventually ordered us to fly. We had to fly.*

An operator of the Ground Control Centre explains similar problems with regard to flying with dangerous weather conditions (G-5):

> *I told them that we had severe "icing" conditions and that we could not fly. Not that we did not want to, but the weather conditions were simply too unsafe. They just wanted us to fly; well then it becomes a safety problem.*

For such occasions, the quality and safety department of 107 ASBt employed an interpretation of Operational Risk Management (ORM). A manager from the quality and safety department explains what ORM looked like for 107 ASBt (S-3):

> *When we are on an operational mission, we have an "escape" for any commanding officer: operational risk management. Sometimes the operational priorities of an assignment can be more important than its safety consequences. Then, safety rules may be violated if all potential risks are acknowledged. But, the most important thing*

of ORM is that you allocate authority where it should be, so that if something does go wrong the operator is not punished. Then, the commanding officer of the Task Force had to sign a document with which he assumed all responsibility for possible damages.

Due to the aforementioned problems and misunderstandings, there were a number of assignments declined during 107 ASBt's 2006 mission, as an operator from the Ground Control Centre explicates (G-5):

It remained to be a battle [between 107 ASBt and other TFU units]. *At a certain moment, the assignments declined and the UAVs were just standing there. Well, then they said: go and look at the qualas again.*

During the second and third mission of 107 ASBt within TFU in 2008 and 2009, the discovery process between 107 ASBt and the other units of TFU went faster because 107 ASBt's operators used their experience from the 2006 mission. However, although assignments were initially similar to the assignments in 2006, along the way, units within TFU began experimenting with the Sperwer-UAV. Over time, the Sperwer was employed for a wide variety of assignments that ranged from guarding troops that had to rest overnight in the field, flying reconnaissance missions combined with Apache helicopters to deterring Taliban forces. An employee from 107 ASBt's assembly team explains "rest overnight" missions (A-3):

When ground troops were outside and had to stay in the field during the night it was discovered that when we flew above their campsite, the Taliban did not attack them.

The same employee describes that Taliban activity declined when the Sperwer was in the air (A-3):

They knew when we were in the air. . . . Also, the Canadians told us that: when we were in the air, it was much quieter.

With regard to the combined reconnaissance missions with Apache helicopters, an employee of the maintenance crew explains that the Sperwer explored where Taliban-ambushes for ground troops were located so that Apache helicopters could be tasked to attack these ambushes (M-2):

We could see where Taliban ambushes were located, and we could advise ground troops to take a different route. Sometimes it was not possible to take an alternative route and then we flew low over these Taliban troops. They mostly disappeared after that because they knew that Apaches were coming quickly after us to terminate them.

Due to this experimentation with the Sperwer-UAV, demand for Sperwer operations within TFU increased. As a result, 107 ASBt had to cope with an increasing number of assignments. Strategies for dealing with too many assignments are therefore detailed in the next section.

3.5.1.2 Dealing With Too Many Assignments

An employee from the assembly team explains that the number of assignments during the second and third mission in Uruzgan was much higher than planned (A-3):

> *Instead of doing four assignments in one week, they told us that we had to do seven. . . . Our "asset" was discovered within TFU. They increasingly valued the capacities of the Sperwer.*

The liaison officer (LSO) of 107 ASBt was an important link between 107 ASBt and the other units of TFU. During the second mission, other units regularly approached the LSO "horizontally". That is to say, these units "skipped" the formal ISTAR chain of command and made direct contact with 107 ASBt's LSO for assignments, as a commanding officer explains (C-2):

> *For example, they asked whether we could you fly over a particular location near Chora. Well we were going to Chora the day after, so we included that in our schedule. . . . That was arranged horizontally.*

A contributing factor to the dramatic increase in assignments during the second and third mission was the live stream of the Sperwer, which was shown on a TV screen in the Operations Room of TFU (TFU-OPS). To manage the increasing amount of assignments, 107 ASBt's LSO simply turned the TV screen off, as a commanding officer describes (C-2):

> *Well, there was this TV screen with a live feed of the Sperwer's camera. When there was some action on the ground it became crowded with people very quickly. (. . .) A disadvantage of this is that these people are inclined to ask for a lot of things: fly over this . . . fly over that. . . . And whether it is a Colonel or General, these people are not trained to give us assignments. . . . We then simply turned the TV-screen off, to limit the number of these assignments.*

The number of assignments was associated with problems regarding 107 ASBt's personnel, as an operator of the Ground Control Centre explains (G-6):

> *At a certain point in time, they wanted to increase to two flights a day. (. . .) That results in problems because we planned our personnel to do one flight a day. . . . So, we had personnel to do one flight a day.*

Next to these problems related to personnel of the Ground Control Centre, the number of assignments resulted in maintenance issues, as an employee from the assembly crew explains (A-3):

> *We conducted much more flights than planned. That result in much more stress on the UAVs. The UAVs therefore required much more maintenance than planned. Also, spare parts were worn out much quicker.* (. . .) *We were pushed to our limits. . . . And at a given time the UAVs were simply used up.*

Due to these maintenance issues, spare parts such as parachutes were used up as well. A problem with the parachutes of the Sperwer was that safety regulations prescribed that they should be washed after three flights. This seemed particularly relevant because of the amount of dust and sand in Uruzgan. However, due to the number of assignments, parachutes had to be "recycled" more than three times to meet the increased demand for the UAV, as an employee from maintenance explains (M-1):

> *We told them that the parachutes were getting too thick because of the sand. They had to be washed again in the Netherlands. They could be used two or three times and then they were used up. . . . But I think they used* ORM [Operational Risk Management] *to fly with these parachutes anyway. . . . At a certain moment, we also had too few parachutes.*

The number of assignments clearly affected maintenance schedules. A maintenance manager explains that he dealt with these issues by restricting flight time of UAVs (M-2):

> *I dealt with these things by planning assignments differently. I told the LSO and the crew in the Ground Control station that some UAVs had time limits. The LSO consequently planned the assignments according to these limits until all spare parts arrived.*

This implicates that maintenance and operational sub-units within 107 ASBt had to align plans more frequently, as an employee of the assembly group explains (A-3):

> *Look, flying has priority. But it cannot be that maintenance lags behind when the amount of flights increases. Operators wanted to fly and fly and fly while they had no insight in whether the UAVs are maintained . . . so that had to be coordinated.*

The "system expert" from 107 ASBt's assembly group was responsible for such coordination. Because the need to coordinate between operations and maintenance increased due to the increased number of flights and assignments, the system expert was put under increasing pressure and stress, as an employee from the assembly group describes (A-3):

> *At a certain moment, sweat was pouring from my back . . . because I had to coordinate maintenance and operations. . . . I became a central player for the unit. I had to decide whether flying was possible. That resulted in increased pressure on the entire assembly group but also on me personally. . . . I just tried to keep myself on my feet.*

Over time, some form of a pattern started to appear with regard to the number of assignments. This provided some grip for maintenance, as the same employee from 107 ASBt's assembly group explains (A-3):

> *After some time, assignments became structured. Initially they planned that we would be flying in the morning or in the evening and that we had the Sunday off. . . . Well most of the time we did three flights on Sunday and we had no assignments in the morning. . . . So at a certain moment we knew that we should prepare the UAVs for the afternoon and Sundays.*

During a particular assignment, it often happened that the UAV was needed for ad-hoc situations such as "troops in contact" (TIC) when ground troops encountered Taliban fire. In such situations, the Sperwer was often "re-tasked" during flight. Dealing with re-tasks will be detailed in the next section.

3.5.1.3 Dealing With Re-Tasks

An operator of 107 ASBt's Ground Control Station describes that re-tasks were happening all the time during the 2008–2009 missions in Uruzgan (G-5):

> *Re-tasks were standard during every flight. . . . From the moment we launched the UAV, it was just a matter of time before we were ordered to re-task. (. . .) Most of the time this was due to "troops in contact", but it also happened when the Battle Group needed reconnaissance of a certain area.*

Another operator from 107 ASBt's Ground Control Station explains that the navigation equipment in the Ground Control Station was not suitable for such re-tasks and that re-tasking the UAV during a pre-programmed flight resulted in the inability to control the UAV during an emergency (G-1):

> *Re-tasking was dangerous because re-tasking the UAV meant that the pre-programmed flight plan had to be abandoned. The problem with the Sperwer was that it often lost its radio connection with the base. In such situations, I normally quickly selected the pre-programmed*

flight plan on the digital map. However, this could only be done when the UAV flew close to its original flight plan and was therefore impossible during re-tasks because the UAV was flying miles from its planned location. I could not select the flight plan on the digital map during signal loss because I had to scroll endlessly in the digital map to find the original flight plan.

Because of these issues, operators in the Ground Control Station tried to reduce the number of re-tasks, as a Ground Control Station operator describes (G-1):

It was hard to convince other people of the danger of re-tasks. When we said to the LSO that he should stop with ordering re-tasks he said: "well, it never goes wrong, right?". That's the difficulty with danger and risk, it goes right until the moment that it doesn't.

According to 107 ASBt's operators, after a while, the Sperwer-UAV was regarded as an asset that could not be missed within TFU. Therefore, their second mission to Uruzgan was extended for several months until May 2009. This period is regarded as the third mission in this chapter. Within 107 ASBt this period is also referred to as the "bonus detachment". The next section details how 107 ASBt's operators dealt with extending the second mission.

3.5.1.4 Dealing With Extension of the Mission

Although 107 ASBt was pushed to and over its limits during the second mission in Uruzgan, the mission was extended for four months. A commanding officer of 107 ASBt describes what this extension looked like (C-2):

In fact, we executed 2,5 missions in Uruzgan: the first in 2006 and 2007, the second in 2008 and 2009, and again in 2009. I was detachment commander in 2008 and we had planned that the mission would take 6 months. Everything was prepared for a six-month period. During the mission, it became clear that we were required to stay longer.

The extension resulted in personnel planning problems, as an operator of 107 ASBt's Ground Control Station describes (G-1):

As the mission duration became longer and longer we had two options: employees that were already in Uruzgan could serve longer or they had to assemble a new detachment to relieve us. But assembling a new detachment meant that everybody that ever served at 107 ASBt and now worked somewhere else in the Army had to be recalled to serve with us again.

Next to personnel planning problems, extending the mission had consequences for the planning and stock of spare parts, as a maintenance manager explains (M-2):

> *We never anticipated on this "bonus detachment". My predecessor heard of this extension only several days or maybe one week in advance and it was also unknown how long the extension would be! So, he tried to make a planning of spare parts as best as possible. When I relieved him, a lot of spare parts were coming in based on his planning. But I had to order a lot of extra spare parts as well. And some parts were not on stock in Holland or at the factory so we had to ground some UAVs.*

An employee of the assembly group describes that, due to the extension and the number of assignments, 107 ASBt was operating on its limits (A-3):

> *We had planned to do a six-month mission and extending that means that all equipment—not only UAV's but also ground equipment—has to operate longer in Uruzgan circumstances with heat and dust. That meant that we were confronted with the limits of what could be tolerated.*

Next to discovering what kind of assignments had to be conducted within TFU, 107 ASBt's operators had to discover how to operate in airspace in which other airplanes were flying. Therefore, the next section explicates how they dealt with these other airspace users.

3.5.2 Dealing With Other Airspace Users

As was highlighted in section 3.3, 107 ASBt mainly trained isolated from other airspace users. This training situation was significantly different from the situation in Uruzgan. The airspace in Uruzgan was crowded with flying assets from Task Force Uruzgan itself, the Australian Army and other airplanes, such as commercial transport helicopters and American medical evacuation flights. An operator from 107 ASbt's Ground Control Centre describes that dealing with other airspace users in the airspace over Uruzgan was "one big surprise" for 107 ASBt. In particular, he mentions that, in Uruzgan, 107 ASBt had to deal with rules and procedures for avoiding collision ("deconfliction") for the first time (G-6):

> *We always assumed that we would operate on our "post stamp",*[19] *and that we always operate in restricted airspace that we own. We were not used to operate with other airspace users (. . .) and in Uruzgan we encountered things that we had not anticipated. To be honest, it was one big surprise over there. . . . We had to invent everything on the spot. . . . That was the first time that we had to deal with deconfliction.*

Dealing with airspace users is divided into three sections: dealing with airspace users within the area of the air traffic control tower, dealing with airspace users outside the area of the air traffic control tower and dealing with airspace users during ad-hoc operations.

3.5.2.1 Dealing With Airspace Users Within the Area of the Air Traffic Control Tower

The air traffic control tower of Tarin Kowt airfield ("TK-tower") was one of the most important players with regard to deconfliction in Uruzgan, as it controlled a circle of about 10 kilometers around Camp Holland. This imaginary circle was divided into "cake-wedges". An employee from the quality and safety department explains how he tried to familiarize himself with the rules and procedures of the air control tower ("TK-Tower") (S-3):

> *The control tower was an important player . . . manned by Air Force employees . . . they had been there from day one. On a regular basis, they had a tower meeting* (. . .) *and at a certain moment you learn with whom you have to coordinate, like: "this is the liaison officer from the Australian Army, how do you do . . . " And the Dutch Air Force was stationed one door further . . . nobody told us what to do . . . we had to discover everything ourselves.*

Learning to deal with the rules and procedures of TK-tower while operating resulted in problematic interaction between 107 ASBt and TK-tower. This was highlighted by an incident in which a Sperwer-UAV was launched while other air traffic was still approaching Camp Holland's airstrip. As an operator from 107 ASBt's Ground Control Centre explains, this incident resulted from misunderstanding in communication between 107 ASBt and TK-tower (G-1):

> *We were used to announce our launch by saying: "launch within ten minutes". TK-tower, however, thought that we were launching over exactly ten minutes. . . . So they thought that there was time for another airplane to land, whereas we decided to launch the UAV after five minutes.*

After this incident, an employee from the quality and safety department of 107 ASBt decided to inform TK-tower on the UAV's launching procedure, as an operator from the Ground Control Centre describes (G-6):

> *After that he*[20] *decided that we had to show each other our ways of working. Why some things are important to us and why some things are important to them. Tower personnel changed every eight weeks, and every time they changed we were introduced again. That was how we solved that with TK-tower. After a couple of times that went smooth.*

Another issue in dealing with TK-tower that 107 ASBt's operators had to cope with was that some aircrafts did not notify TK-tower of their approach. Also, during the first mission TK-tower had no directive role and was only able to provide non-binding advice due to legal restrictions in Uruzgan, as an operator of 107 ASBt's Ground Control Centre explains (G-1):

> *Sometimes we experienced that some aircrafts did not work with TK-tower at all. That we were landing and Afghan or Russian airplanes did not care about anything. . . . TK-tower tried to arrange everything but they had no directive role, they could not hold people accountable when the rules were not obeyed.*

Most of the time, however, the Sperwer was deployed outside the circle that was controlled by TK-tower. Outside this circle, other rules and regulations applied, that also had to be discovered by employees of 107 ASBt. Dealing with airspace users outside the circle controlled by TK-tower is detailed in the next section.

3.5.2.2 Dealing With Airspace Users Outside the Area of the Air Traffic Control Tower

Although the airspace outside the circle controlled by the air traffic control tower was designated as "uncontrolled airspace", the units within TFU employed several methods of "deconfliction"[21] to avoid conflicts and collision. Coordination between airspace users took mainly place within TFU's operations room (TFU-OPS). Within 107 ASBt the liaison officer (LSO) was responsible for coordinating with other units within TFU. During UAV flights, the liaison officer was seated in the TFU-OPS. Consequently, the LSO was a key player in discovering how things worked within TFU, as a commanding officer of 107 ASBt states (C-2):

> *While I was busy building our camp, the LSO went to the OPS-room and just asked: "how do things work around here?". And they explained it to him. He was also introduced to the Task Force Air Management Element* [TAME]. *He just made his own deals with everybody and constructed a couple of scenarios for particular operations. That is how agreements were made.*

The Task Force Air Management Element (TAME) was important for the coordination and planning of TFU's flying assets outside the circle that was controlled by TK-tower. All flying assets within TFU had a representative who took seating in TAME and agreements were made on where and when operations took place. By means of TAME, however, it was not possible to reserve pieces of airspace. Airspace had to be requested at the Combined Air Operations Centre in Bahrain (CAOC). This was done by means of requesting pieces of airspace, "keypads", through a computer program based on the instant messaging program mIRC, as the same commanding officer explains (C-2):

> *Before launching, airspace had to be requested. In TAME, no airspace is assigned. . . . There was a mIRC computer in the TFU OPS-room on which all messages for Regional Command South*[22] *were shown. On that computer, I also requested air space by typing "skyview airspace request". . . . And then I requested "keypads". They had put a raster over Uruzgan that divided the province in squares. I picked the particular keypads that we needed for an operation and chose a particular altitude. Those keypads were then reserved at that particular altitude. We also had to post our VHF frequency, so that other aircraft could contact us directly when they had fly through our airspace.*

Due to the nature of assignments, deconflicting the operations of the Sperwer-UAV with other flying assets of TFU by means of TAME and keypads, however, was associated with problems because the piece of airspace that was requested was by the Sperwer crew was very large, as a commanding officer describes (C-2):

> *We requested keypads that were several kilometers wide. And we mostly requested a space of eight by four keypads. It was impossible for other aircraft to know in which particular keypad we were at a certain point in time.*

As a result, deconfliction between aircraft outside the circle controlled by TK-tower relied mostly on local coordination by means of the VHF radio and "see and avoid", which are commonly used deconfliction methods for "regular" military aircraft. The Sperwer, however was not able to participate in these methods. With regard to "see and avoid" an operator of 107 ASBt's Ground Control Centre explains that the Sperwer-UAV was blind with regard to other aircraft in the airspace (G-1):

> *We were flying blind . . . I mean, the Sperwer does not have any eyes . . . We had a camera but that camera looks to the ground.*

In addition, most of the time the Sperwer-UAV operated outside the range of 107 ASBt's VHF radio that was located in the Ground Control Centre. It was therefore impossible for other aircraft to make contact with the Sperwer, as a commanding officer explains (C-2):

> *We flew on a particular altitude that was reserved for us only, and when other aircraft wanted to use that altitude they had to contact us by radio. . . . But they could not reach us. . . . The Sperwer was*

> *able to operate at a distance of 90 kilometers from the base, but the range of our VHF radio was much smaller. So, when we operated in Chora, for example, we did not know whether Apaches were also flying there.*

Consequently, deconflicting with other aircraft outside the circle controlled by TK-tower was impossible for 107 ASBt's operators. The same commanding officer of 107 ASBt states that the area outside TK-tower's circle looked like the "Wild West" (C-2):

> *Outside* (TK-tower's circle) *it was the Wild West. . . . We could not reach other aircraft. For example, we could not inform Apaches on our location . . . we were unable to contact anyone.*

These problems with regard to deconflicting outside TK-tower's circle had consequences for safety of operations within TFU, which is highlighted by a near miss between the Sperwer and two Dutch Apache helicopters, as a commanding officer explains (C-2):

> *We may have had countless near misses. . . . An Apache pilot thought that he had a near-miss with a French Mirage fighter jet . . . But at that time there were no French in that area. When they looked into that incident they found out that it was us.*

This section explicated how 107 ASBt dealt with other aircraft outside TK-tower's circle during flights that were scheduled. The next section will explicate how they dealt with other aircraft during ad-hoc operations and re-tasks.

3.5.2.3 Dealing With Airspace Users During Ad-Hoc Operations and Re-Tasks

As was highlighted previously, the Sperwer was often re-tasked during an ad-hoc event such as "troops in contact". During such ad-hoc events, many flying assets were directed to the same location to assist ground troops, which also that pre-defined plans of deconfliction needed to be abandoned. Deconflicting these assets during such ad-hoc operations was done by means of mutual communication in the Operations Room of Task Force Uruzgan (TFU-OPS). As is shown schematically in Figure 3.10, some units of TFU had their own section within TFU-OPS. A watch officer monitored ongoing operations ("Current").

For deconfliction between the Sperwer and other airspace users within TFU during ad-hoc operations, not only 107 ASBt's liaison officer (LSO) was seated in the TFU-OPS. An air liaison officer (ALO) was the representative for the assets of the Dutch Air Force such as Apaches and F16s.

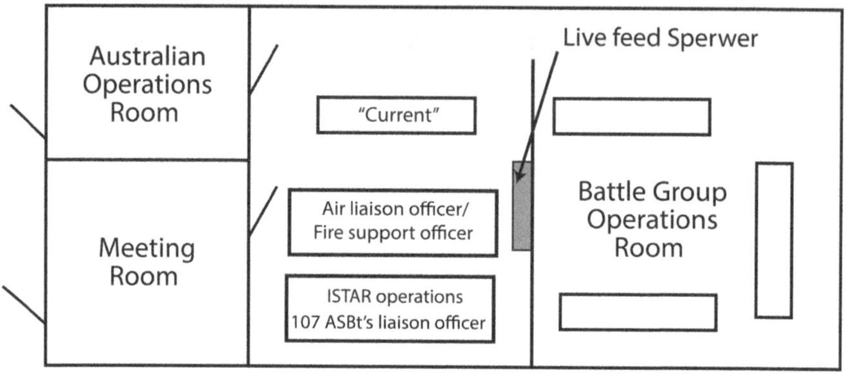

Figure 3.10 Schematic layout of the Operations Room of Task Force Uruzgan in 2008

A fire support officer (FSO) was the representative for the Battle Group.[23] Although the Battle Group was an Army unit, the Battle Group was an important airspace user as they operated with artillery.[24] The Dutch Air Force had a separate OPS-room at Camp Holland. Within the Air Force OPS-room a Ground Liaison Officer (GLO) represented the Army. Also, an Australian detachment was part of TFU, they had a separate room within TFU-OPS, as is shown in Figure 3.10.

During ad-hoc operations, a "Forward Air Controller" (FAC-er) managed the airspace around these operations. Mostly a FAC-er closed the airspace above ground operations for all non-essential aircraft by means of declaring a "Restricted Operations Zone" (ROZ). A commanding officer explains how he dealt with this seemingly complicated deconfliction process between flying units during ad-hoc operations (C-2):

> *When we had a re-task in an area that was not deconflicted beforehand, we arranged that on the spot. Then I went to the fire support officer and asked: "are you shooting over there?", "is there a ROZ"? Then I went to the ALO . . . and so I talked with all the important people.*

Although the Sperwer was directed to a ROZ many times to assist ground troops, there was no direct communication between the operator of the Sperwer in the Ground Control Centre and the FAC-er, as an operator explicates (G-6):

> *When we were tasked to assist troops in contact, the Apaches were mostly also there. But when F16 or F-18 fighter jets arrived we were*

almost always removed from the ROZ. That was all dealt with by the LSO. I never had direct contact with a FAC-er.

A commanding officer explains that one of the main reasons that the Sperwer operator could not communicate with a FAC-er was that both the operator of the Sperwer and the FAC-er would become overloaded with information (C-2):

When we were sent to such operations, I talked with the fire support officer and he then contacted the FAC-er. (. . .) It is good to have a couple of layers because a FAC-er does not want to listen to eight radios (. . .) and otherwise everybody would also start bothering the Sperwer operator.

3.5.3 Dealing With Units at Camp Holland

At the start of both missions, 107 ASBt had to build its camp in order to start operations. To do so, 107 ASBt had to work together with other units at Camp Holland such as the Engineers and Logistics. Dealing with units at Camp Holland is divided into two sections: dealing with units at Camp Holland at the beginning of both missions and dealing with constantly changing units at Camp Holland.

3.5.3.1 Dealing With Units at Camp Holland at the Beginning of Both Missions

At the beginning of the first mission 107 ASBt had to negotiate quite firmly to obtain a suitable place for deployment at Camp Holland, as an operator of 107 ASBt Ground Control Station describes (G-5):

Our place was hard earned by. . . . .[25] *He fought really hard for that spot. . . . And it was only dust and sand.*

However, the place at Camp Holland at which the Sperwer's launching device was located crossed the landing strip of Tarin Kowt airfield during launches of the UAV, as is schematically presented in Figure 3.11.

Consequently, 107 ASBt was confronted with landing and departing aircraft at every launch of the Sperwer. An operator of 107 ASBt Ground Control Station describes this launching situation (G-5):

We could only launch in one direction . . . and we could not launch in the opposite direction because then we would be launching over Camp Holland's barracks. We were launching over the landing strip, which was not helpful.

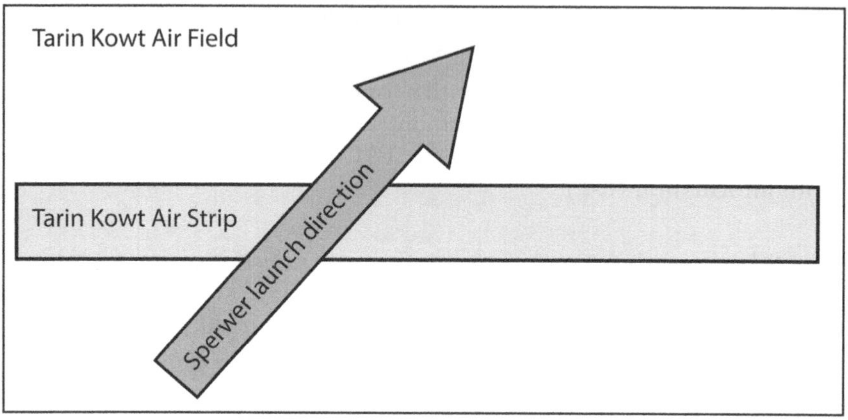

Figure 3.11 Schematic representation of Sperwer launches at Tarin Kowt airfield

Not only the place of the launching device was associated with problems. The launching device was also placed next to a so-called HESCO-wall, a big wall that was built to protect Camp Holland from enemy fire. This wall prevented the crew from having sight on the launching direction and incoming air traffic. Also, on the other side of the HESCO-wall was a road for military vehicles. To deal with incoming air traffic and traffic on the road next to the HESCO-wall, it was decided to put the Ground Safety Officer who was in charge of safety of ground operations of 107 ASBt, such as launching, on the HESCO-wall. In this way, he could be on the lookout for any problems during launching, as an operator of 107 ASBt's Ground Control Station explains (G-6):

> *He kept an eye on air traffic and other things. . . . We could not see that because we were launching over the HESCO-wall, so we put somebody up there. When he spotted any air traffic, the flight was aborted.*

An employee from 107 ASBt's quality and safety department acknowledges these tasks for the ground safety officer (S-2):

> *My main task was to monitor the surroundings, to look for any aircraft, personnel or cars. . . . When that happened, I aborted the launch and made sure that the incoming aircraft could land safely. . . . We experienced once that the UAV had a technical problem and dove into the airstrip after launch. . . . When there would have been a helicopter flying there, we would have had a serious problem.*

During the startup phase of 107 ASBt's first mission within TFU, the unit had to improvise at Camp Holland. Next to dealing with the launching location, maintenance of the Sperwer's parachutes was also characterized by improvisation, as an employee from 107 ASBt's quality and safety department describes (S-2):

> *When we arrived in Uruzgan, we had no water, no electricity and the location was problematic. We also discovered that our parachute-drying tower, which was 24 meters high, could not be placed at Camp Holland, and then we had to improvise. This had consequences . . . we lost electric power a couple of times and we also had shortage of water.*[26] (. . .) *In order to comply with safety rules and regulations we have to attain the right conditions. . . . Eventually we succeeded, but I doubt whether we operated optimally.*

The same employee from 107 ASBt's quality and safety department points out that the startup phase of the second mission resembled the startup phase of the first mission, but that it was easier for 107 ASBt to cope with units at Camp Holland because they had learned from previous experiences (S-2):

> *The problems started all over again. . . . They had not anticipated on our arrival again. . . . But it was easier for us because we had done it before. . . . We had to put a lot of effort in it.*

During 107 ASBt's missions, TFU's units at Camp Holland changed frequently. How 107 ASBt dealt with constantly changing TFU-personnel is explicated in the next section.

3.5.3.2 Dealing With "Rotating" Units at Camp Holland

Dealing with units at Camp Holland was complicated by the frequency in which units within TFU were relieved and replaced by "new" units from the Netherlands. Within the Dutch defense organization, the process of relieving and replacing units is also referred to as "rotation". An employee from 107 ASBt's Ground Control Station explains that every time the Battle Group "rotated", 107 ASBt was confronted with a "new" Battle Group that had to learn to work with an UAV all over again (G-5):

> *We invited the new Battle Group and showed them everything all over again. . . . How we worked and what we could and could not do.*

To deal with rotations, the units that were relieved tried to transfer as much knowledge as possible to the new units in a period of one or two weeks. This process of transferring knowledge is referred to as a

"HOTO" (hand-over-take-over). An operator from 107 ASBt's Ground Control Centre describes, however, that the HOTO-process of TK-tower were not sufficient to transfer all details of working with a Sperwer-UAV (G-1):

> *These HOTO's were not sufficient to learn everything about operating with a Sperwer. So, we knew that personnel of TK-tower changed every eight weeks. Then, we used to visit new TK-tower personnel to check up on any problems.*

TFU's Battle Group had a similar HOTO-process. However, when asked whether these HOTO's were sufficient to transfer all knowledge on operating with a Sperwer, an employee from 107 ASBt maintenance crew answers that this was not the case (M-2):

> *No, HOTO's are incredibly busy. There are twice as many people on the camp and they are constantly deliberating on how to do this and that. . . . And the people that are leaving have their minds already set at going home.*

"Rotating" was associated with safety issues because new units and employees within TFU had to learn to operate with the limitations and possibilities of a Sperwer-UAV all over again, as a commanding officer of 107 ASBt explains (C-2):

> *One of the issues was that a new commander did not understand our safety limitations. (. . .) One such as safety rule is that our landing zone had to be free of any obstacles. And the new commander decided that it would be convenient to build a new watchtower in that area . . . then we cannot fly anymore. . . . And also, he decided to place iron markers along a road in our landing zone . . . then we cannot fly anymore either because when a UAV hits those markers during landing, it's total-loss.*

On this particular issue, it was decided to start an "ORM-procedure", which was already mentioned previously. The same commanding officer explains this procedure on this particular issue (C-2):

> *We were already airborne when we heard that they had put iron markers in our landing zone. Then we had to start an ORM-procedure really quick. We had to weigh the risks of landing outside the camp risking that Taliban fighters would capture the UAV or risking substantial damage to the UAV by landing between the markers. Eventually the TFU-commander had to decide because that responsibility is above my pay grade. Losing the UAV would have cost us one million Euros.*

Operating in Uruzgan also meant that 107 ASBt had to deal with environmental circumstances regarding the weather and the landscape. These circumstances differed substantially when compared to their training circumstances. Strategies that concern dealing with such circumstances are reported in the next section.

3.5.4 Dealing With Environmental Circumstances in Uruzgan[27]

Environmental circumstances in Uruzgan differed substantially from 107 ASBt's training circumstances. For example, temperatures in Uruzgan ware much higher during the summer and the landscape in Uruzgan was characterized by mountains and a sandy and dusty soil. This section is divided into two sections: dealing with environmental circumstances during take-off and flight and dealing with environmental circumstances during landing.

3.5.4.1 Dealing With Environmental Circumstances During Take-Off and Flight

Camp Holland was located at a height of approximately 1300 meters. This meant that the air density was much lower when compared to 107 ASBt's training conditions. The difference in air density had a significant effect on the way the Sperwer was launched, as an employee from 107 ASBt's maintenance crew explains (M-2):

> *Here* [in the Netherlands] *we have an air density of 1013 at sea level. Over there we had an air density of 890 hecto Pascal. We had to adjust our launching speed because lower air density decreases lift of the UAV. Also, we the maximum altitude of the UAV was lower over there.*

The lower air density resulted in problems at the begin of the first mission that had to be solved to launch the UAV safely, as another employee of the maintenance crew describes (M-1):

> *Operators were not familiar with the difference in air pressure . . . it was a learning process.* (. . .) *At the beginning we saw that the UAV descended after launch . . . it just dropped.*

Along the way, a solution for this specific problem was found. An employee of 107 ASBt's maintenance crew explains that solving this problem involved considering many parameters (M-2):

> *One can solve that by making the UAV lighter, increasing the launching pressure and increasing the amount of RPM's of the Sperwer's engine. The launching pressure could only be increased until 9,8*

bar and making the UAV lighter by reducing the amount of fuel has implications for the range.

Mountains characterize the Uruzgan landscape, which is rather different than the landscape in which 107 ASBt used to train. Flying in this landscape resulted in problems with regard to the connection of the Ground Control Station with the Sperwer. When the Sperwer flew behind mountains, the connection with the Ground Control Station was lost. An employee from 107 ASBt's maintenance crew (M-1) explains that navigators were not familiar with this problem at the beginning. To prevent faulty maintenance orders due to these problems, he decided to coach the crew in the Ground Control Centre on the effects of mountains on the Sperwer's signal.

It occurred that the operator had communication problems with the UAV, that the images of the Sperwer's camera were not transmitted properly. That could result in aborting the mission and writing a maintenance order to find that communication problem. But what we did was when the operator encountered a communication problem they called me. I looked over their shoulder and asked things like: where are you flying? Then I saw that they were flying behind a mountain. . . . The navigator had also seen that but they do not understand that the communication link works on a line-of-sight principle. The aircraft must be in a direct line with our antennas. So, I told them to fly to the right . . . problem solved. And the operator will know about this problem in the future. . . . In this way, I saved maintenance a lot of extra and unnecessary work.

The same employee from 107 ASBt's maintenance crew (M-1) describes that such informal contacts were often established within the unit and that this way of working prevented a lot of unnecessary work and maintenance delays.

When they encountered a problem they first called the system expert.[28] And when he didn't understand the problem they called us. (. . .) In this way, we could catch up a lot of delays because many problems were prevented.

Also, during landing the Sperwer, 107 ASBt had to deal with local conditions. Strategies for dealing with such conditions during landing are explicated in the next section.

3.5.4.2 Dealing With Environmental Circumstances During Landing

High temperatures in Uruzgan had consequences for landing the aircraft safely because high temperatures result in even lower air density. Landing during daytime consequently resulted in rough landings that caused substantial damage to the UAVs, as an employee from 107 ASBt's assembly crew explains (A-3):

> *The UAVs came down pretty rough and that resulted in substantial damage. . . . At a certain point in time there were not many UAVs left to fly with. . . . And I told them that continuing flights during daytime would leave us with no UAVs left.*

By trying to coordinate maintenance and operations, flights were planned in the morning or evening as much as possible. Aligning maintenance and operations, however, was not easy as the same employee from 107 ASBt's assembly crew describes (A-3):

> *In the beginning coordination was difficult. We wanted to prove ourselves because we are relatively new Army unit. And it took a while before I had convinced the LSO that he should not accept assignments during daytime because those flights resulted in serious damages.*

Apart from high temperatures, characteristics of the Uruzgan landscape also resulted in problems during landing. Because of the rough and rocky soil, "belly pods"[29] were severely damaged. This caused maintenance problems as an employee from 107 ASBt's maintenance crew states (M-1):

> *We had a lot of damage . . . and therefore we could not keep up with the maintenance work. Then we decided to inspect the landing zone and we discovered that the zone was swamped with rocks . . . and there was even a large iron pole sticking out the ground. . . . They did not look at that at all.*

Dealing with these issues was also associated with internal tension and problems in the coordination between the sub-units of 107 ASBt, as the same maintenance employee describes (M-1):

> *There was a giant iron pole in the middle of the landing zone sticking out the ground. . . . Ground-OPS used that pole as a centering tool to build the landing zone. . . . They did not pay any attention to the consequences. . . . Things like that happened a lot.*

During the second mission, it was eventually decided to relocate the landing zone, as an employee from 107 ASBt's maintenance crew explains (M-2):

> *We were repairing "belly pods" continuously. (. . .) Eventually we decided to relocate the landing zone and we used the Engineer's*

> *salvage tank to even the ground and remove rocks. After that, things improved substantially.*

As highlighted previously, accumulating dust and sand was associated with problems with the Sperwer's parachutes. However, it took a while before this problem was discovered. Different parachute-related activities, such as cleaning, folding and assembling, were divided over separate departments within 107 ASBt. At first sight, the parachute problems were attributed to human errors during the parachute-folding process and technical problems. Eventually they discovered that accumulating dust and sand caused the parachute problem. An employee from 107 ASBt's maintenance crew explains that this was discovered through establishing coordination between 107 ASBt's maintenance and assembly departments (M-1):

> *We did the first investigation on the parachute problem. . . . And we saw that the parachute was stuck in the parachute bay. But at that time, we could not say whether that was due to human error or mechanical problems. . . . Until we talked to the system expert and he said that they had problems putting the parachute into the UAV. Then I got the idea that the parachutes must have been too big to fit in the parachute bay. . . . After the second crash, we were able to conclude that there must have been too much sand and dust in the parachutes. . . . They were simply too big.*

3.6 Analysis

In this section, the results of the reduction and integration phase are presented. In the reduction phase, the results of the previous section are analyzed in order to develop hypotheses on the influence of organizational design on self-organization and the emergence of safety for 107 ASBt within TFU. In the integration phase, conclusions are drawn on the influence of structural design characteristics on the emergence of safety during 107 ASBt's expeditionary operations within TFU. As such, this section presents the grounded theory that is developed in this chapter.

3.6.1 Reduction Phase

In the previous section, it became clear that interacting with TFU's units was associated with numerous safety problems. Also, interactions within 107 ASBt can be interpreted as being problematic, as these were associated with safety issues too. Subsequently, 107 ASBt's operators developed strategies that were aimed at discovering, creating and shaping the interaction network both within their own unit and within TFU. It was also shown, however, that such efforts sometimes were initiated after incidents had already occurred. Also, it sometimes seemed impossible to change the interaction network in such a way to create safe operations within TFU.

Subsequently, by combining the results with the "compass directions", this section firstly aims to reconstruct the relation between TFU's design on self-organization of 107 ASBt's operators and emergence of safety within TFU. After that, the relation between design of 107 ASBt, self-organization and emergence of safety of their operations within TFU is detailed. In this reconstruction, as was pointed out earlier, analytical abduction (cf. Kramer, 2004) is used to combine data of the specification phase with the "conceptual compass" in order to derive analytical statements on the relationship between organizational design self-organization and the emergence of safety for 107 ASBt's operations within TFU.

3.6.1.1 The Influence of Structural Characteristics of TFU

From the results outlined in the previous section, it can be firstly inferred that interaction between 107 ASBt and TFU's units was often characterized by missing integration between 107 ASBt and other units within TFU. This was highlighted in the section on dealing with assignments, dealing with airspace users and dealing with units at Camp Holland. Such missing integration consisted of two parts. At the one hand, 107 ASBt seemed to be poorly integrated into the operations of TFU, as it was shown that both TFU units' and 107 ASBt's operators did not know, at the start of TFU's operations, what place the UAV could take within TFU's operations. On the other hand, such missing integration was witnessed in the absence of agreements, or rules, between 107 ASBt and TFU's units. Along the concepts outlined in the conceptual "compass" this would point to an organization in which both the production and control structure was characterized by *limited structural coupling* (cf. De Sitter, 1994, p. 79) between its workstations. That is to say, from the start of the mission, input-output relations between 107 ASBt and TFU's units and accompanying agreements or control mechanisms, seemed to be missing. As structural coupling between workstations (i.e. units) can be regarded as a basis of any organization's structure, it can be questioned whether, from the perspective of 107 ASBt, TFU had a structure from the start of their operations.

Furthermore, it is argued that such limited structural coupling between 107 ASBt and TFU's other units can be related to the way TFU was "mixed and matched". As stated before, 107 ASBt was grouped with other Army and Air Force units in a large expeditionary configuration within TFU. This configuration differed substantially from the organizational configuration in which they were training in The Netherlands. In their training situation, 107 ASBt conducted assignments alone, whereas within TFU the unit was planned to operate as an intelligence unit that was meant to be part of a broader primary process of TFU that operated within the Uruzgan environment. As a result, the first hypothesis is formulated as follows:

Hypothesis 1: From the perspective of 107 ASBt, using a "mixing and matching" strategy to design TFU resulted in an expeditionary organization that was characterized by missing structural coupling between units.

It was witnessed in the case description that due to such missing integration, safety incidents occurred. This was highlighted by assignments that were ordered during lightning and with icy conditions, which confronted 107 ASBt and the Sperwer-UAV with dangers, a near miss with Apache helicopters and problems during take-off at Camp Hollands airstrip. It can be argued that, from the perspective of 107 ASBt, such safety issues came into existence as a direct result of TFU's structural layout and enactment (cf. Weick, 1979) of TFU in its dynamic complex mission environment. That is to say, at the one hand, from the perspective of 107 ASBt, TFU's "mixed and matched" organizational design resulted in missing integration between 107 ASBt and other units. On the other hand, because TFU operated in a dynamically complex operating environment, the only way of discovering what needed to be done in that environment was by acting. This means that TFU's units could not wait behind closed fences in order to find out what needed to be done and what rules to use in order to do so safely, they had to discover this along the way by enacting their environment. Due to such enactment, it can be argued that there was simply not enough time for 107 ASBt's operators find out how to operate with other units within TFU. Along Thompson's concepts, they indeed had to "swing into action". This resulted in operations with underdeveloped integration for critical interdependencies within TFU, which had safety consequences for both 107 ASBt and TFU.

Trying to explain these safety issues from an IOR perspective, however, seems to be challenging for the following reasons. Although safety incidents indeed seem to be directly associated with design of the expeditionary organization, they cannot be solely defined as a lack of control capacity or the result of structural complexity. Instead, from the perspective of 107 ASBt, the disturbances described previously were related to the absence of structural coupling between workstations within TFU and TFU's enactment in its operating environment. The absence of structural coupling is not part of the seven "design parameters" described in the section on the conceptual compass (3.2). This difference between the results found in this chapter and the premises of IOR may be attributed to the observation, which was also made earlier in this chapter, that IOR is mainly built for "Mainstream Holland Inc." instead of expeditionary organizations.

According to De Sitter (1994), Mainstream Holland Inc. is characterized by standard bureaucratic designs. Within such designs, coupling between workstations is already specified, which from the perspective of 107 ASBt is in contrast to expeditionary organizations in which coupling seems to be missing at the start of operations.[30] Nevertheless, based on the results of this chapter, the following hypothesis is formulated:

Hypothesis 2: A combination of missing structural coupling within TFU and TFU's enactment threatened safety of 107 ASBt and TFU during operations.

Due to missing structural coupling, self-organizing strategies of 107 ASBt's operators were initially characterized by finding ways to discover what assignments they had to do, with whom they had to cooperate and what rules and procedure applied within TFU. Sometimes they initiated such strategies after safety incidents had already occurred. In order to get to know other units and to find out what assignments could be done, "sales pitches" were organized by some of 107 ASBt's operators for other TFU units and TFU commanders. Subsequently, agreements had to be developed with these other units on what kind of assignments could be done and what could not be done with a Sperwer-UAV. Such activities can be interpreted as *self-design* (cf. Weick, 1977). Based on De Sitter's definition of structural coupling (1994, p. 79), 107 ASBt's activities can be interpreted as *creating* structural coupling within TFU's production structure. That is to say they were aimed at establishing input-output relationships and accompanying agreements between themselves and other TFU workstations. As structural coupling between units can be interpreted as the basis of any organizational structure, it can hence be interpreted that, from the perspective of 107 ASBt, operators were trying to self-design the unit into TFU's organizational structure.

In contrast to their self-organizing strategies for dealing with assignments, the strategies of 107 ASBt's operators for dealing with airspace users were not aimed at creating input-output relations. Instead, they were aimed at discovering, establishing and refining rules and procedures for safety-critical interdependencies, such as rules for "deconfliction" with other airplanes and procedures with TK-tower. Following De Sitter (1994), these strategies can be interpreted as attempts to integrate 107 ASBt into TFU's control structure. Yet, most airspace (safety-related) rules and procedures within TFU were based on existing NATO procedures. Consequently, most discovery efforts of 107 ASBt for dealing with airspace users seemed directed towards exploring an "already explored terrain". Therefore, the third hypothesis is formulated as follows:

Hypothesis 3: Self-organization of 107 ASBt's operators was mainly aimed at self-designing 107 ASBt into TFU's organizational structure.

Also, it can be argued that, due to enactment, it was gradually discovered within TFU in what ways the Sperwer could be best deployed to deal with the dynamically complex mission area in Uruzgan. This resulted in new and innovative ways to operate with the Sperwer-UAV. For example, after some time the UAV was "tasked" for rest-overnight operations and assignments together with Apache helicopters. However, as a result, 107 ASBt had to operate in changing configurations of other units within TFU with which integration turned out to be absent. Therefore, the fourth hypothesis is formulated as follows:

Hypothesis 4: Enactment of TFU in its environment and accompanying innovation of TFU's units with the Sperwer-UAV resulted in ongoing integration issues because of the changing configurations of units in which 107 ASBt operated.

Despite the occurrence of safety issues, 107 ASBt's operators reported that operating within TFU became less problematic after some time. In this sense, self-designing efforts of 107 ASBt's operators improved safety of UAV operations within TFU. These efforts of 107 ASBt's operators were, however, complicated by the frequency in which TFU's other units were relieved by "new" units from the Netherlands (i.e. "rotation"). These new units had to learn to operate with a Sperwer-UAV all over again, for which the Hand-Over-Take-Over procedure seemed too short. This resulted in safety issues, which was for example illustrated by problems on the Sperwers landing zone that resulted from orders of a Task Force Commander. Hence, the fifth hypothesis is formulated:

Hypothesis 5: Self-designing efforts of 107 ASBt's operators were complicated by "rotation" of units within TFU, which was associated with safety threats.

Lastly, 107 ASBt's operators found out that existing (NATO) rules and procedures did not fit their operations, which resulted in safety issues that were unsolvable for 107 ASBt's operators. This was highlighted by the inability of the Sperwer-UAV to participate in "see-and-avoid" and local deconfliction outside the area of TK-tower. Apparently, these rules and procedures did not fit the nature of UAV operations in Uruzgan. As a result, these aspects of TFU's control structure presented permanent safety threats to 107 ASBt's operations within TFU. Consequently, the sixth hypothesis is developed:

Hypothesis 6: Due to incompatible rules and procedures, 107 ASBt and TFU were confronted with permanent safety threats during UAV operations.

3.6.1.2 The Influence of Structural Characteristics of 107 ASBt

Next to the substantial influence TFU's interaction network had on self-organization and the emergence of safety, the interaction network within 107 ASBt also had a substantial influence on this.

During the 2008 and 2009 missions, TFU discovered that the Sperwer-UAV was a valuable asset in its operations in Uruzgan. This, however, increased the number of assignments substantially. As was stated in the specification phase, the increased number of assignments resulted in maintenance delays, shortage of spare parts, stress for individual operators and UAVs that were not fully operational. Especially shortage of spare parts combined with environmental circumstances in Uruzgan had safety consequences because parachutes needed to be "recycled" beyond their regular maintenance interval. This resulted in the accumulation of sand and dust, which turned out to be detrimental for the Sperwer's ability to land without damage. Although the assembly department had experienced that it was difficult to put the parachutes into the UAVs and the maintenance department had discovered that dust and sand had accumulated in the parachutes, it took two accidents to relate these findings to another. Therefore, it can be stated that interaction and coordination between the departments of 107 ASBt became problematic and this influenced the way operators within the unit could develop safety substantially. Similar internal problems can also be seen from the way departments of 107 ASBt interacted while creating a landing zone for the Sperwer on Uruzgan's rocky landscape. For example, 107 ASBt's Ground-OPS team was responsible for creating a landing zone. However, they did not seem to be aware of the requirements that were needed for a safe landing of Sperwers until maintenance employees decided to find out where substantial damages during landing came from. Although some may interpret these problems as a problem of communication within 107 ASBt, such lack of process oversight can be related to design of 107 ASBt's organizational structure.

De Sitter (1994; De Sitter et al., 1997) points out that grouping specific activities at specialist departments, which he refers to as a high degree of functional concentration, has a negative effect on process oversight within these different specialized departments. Decreased process oversight, on its turn negatively influences the ability of operators to solve disturbances and hinders outcomes at the organizational level. As can be seen in Figures 3.2 and 3.5, most activities of 107 ASBt are grouped at different specialist departments. Following De Sitter, therefore, 107 ASBt's structure can be interpreted an example of a functionally concentrated organizational structure.[31] It can thus be argued that problematic process oversight can be attributed to functional concentration within the unit. For 107 ASBt, it can consequently be posed that dividing 107 ASBt's activities over different specialist workstations had a negative effect on the ability of 107

ASBt's operators' self-organizing abilities and subsequently hindered the emergence of safety. Hence, the seventh hypothesis is developed:

Hypothesis 7: A high degree of functional concentration within 107 ASBt negatively influenced operators' self-organizing abilities and hindered the emergence of safety within the unit.

The 107 ASBt operators tried to deal with these issues by planning the UAVs differently, by recycling spare parts such as parachutes and by coordinating more intensively between operations and maintenance departments. Next to this, reshaping internal procedures was used as a strategy for dealing with changes in air density and temperatures, which were dangerous when launching the Sperwer. Following De Sitter's distinction between production and control, structure, these efforts can be interpreted as ad-hoc changes to 107 ASBt's control structure (i.e. redesign of 107 ASBt's control loops). It can be argued that, in this way, 107 ASBt's operators tried to adapt the unit to operating within TFU and environmental circumstances in Uruzgan. In line with the preceding section, the eighth hypothesis can be formulated:

Hypothesis 8: Self-organizing strategies within 107 ASBt partly consisted of redesigning control loops in an attempt to adapt their organization to demands of TFU and the Uruzgan environment.

In the next section, the results of the integration phase of this chapter are presented.

3.6.2 The Integration Phase

In this section, conclusions are drawn on the relation between organizational design, self-organization and the emergence of safety for 107 ASBt within TFU. A noteworthy result of the analysis is that organizational design of both TFU and 107 ASBt impacted self-organization and the subsequent emergence of safety substantially. Apparently from the beginning, TFU's design was characterized by missing structural coupling of 107 ASBt into TFU's production and control structure, which could be related to the way 107 ASBt was mixed and matched with other units within TFU. From the perspective of 107 ASBt, it can be stated that, from the beginning of their operations within TFU, a coherent expeditionary organization seemed to be absent. Because of TFU's necessity to act in its operating environment, however, 107 ASBt had to conduct its operations within TFU with an underdeveloped organizational structure, which had safety consequences for both 107 ASBt and TFU. As a reaction, 107 ASBt's operators began to improvise and pioneer within TFU in order to self-design the unit into TFU. Along the way and due to their efforts to integrate 107 ASBt within TFU, 107 ASBt's operators reported that operating within TFU became less problematic. However, due to "rotation" and incompatible rules and procedures for deconfliction in the air some issues were unsolvable for 107 ASBt's operators, which resulted in permanent safety threats to TFU. In this way, it can be argued that TFU's design presented 107 ASBt with safety issues problem that, at least partly, could not be solved. This consequently resulted in safety issues at the level of TFU that could not be avoided. Emergence of safety therefore seemed inherently compromised.

Furthermore, related to influence of 107 ASBt's design on safety it was found that poor process oversight and associated safety issues could be related to high degrees of functional concentration within 107 ASBt. Apparently, the way 107 ASBt was designed did not match expeditionary demands, which resulted in safety threats. As a reaction, 107 ASBt's operators tried to adapt their organization to demands within TFU and Uruzgan by reshaping control loops. This eventually increased the ability of 107 ASBt to operate safely in Uruzgan. Nevertheless, this was more or less achieved after safety incidents had already occurred.

3.7 Conclusion

This chapter aimed to explore the relationship between organizational design, self-organization and the emergence of safety within TFU by taking a specific "normal work" approach and using a grounded theory methodology. It was found that self-organization and the emergence of safety of 107 ASBt's operations within TFU was significantly and in multiple ways impacted by design of the unit itself and that of TFU. The exploration carried out in this chapter has provided a first but detailed understanding of the relationship between organizational design self-organization and the emergence of safety in an expeditionary organization. As was stated in Chapter 1, the results of this chapter will be used develop and understanding of the relationship between organizational design, self-organization and the emergence of safety in expeditionary organizations that can be used for building the theory at which this book is aimed. This means that findings from the perspective of 107 ASBt have to be generalized to the level of TFU and validated for expeditionary organizations in general. This is done in Chapters 4 and 5 of this book.

Notes

1. This chapter is partly developed from: Moorkamp, M., Wybo, J. L., & Kramer, E. H. (2016). Pioneering with UAVs at the battlefield: The influence of organizational design on self-organization and the emergence of safety. *Safety Science*. doi:10.1016/j.ssci.2015.09.029 and Moorkamp, M., Kramer,

E. H., Gulijk van, C., & Ale, B. J. M. (2014). Safety management within task force Uruzgan: A report on working with unmanned aerial vehicles. In R. D. J. M. Steenbergen, P. H. A. J. M. Van Gelder, S. Miraglia, & A. C. W. M. Vrouwenvelder (Eds.), *Safety, reliability and risk analysis: Beyond the horizon*. Boca Raton, FL: CRC Press.

2. This definition is literally translated from Dutch to English, based on De Sitter (1994).
3. IOR uses the concept of "control capacity" to refer to operator's options to deal with problems themselves (internal control capacity) or pass them on to another department/ workstation (external control capacity).
4. In recent developments of IOR written in Dutch, see for example Kuipers et al. (2010); eight parameters are used to characterize the production and control structure within an organization. However, the seven parameters presented in this section are adopted from an English article by De Sitter et al. (1997) and possess enough detail that suffice the purposes of this section of the book.
5. It has to be noted that production structure and control structure are concepts to understand and analyze the way activities are grouped and coupled, they do not refer to different "structures" within an organization. Only in bureaucratic organizations that are known for a maximum division of labor, production and control structure may refer to different and distinguishable organizational parts.
6. This is a major argument for preferring IOR concepts over HRT or resilience engineering concepts as a conceptual compass for the empirical studies in this book. The latter were critiqued in Chapter 2 for their inconsistency in dealing with assumptions from systems theory and organization design concepts.
7. The goal of this section is not to give an exhaustive and detailed overview of the different outcome "variables" at which De Sitter's theory is aimed at. The aim of this section is to evaluate IOR on its main premises. For a detailed overview see: Achterbergh and Vriens (2010).
8. This term is literally translated from the De Sitter's Dutch phrase "Doorsnee-Nederland B.V.".
9. 107 ASBt was named 101 Remotely Piloted Vehicle Battery until 2011. In this chapter, the unit will be referred to as 107 ASBt.
10. ISAF: International Security Assistance Force.
11. Soesterberg Air Force Base was closed in 2008. In 2006 however, it was still operational and provided operations in Uruzgan with Chinook transport helicopters.
12. It should be noted here that the operationalization presented in this section is more closely linked to a sensemaking approach to self-organization, as advocated by Weick (2012), than a complexity science interpretation of self-organization. Operationalization of the latter can be found in Comfort (1994) and Kauffman (1993), for example.
13. In this book, the words "organization design" and "organizational structure" are used interchangeably. This is done because, although other organization design approaches may contest this (see for example Burton et al., 2015), to IOR organization design is all about organizational structures.
14. This fallacy is often used in relation Bayesian statistics (see Villejoubert & Mandel, 2002) but seems to be relevant to the argument built here.
15. Some might argue that an inherent, and reliability enhancing, part of analyzing qualitative data is to replicate coding by a second "coder". Such efforts are thought to establish "inter-rater reliability". However, Morse (1997) points out that duplicating coding is only suitable for structured or semi-

structured interview techniques. For "open" interviews, it is impossible for a second "coder" to replicate the categories coded by the first coder. This is due to the gradual process of "open" interviews in which a better understanding of the phenomenon of interest is reached in the course of the entire interview process. In line with Morse, in this study it is not attempted to replicate coding of the categories by a second coder. Instead, a second interviewer was present during the first seven interviews presented in this study in order to ensure progress in understanding the phenomenon of interest during the interview process.

16. A difference between Yin and Wester and Peters can be found in their definition of reliability. Where Yin points out that reliability of a study should ensure that the same study can be can conducted all over again, Wester and Peters (2004, p. 129) point out that doing the exact same study over again might be impossible due to the fact that the study (for example interviewing respondents) has already been done. Instead they point out that reliability of a grounded theory study refers to the ability to trace research steps (in Dutch: navolgbaarheid).
17. In adhering to this advice from Yin, it is argued that the possibility to trace research steps is made possible. Hence, complying with the argument made by Wester and Peters presented in the earlier endnote.
18. IED: Improvised Explosive Device (roadside bomb)
19. This is how employees refer to their training area in 't Harde, the Netherlands.
20. The interviewee refers to the already mentioned employee from 107 ASBt's quality and safety department.
21. The rules and procedures that were employed to avoid conflicts and collision in the air, are referred to as "deconfliction measures".
22. Regional Command South was located in Kandahar and responsible for the south of Afghanistan, including Uruzgan.
23. The Battle Group mostly consisted of an Army infantry battalion and an Army artillery platoon. During the Uruzgan mission however, Battle Groups were also assembled from Marine units.
24. Artillery units are able to shoot with grenades over distances of approximately 20 kilometers and consequently use significant pieces of airspace during their operations.
25. The name is omitted to respect anonymity.
26. The Sperwer's parachutes had to be dried under specific atmospheric conditions, which required a certain humidity level. Water was needed to reach the required level of humidity.
27. Note that the term "environmental" employed in this section refers to atmospheric conditions and characteristics of the Uruzgan landscape. This is not to be confused with the term dynamic complex "environment" as it is used in section 3.2. The latter refers to the degree of environmental variation, that is to say the degree in which tasks and goals that an organization has to conduct in its operating environment, varies.
28. The system expert was the technical expert of the Sperwer-UAV and part of 107 ASBt's assembly crew.
29. "Belly pods" were located at the underside of the Sperwer and contained the UAV's camera.
30. This observation may pose an opportunity to contribute to IOR and Sociotechnical Systems Design theory. Therefore, this aspect is also addressed in the chapters later on in this book.

31. By using IOR's "design parameters", it can be argued that 107 ASBt's production structure is also characterized by a high degree of division between performance, preparing and supporting activities (parameter 2). It can be argued however, that such a division is a more detailed translation of "functional concentration". Hence, the term "functional concentration" is employed in the seventh hypothesis.

References

Achterbergh, J., & Vriens, D. (2010). *Organizations: Social systems conducting experiments*. Berlin: Springer Verlag.

Blumer, H. (1986). *Symbolic interactionism: Perspective and method*. Berkeley, CA: University of California Press.

Boeije, H. R. (2005). *Analyseren in kwalitatief onderzoek: denken en doen*. Amsterdam: Boom bestuurskunde.

Bourrier, M. (2002). Bridging research and practice: The challenge of "Normal Operations" studies. *Journal of Contingencies and Crisis Management*, *10*(4), 173–180.

Burton, R., Obel, B., & Håkonsson, D. (2015). *Organizational design: A step-by-step approach*. Cambridge: Cambridge University Press.

Comfort, L. K. (1994). Self-organization in complex systems. *Journal of Public Administration Research and Theory: J-PART*, *4*(3), 393–410.

Dekker, S. W. A. (2005). *Ten questions about human error*. New York: Lawrence Erlbaum.

International Civil Aviation Organization. (2006). *Doc 9859 AN/474: Safety management manual* (1st ed.). Montreal: ICAO.

Kauffmann, S. (1993). *The origins of order: Self-organization and selection in evolution*. New York: Oxford University Press.

Kramer, E. H. (2004). *Organizing doubt: Self-organization and army units in crisis operations*. Eindhoven: Eindhoven University of Technology.

Kuipers, H. (1998). The socio-technical designer as Wizard and Juggler. *Concepts and Transformation*, *3*(3), 229–254.

Kuipers, H., van Amelsvoort, P., & Kramer, E. H. (2010). *Het Nieuwe Organiseren: alternatieven voor de bureaucratie*. The Hague: Acco.

Moorkamp, M., & Kramer, E. H. (2014). *Veiligheid van expeditionair organiseren binnen Task Force Uruagan*. Breda: Netherlands Defense Academy.

Moorkamp, M., Kramer, E. H., van Gulijk, C., & Ale, B. J. M. (2014). Safety management within task force Uruzgan: A report on working with unmanned aerial vehicles. In R. D. J. M. Steenbergen, P. H. A. J. Van Gelder, S. Miraglia, & A. C. W. M. Vrouwenvelder (Eds.), *Safety, reliability and risk analysis: Beyond the horizon*. Boca Raton, FL: CRC Press.

Moorkamp, M., Wybo, J-L., & Kramer, E. H. (2016). Pioneering with UAVs at the battlefield: The influence of organizational design on self-organization and the emergence of safety. *Safety Science*, *88*, 251–260.

Morse, J. M. (1997). Perfectly healthy, but dead: The myth of inter-rater reliability. *Qualitative Health Research*, *7*, 445–447.

Royal Netherlands Army. (2002). *Armyplan 1341*. Internal document Royal Netherlands Army. The Hague: Ministry of Defense.

Royal Netherlands Army. (2003). *Armyplan 1342*. Internal document Royal Netherlands Army. The Hague: Ministry of Defense.

Royal Netherlands Army. (2007). *Armyplan 1522*. Internal document Royal Netherlands Army. The Hague: Ministry of Defense.

Sitter, L. U. de. (1994). *Synergetisch produceren: Human Resources Mobilisation in de produktie een inleiding in structuurbouw*. Assen: Uitgeverij Van Gorcum.

Sitter, L. U. de, Hertog, J. F. den, & Dankbaar, B. (1997). From complex organizations with simple jobs to simple organizations with complex jobs. *Human Relations*, *50*(5), 497–534.

Strauss, A., & Corbin, J. M. (1990). *Basics of qualitative research: Grounded theory procedures and techniques*. Newbury Park, CA: Sage Publications, Inc.

van Eijnatten, F. M., & Van Der Zwaan, A. H. (1998). The Dutch IOR approach to organizational design: An alternative to business process re-engineering? *Human Relations*, *51*(3), 289–318.

Villejoubert, G., & Mandel, D. R. (2002). The inverse fallacy: An account of deviations from Bayes's theorem and the additivity principle. *Memory & Cognition*, *30*(2), 171–178.

Weick, K. E. (1977). Organization design: Organizations as self-designing systems. *Organizational Dynamics*, *6*(2), 31–46.

Weick, K. E. (1979). *The social psychology of organizing*. New York: McGraw-Hill.

Weick, K. E. (2012). *Making sense of the organization volume 2: The impermanent organization*. Hoboken, NJ: John Wiley & Sons, Inc.

Wester, F. (1987). *Strategieën voor kwalitatief onderzoek*. Bussum: Coutinho.

Wester, F., & Peters, V. (2004). *Kwalitatieve analyse: uitgangspunten en procedures*. Bussum: Coutinho.

Yin, R. K. (2003). *Case study research: Design and methods* (Vol. 5). Thousand Oaks, CA: Sage.

4 The Influence of Temporary Organization Design on the Operations of Task Force Uruzgan

4.1 Introduction

In the previous chapter, hypotheses were developed on the relationship between organization design, self-organization and the emergence of safety for 107 ASBt's operations within Task Force Uruzgan. However, in order to "fill" the theoretical gap that was identified in Chapter 2, the "conceptual map" that is developed in the course of this book needs to get beyond the exploration stage. For this, an understanding of the relationship between organizational design, self-organization and the emergence of safety has to be developed for expeditionary organizations in general. This chapter will therefore present the third study of this book in which the following research question will be addressed:

> **What hypotheses on the relation between organization design, self-organization and the emergence of safety in expeditionary organizations can be formulated?**

Chapter 3 showed a substantial relation between organizational design and the emergence of safety at two organizational levels, that of 107 ASBt and that of TFU. However, a number of generalization issues arise in translating these results to the level of TFU and expeditionary organizations in general. That is to say, the study in Chapter 3 was conducted only from the perspective of 107 ASBt. The particular influence of organizational design on the emergence of safety found within the 107 ASBt case may, therefore, have been unique for them and not symptomatic for either Task Force Uruzgan or expeditionary organizations in general. It was already highlighted in Chapter 3 that some characteristics of 107 ASBt made the unit unique within the Royal Netherlands Army. For example, 107 ASBt could not train with other units due to legal restrictions on the UAV, which could have played a major role in the integration issues they experienced within TFU. Also, 107 ASBt was operating as a particular intelligence unit that, due to the unmanned nature of the UAV, did not directly engage in the dynamics of the Uruzgan operating

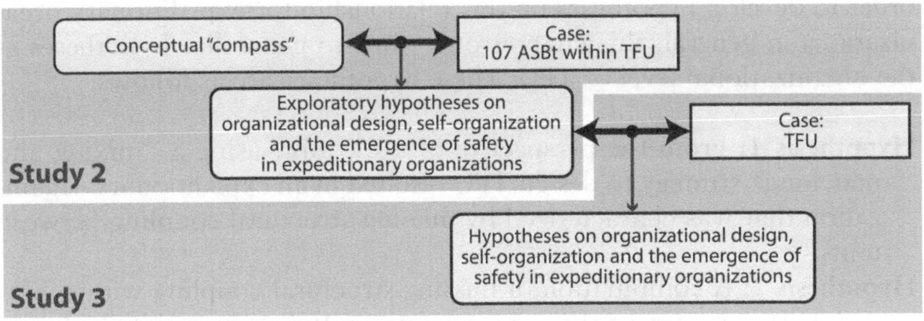

Figure 4.1 Research model of study 3

environment. This might have had consequences for the type and amount of safety related issues that were found in Chapter 3. Hence, findings within 107 ASBt cannot be translated one-on-one to the level of TFU or expeditionary organizations in general.

Therefore, to be useful for the goal of this book, findings on the relationship between TFU's organizational design and the emergence of safety from the perspective of 107 ASBt have to be firstly verified by studying other units within TFU in such a way that statements can be made on the relation between organizational design and the emergence of safety at the level of TFU. After that, it has to be elaborated how these findings can be generalized to the level of expeditionary organizations in general, at Van Strien's level B.

In this chapter therefore, by conducting a second case study in which other units within TFU are studied, it is firstly attempted to generalize hypotheses on the relationship between organizational design and the emergence of safety within TFU. After that, analytical generalization (cf. Yin, 2003) is used to construct hypotheses on the influence of organizational design on the emergence of safety for expeditionary organizations in general. These steps can be visualized by means of Figure 4.1.

This chapter is subsequently divided into several sections. Firstly, the hypotheses developed in Chapter 3 that this chapter aims to verify are presented. Secondly, more background information is given on Task Force Uruzgan. Secondly, the methodology that is used in this chapter is presented. Thirdly, the results and analysis are explicated. Finally, the chapter ends with a conclusion.

4.2 Hypotheses Derived From the Perspective of 107 ASBt

In this section the hypotheses developed in Chapter 3 on the relationship between TFU's organizational design, self-organization and the emergence of safety are presented only. The reason for this is that in order to develop hypotheses on this relationship for expeditionary organizations in general, this chapter only aims to generalize hypotheses at the organizational level of TFU. These hypotheses are as follows:

Hypothesis 1: From the perspective of 107 ASBt, using a "mixing and matching" strategy to design TFU resulted in an expeditionary organization that was characterized by missing structural coupling between units.

Hypothesis 2: A combination of missing structural coupling within TFU and TFU's enactment threatened safety of 107 ASBt and TFU during operations.

Hypothesis 3: Self-organization of 107 ASBt's operators was mainly aimed at self-designing 107 ASBt into TFU's organizational structure.

Hypothesis 4: Enactment of TFU in its environment and accompanying innovation of TFU's units with the Sperwer-UAV resulted in ongoing integration issues because of the changing configurations of units in which 107 ASBt operated.

Hypothesis 5: Self-designing efforts of 107 ASBt's operators were complicated by "rotation" of units within TFU, which was associated with safety threats.

Hypothesis 6: Due to incompatible rules and procedures, 107 ASBt and TFU were confronted with permanent safety threats during UAV operations.

4.3 Task Force Uruzgan and the Development of Smallest Units of Action[1]

Initially, in 2006, the Dutch government depicted the operation in Uruzgan as a reconstruction operation. However, over the four years of its deployment, TFU has engaged in numerous combat activities with opposing parties in the Uruzgan province. Along the way an assembly process was developed within TFU to create operational units that could match these demands. These units were called Smallest Units of Action (SUAs) or Combined Arms Teams (CATs). Because assignments could practically vary per mission, the SUAs within TFU differed substantially from each other in composition (Kramer et al., 2012). The bottom-up design process of SUAs within TFU is schematically presented Figure 4.2. The dotted lines in this Figure reflect that TFU staff had limited command and control over the Air Task Force, the Military Police and the Special Forces.

4.4 Methodology

To verify the hypotheses developed in Chapter 3 and subsequently develop hypotheses at the level of expeditionary organizations in general,

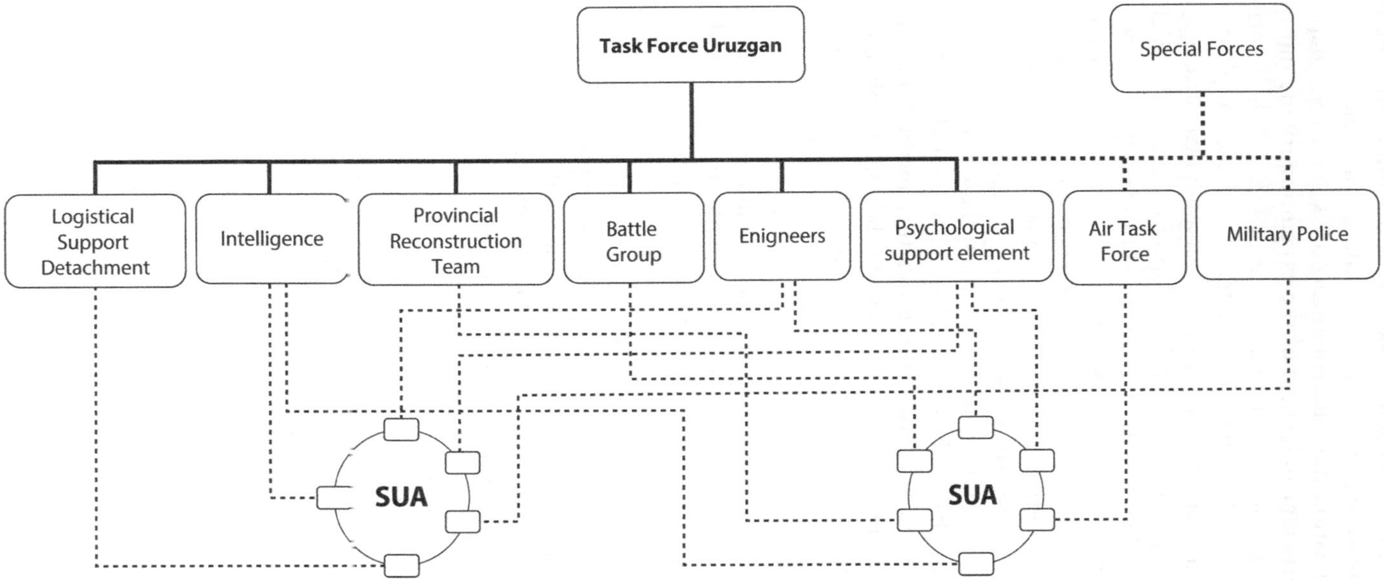

Figure 4.2 Task Force Uruzgan's Smallest Units of Action (SUA) assembly process

a "normal work" approach is taken that resembles the one outlined in Chapter 3. However, instead of exploring the influence of TFU's design on self-organization and the emergence of safety, this chapter aims to search for particular influences of the expeditionary organization design on self-organization and the emergence of safety. The "normal work" approach as was described in Chapter 3, is hence applied in a rather "deductive" fashion. That is to say, as an analytical strategy, deduction is aimed at "applying general rules to specific cases" (cf. Richardson & Kramer, 2006). Yet, the study presented in this chapter is not to be interpreted as "purely" deductive because during the analysis room is left for other experiences from respondents. Hence, the approach taken in this chapter can be interpreted as taking an approach that resembles analytical abduction, as the "rules" derived from Chapter 3 are verified with the possibility for respondents to diverge from these "rules".

To carry out the study in this chapter, a second case study will be conducted. The main reason for using this methodological approach is that is applicable to study phenomena that are highly contextualized (Strauss & Corbin, 1990), which still is the case for operations of expeditionary organizations. Also, as was also highlighted in the previous chapter, a case study approach is able to map interactions and the way these interactions give meaning to experiences of individuals. However, based on the points stressed in this section, a qualitative case study approach has to be applied in a particular way to verify the hypotheses developed in Chapter 3. That is to say, based on the goal of this chapter and the potential problems of generalization highlighted in the introduction, three criteria for such a methodology can be emphasized.

Firstly, the relationship between organizational design, self-organization and the emergence of safety within TFU that was found from the perspective of 107 ASBt needs to be generalized to the level of TFU. To do so, it has to be verified whether the nature of the interaction network of TFU as experienced from the perspective of 107 ASBt, can be attributed to their uniqueness or that these influences are exemplary for the way other units within experienced operating within their interaction network. Determining whether the results from Chapter 3 can be attributed to 107 ASBt's uniqueness or not, implies that it has to be investigated whether interaction of other units with 107 ASBt can be interpreted as being similar to the way these other units dealt with other interaction partners. Subsequently, when this is the case, it can be concluded that 107 ASBt's experiences were not that unique within TFU. This may subsequently imply that other units had experiences within TFU similar to 107 ASBt's experiences, which may suggest that a similar relationship between organizational design, self-organization and the emergence safety can be analytically reconstructed. This subsequently may make attempting to verify the hypotheses developed in Chapter 3, and generalize these to the level of TFU, a road worthwhile to take. Only after these steps have been taken, it seems to be valid to investigate whether and how such findings from within TFU are relevant for expeditionary organizations in general.

To conduct a qualitative case study that enables taking the steps highlighted above, the next sections explicates research design, data collection and data analysis of the study presented in this chapter.

4.4.1 Research Design

To verify whether 107 ASBt's experiences within TFU's interaction network can be attributed to the unique character of their operations or that they are exemplary for the way other units developed safety within TFU, 11 in-depth interviews are analyzed in this chapter. Nine in-depth interviews were conducted with representatives of various units within TFU with which 107 ASBt needed to interact during their operations within TFU in the period between 2006 and 2010. In addition, two interviews with representatives of 107 ASBt, who coordinated frequently with TFU's units were used to place experiences of other units with 107 ASBt into context.

By selecting respondents in this way, it can be studied how these units dealt with 107 ASBt, how they dealt with other interaction partners and whether they experienced influences from the TFU's interaction network in a way similar to 107 ASBt's experiences. According to Yin, this strategy can be called a single-case study in which multiple sub-units are embedded (2003, p. 40). A visual representation of the units studied within TFU is presented later.

4.4.2 Data Collection

During the interviews respondents were firstly asked how they dealt with 107 ASBt during their operations and what strategies they used to deal with other interaction partners in developing safety of their own operations within TFU. Subsequently, the interview was directed to investigating whether these strategies resembled the strategies of 107 ASBt. As such, the interviews were not "open" but guided by the results from Chapter 3. To refer to respondents in the results section of this chapter, respondents were given a "code" that represents to their function within TFU. These codes are shown in Table 4.1. In this way anonymity is guaranteed because results are not traceable to individual respondents.

4.4.3 Data Analysis

To verify the hypotheses that were developed for the organizational level of TFU in Chapter 3 and generalize these to the level of expeditionary organizations in general, this chapter also uses the research steps Wester and Peters (2004) proposed for developing a grounded theory. This methodology is chosen because it gives the possibility to use the proposed

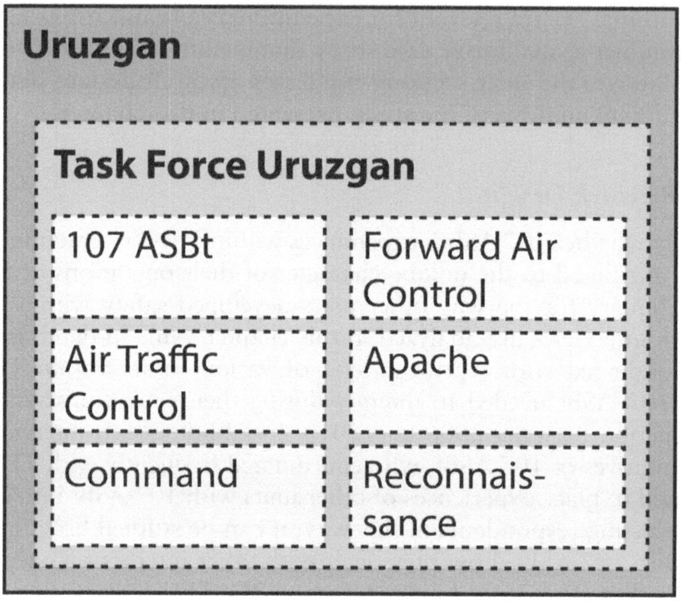

Figure 4.3 Research strategy of Study 3

Table 4.1 Coding respondents of study 3

Respondent	*Code*
Commanders	C
Air Traffic Controllers	ATC
Reconnaissance Operators	REC
Forward Air Controllers	F
Air Liaison Officers	ALO
Apache Pilots	AP

research steps to systematically combine (cf. Dubois & Gadde, 2002) the experiences of units within TFU with the results from Chapter 3. Also, application of their research steps gives the opportunity to apply analytic generalization to generalize results from the level of TFU to the level of expeditionary organizations in general. To do so, the research steps proposed by Wester and Peters are not applied straightforward, but in the following way:

Firstly, the exploration phase is aimed at exploring ways in which the units studied in this chapter dealt with 107 ASBt and whether this had similar consequences for safety as compared to the results of Chapter 3. After that it is investigated how they dealt with other units within TFU and what influence this had on the type and amount of safety issues and their ability to solve safety issues. Subsequently, coding the interviews was done by "axial coding" (cf. Boeije, 2005) in which it was firstly investigated whether they dealt with 107 ASBt in a way similar to the way in which they dealt with other units. Secondly, in the specification phase, the experiences of other units were linked to those found from the perspective of 107 ASBt. After that, verifying the hypotheses that were derived from the perspective of 107 ASBt becomes possible. As such, thirdly, in the reduction phase, the findings of the specification phase are confronted with the hypotheses developed in Chapter 3. Fourthly, in the integration phase, it is established whether these findings can be analytically generalized beyond TFU, to expeditionary organizations in general. As a result of the integration phase, new hypotheses are developed on influences of organizational design, self-organization and the emergence of safety in expeditionary organization that are located at Van Strien's level B.

4.4.4 Reliability and Validity

The methodological choices made in this chapter have consequences for reliability and validity of the results and analyses. The procedures used in this chapter resemble those in Chapter 3. However, as the research goal of this chapter is substantially different than the goal of Chapter 3, the procedures followed in this chapter are different as well. Therefore, this section explicates the measures taken to attain reliability and validity of the results and analyses of this chapter.

For attaining reliability, Yin (2003, p. 37) advises to document as many research steps as possible. Therefore, in addition to the procedure followed for documenting interviews conducted within 107 ASBt, interviews were also recorded digitally by means of a voice recorder and subsequently transcribed word-for-word. Internal validity refers to the ability of the study to detect possible intervening variables in making casual claims. The methodological steps proposed in the previous sections, which are an application of the grounded theory methodology developed by Wester and Peters, are aimed at detecting possible intervening variables. Especially in the exploration and specification phase are characterized by going back and forth between data, and the results from Chapter 3. With regard to attaining construct validity, it has to be shown in this chapter that changes in safety within TFU are due to aspects of the expeditionary organization's structural design that influences the amount and type of safety issues and the way operators could solve safety issues. In order to do so, as was mentioned before, structural influences have to be reconstructed analytically. That is to say, these influences cannot be "seen" directly and therefore have to be "built" analytically from combining operators' experiences with theoretical constructs along the "normal work" approach outlined in Chapter 3.

External validity is particularly relevant for this chapter because the goal of this chapter was to develop hypotheses for expeditionary organizations in general, whereas data is gathered within a particular expeditionary organization, TFU, guided by hypotheses developed from the perspective of 107 ASBt. Several steps are taken in the analysis of this chapter to enable generalization. Firstly, it is verified how the units studied within TFU dealt with 107 ASBt and whether this resembled the way in which they dealt with units in their own interaction network. From this step, it becomes clear whether 107 ASBt is to be treated as a unique unit within TFU or that similarities can be detected between 107 ASBt and other units within TFU. When the latter is the case, results derived from the perspective of 107 ASBt may be relevant more broadly within TFU. Only after establishing this, it can be attempted to verify hypotheses derived from the perspective of 107 ASBt at the level of TFU. Thirdly, analytical generalization (cf. Yin, 2003) is used to elaborate on the relevance of these findings for expeditionary organizations in general.

An aspect that may hinder external validity in this chapter is that the results of Chapter 3 steer the way other units within TFU are researched. Because of this strategy, the study in this chapter may not "see" that other units within TFU may have experienced other influences on safety from their interaction network, which may point to other influences of organizational design. A counterargument to this is, however, that analytical abduction, or systematic combining—in terms of Dubois and Gadde (2002)—is used as an analytical strategy in studying these other units. By means of this analytical strategy, empirical data and the results from Chapter 3 are constantly confronted with each other. This ensures that at the one hand, enough room was left in the interviews for the respondents to elaborate on potential other influences of the organizational network within TFU. On the other hand, it ensures that potential other influences of organizational design are not missed. Lastly, in the step in which analytical generalization takes place, findings are generalized to expeditionary organizations in general with help from existing theory. This makes sure that hypotheses developed for expeditionary organizations in general are connected to issues that can be interpreted as being relevant to the family of expeditionary organizations at which this book is aimed.

4.5 Results

The results are presented in the following way. Firstly, the results of the exploration phase are presented in which it is detailed how the units studied in this chapter interacted with 107 ASBt and whether this has similar consequences for the safety issues that they experienced and the way they could deal with safety issues. After that, it is detailed whether interaction with other partners within TFU influenced the amount of safety issues and the way they could deal with safety issues. Secondly, the results of the specification phase are presented in which it is explicated whether these influences of the interaction network resembled influences experienced by 107 ASBt. Secondly, in the reduction phase, it is attempted to verify hypotheses on the relationship between organizational design, self-organization and the emergence of safety developed in Chapter 3, which were also presented earlier. After that, the integration phase uses analytical generalization to develop hypotheses on the relationship between organizational design, self-organization and the emergence of safety for expeditionary organizations in general.

4.5.1 Exploration Phase: Interacting With 107 ASBt and Other Units Within TFU

This section first describes how the units studied in this chapter interacted with 107 ASBt and whether this, from their perspective, was associated with similar safety issues. After that, it is explicated whether this resembles the way they dealt with other interaction partners within TFU.

4.5.1.1 Interacting With 107 ASBt

From Chapter 3, it became clear that 107 ASBt's operators experienced limited integration between their units and other units within TFU. From the perspective of the units studied in this chapter, integration with 107 ASBt also seemed problematic and resulted in similar safety issues. A Royal Netherlands Air Force air traffic controller explains that it was unclear for air traffic control personnel what to do in the case of an incident or emergency with the Sperwer (ATC-2):

> *I witnessed that they said: "launch within ten minutes". And that we were waiting . . . and that the Sperwer crashed headfirst into the "dirt-strip[2]" immediately after launch. . . . And then I had to coordinate with these guys because I didn't know what do. Is it dangerous? Are the guys from 107 going to retrieve it? What are we going to do? It was just lying there with its nose in the sand.*

Also, from Chapter 3 it became clear that from the perspective of 107 ASBt, the unit was poorly integrated in the Uruzgan airspace as they could not participate in local "deconfliction" and see-and-avoid. In this way 107 ASBt relied on other units for safe operations.[3] An Apache pilot, however, explains that keeping clear of the Sperwer was an issue due to the Apache's limitations, which were discovered during operations in Uruzgan (AP-2):

> *We did not have contact with the Sperwer operator. They were flying blind. So, we had to deconflict that before take-off. (. . .) Then we made agreements based on altitude. They were at altitude X, so*

> *then we had to stay away from that altitude. . . . That was arranged by mIRC. One of the problems with that was when we were in the air, we could not transmit that information to the aircraft. That was problematic because we only had* [VHF] *line of sight connections.*

Along the way, Apache pilots found a way to get information on the whereabouts of other Sperwer-UAVs, and other flying assets of TFU, by contacting Forward Air Controllers in the field with their onboard, line of sight, VHF radio. Forward Air Controllers (FAC-ers) were responsible for tasking and "deconflicting" fire support assets, for supporting patrols on the ground. Within TFU, Dutch Apaches, F16's and artillery mostly provided fire support for these patrols. In addition, American F15 and F18 fighter jets were able to provide fire support in the Uruzgan province. During fire support, TFU staff in the OPS-room assigned a Restricted Operations Zone (ROZ) to FAC-ers. FAC-ers were one of the few operators on the field that had both a VHF radio and a tactical satellite radio (TACSAT). With TACSAT, FAC-ers were able to connect to many other units in the field, CAOC and the TFU operations room. On the question whether they were increasingly employed as a "radio relay station", a FAC-er answers (F-3):

> *That happened a lot. One of the channels was the TAC-P*[4] *admin net. All TAC-P's in Afghanistan were on that channel. It happened that we were in an area that belonged to our Battle Group, but that we were working with units that were controlled by another Task Force. So, my situational awareness (SA) was much better than the SA of my commander.*

However, developing safe operations by means of this strategy did not always succeed. A consequence was that Apaches did not always know where Sperwers were flying. Keeping clear of Sperwers depended consequently on the visual ability of Apache pilots to spot and avoid a Sperwer in the air. Due to the size and color, however, Sperwers were hard to spot, as the same Apache pilot explains (AP-2):

> *Look, Sperwers were a pain in the ass . . . they were hard to spot.*

Also, a Forward Air Controller states that because of these problems to avoid the Sperwer, Apaches and Medevac (medical evacuation) helicopters, with which he had frequent contact, did not like the presence of the Sperwer in their airspace (F-3):

> *Apaches, the Sperwer and Medevacs were not each other's friends.* (. . .) *That went wrong* (. . .) *Sperwers were unable to keep the altitude*

> *to which they were assigned and they were unaware of each other's position in the air.*

In Chapter 3, it was also highlighted that units within TFU started innovating with the UAV, that was found to increase the ability to operate in the dynamic Uruzgan operating environment. A TFU commander underscores this by stating that (C-3):

> *If you want to know what happens at the other side of a hill without a UAV, you have to walk. And when you arrive there and they* [opposing forces such as Taliban] *start to shoot, you are in combat. When you have a UAV, you are able to scout whether opposing forces are present or not before you send your troops to that area. Also, when we conducted operations on roadside bombs, reconnaissance by foot is very time consuming. In addition, we were vulnerable when we stayed at the same place for some time. . . . Then you have to keep an eye on the surrounding area to see whether they* [opposing forces] *were coming for us. . . . That was all possible with a UAV.*

The Sperwer was increasingly tasked to various assignments with various units such as patrolling over ground forces who had to "rest overnight" in the field. A reconnaissance operator explains that in due time, they did not want to go on patrol without the presence of the Sperwer in the air above them to scout for possible dangers (REC-1):

> *When we didn't have a Sperwer during operations in Mirabad, I'm sure that we had overlooked important things. . . . Opposing forces moving in the field . . . And so, we were very happy to have a Sperwer above us because then we were able to see what was going on.* (. . .) *The element of surprise was removed by using a Sperwer.* (. . .) *It* [the Sperwer-UAV] *was very important to us.*

Also, for TFU's OPS-room the Sperwer became important for creating "situational awareness" (SA). As a result, the Sperwer was often tasked to improve SA of TFU's staff despite its negative effects on ground operations, as a FAC-er explains (F-3):

> *Then it happened that when I was in a TIC* [Troops in Contact] *situation a UAV was launched while I asked for fixed wing combat support. Then I said: that is no use to me out here. . . . They answered: the UAV can help improving SA. Well, I didn't need that because I already knew where the enemy was.*

An Apache pilot explains that such innovation with the Sperwer, however, increased safety issues in the Uruzgan airspace because Apaches were sent to areas were a Sperwer was flying because they had to eliminate opposing forces discovered by a Sperwer (AP-2):

> *With regard to safety in the air. . . . What happened a lot was that a Colonel or a General saw something on the Sperwer's live feed* [in TFU's OPS room] *and then decided to send Apache to that area.* (. . .) *In these cases, we were sent to areas were a Sperwer was flying.*

These statements highlight that also from the perspective of other units, integration with 107 ASBt was problematic, that they too attempted to create and shape interaction with the UAV unit but that this was not always successful and led to safety issues that could hardly be solved.

The next question addressed is this: what strategies did the units studied in this chapter use to interact with other units? That for engaging in TFU's operations, interacting with other units may show similarities to the way they had to deal with 107 ASBt was already highlighted briefly by the quoted FAC-er who explains his role as a "radio relay station". This quote reveals that FAC-ers were not only used in this way to create integration with Sperwers, but that they seemed to be contacted many other units for similar issues. This may imply that for more units, integration into TFU was an issue and that they used ad-hoc solutions in attempt to solve these issues. Therefore, in the next section, it is detailed how the units studied in this chapter dealt with their interaction partners in order to develop meaningful and safe operations within TFU and whether this resembles the way they dealt with 107 ASBt.

4.5.1.2 Interacting With Other Units Within TFU

In this section, it is detailed 1) whether the way the units studied in this chapter interacted with 107 ASBt in a way that resembled the way in which they interacted with other units within TFU and 2) whether this had similar influences on the type and amount of safety issues and the way they could deal with safety issues.

With regard to integration within the Task Force, an operator from TFU's reconnaissance unit explains that they also used "sales pitches" to familiarize themselves with other units within TFU (REC-1):

> *Look, I don't need to tell my commander here* [in the Netherlands] *how to work with reconnaissance units. Within TFU, however, commanders were often not used to work with us. So, then I need to tell them what the possibilities and limitations of our unit were.*

Forward Air Controllers, seemed to experience integration issues as a FAC-er explains that, in the beginning of TFU's operations, other units within TFU were not used to operate with fire support assets and that an understanding of the possibilities and limitations of fire support was developed along the way (F-2):

> *It was a challenge for FAC-ers to prove our added value, and that we were included in planning processes. In the beginning, that wasn't the case. (. . .) Within the Battle Group they gradually discovered that we were quite essential . . . a lot of units were unknown and unpopular over there.*

Next to reconnaissance operators and FAC-ers, air traffic controllers also had to discover with whom to operate within TFU, as an air traffic controller explains (ATC-2):

> *We had to work with all kinds of Army people over there, like and S1, S2 and S3.*[5] *. . . When we came there, I had no idea what that meant. . . . At a certain point I made a list on which I noted with what and who we had to work.*

From these quotes, it becomes clear that reconnaissance units, FAC-ers and air traffic controllers also experienced limited integration within the Task Force. Also, it becomes clear that they used ad-hoc solutions in trying to overcome these issues. To highlight that these solutions were sometimes initiated after safety problems already had occurred, an Apache pilot stresses that he was constantly confronted with safety problems in interaction with Army units and that he had to subsequently make agreements with these Army units (AP-2):

> *We were constantly surprised over there by the Army. . . . Everything that is not allowed on an airfield here* [in the Netherlands] *was happening over there. . . . They suddenly decided to put up a large crane, or a balloon or a UAV . . . They were not thinking about the implications for us . . . So we had to train these Army guys in with whom they had to coordinate.*

Related to limited integration and subsequent efforts to create integration, a Task Force commander points out that for TFU, 49 different units were operating in a configuration that substantially differed from the way these units were used to work and train within their parent organizations (C-3):

> *I don't know the exact number, but we had units from 49 different parts of the organization. (. . .) So, we had to create one unit out of 49 different units.*

Of course, before these units were sent abroad, training exercises were organized to train these units in an expeditionary configuration. For TFU, a "formation" exercise and an "integration" exercise were organized. The formation exercise took about four weeks and the integration exercise was about two weeks. However, as the same Task Force commander points out, units were not always all present during these exercises (C-3):

> *About 25 of these units were present from the start of the training period. The remaining units were gradually merged into the expeditionary organization. The last units were added at the beginning of the integration exercise.*

That this way of training did not fully prepare individual units for operating in an expeditionary configuration, as is highlighted by a Forward Air Controller, who states that he was not able to train in "real life" with units that he encountered within TFU (F-2):

> *I was added during the integration exercise. And then I discovered that they did not know what to do with fire support. Also, exercises were mostly "pro memorie": that we had to imagine training with units such as airplanes and helicopters but that they were physically absent. Radio communications were also absent so we had to improvise with cell phones.* (. . .) *Due to that, it was discovered in the mission area what it means to be part of the Task Force.*

Due to these training issues, it seems that to a large degree, integration between the units of TFU had to be developed in the mission area. Forward Air Controllers subsequently experienced that, in shaping interactions with other units within TFU, existing rules and procedures had shortcomings and that application of these rules during operations resulted in safety issues. During training in brigade formation, FAC-ers were used to deconflict fire support with 81-millimeter mortars only at the level of their company[6] and inform battalion-staff afterwards. During brigade operations, this is possible because companies are assigned to separate geographical areas that do not overlap. In Uruzgan, however, companies were not assigned to separate geographical areas, and mission areas overlapped. Deconflicting fire support by means of brigade "rules" consequently, resulted in safety problems, as a FAC-er explains (F-3):

> *My 81 millimeters were deconflicted within the company and the Sperwer was launched on TFU-staff orders. So, it was possible that I ordered 81-millimeter fire support and that nobody of TFU staff knew that.* (. . .) *So, when they launch that UAV, they do not know what my 81-millimeters are doing.*

Not only were TFU's units innovating with the Sperwer-UAV and Apache helicopters, as was shown in the previous section. This was also the case for Forward Air Controllers. Along the way, TFU's units discovered that fire support was an asset that could not be missed during operations in Uruzgan, as a FAC-er explains (F-3):

> *They* [TFU's units] *wanted us to accompany them more and more. Because they discovered that when they were in a TIC* [Troops in Contact] *situation, we could solve that by means of fire support. They were quite happy with us along the way.*

The same FAC-er points out that during operations within TFU he experienced uncontrolled, unexpected and unsafe interactions between fire support assets on which he had no influence (F-3):

> *There were times that I was firing with artillery and that I suddenly heard the sound of a helicopter in the area. (. . .) Also, once I was training with two F18 fighter jets when I suddenly heard something . . . two German Tornado fighter jets soared through my "restricted operations zone" with a speed of 1000 kilometers per hour . . . I got used to it, in the beginning you are stupefied: did that really happen? After two months, you just start to accept that it happens . . . because I could not do anything about it.*

The exploration phase presented in this section has shown how units within TFU interacted with 107 ASBt and whether this resembled the way they interacted with other partners. This clearly seems to be the case, which leads to the conclusion that 107 ASBt was unique to some extent, but not in the way they experienced influences from the interaction network from within TFU on safety issues and their ability to solve safety problems. Therefore, in the next section, it will be investigated in more detail whether these influences can be interpreted as being similar to the influences experienced by 107 ASBt, which is a necessary step before it can be attempted to verify the hypotheses from Chapter 3.

4.5.2 Specification Phase

In this section, it is investigated whether the units studied experienced influences of TFU's interaction network on safety similar to the influence experienced by 107 ASBt. These influences experienced by the units studied in this chapter are subsequently reflected by means of the experiences of 107 ASBt derived from Chapter 3.

Quite clearly, the degree to which limited integration within TFU that was experienced by 107 ASBt was also experienced by the majority of the units studied within this chapter. Also, it was witnessed that ad-hoc solutions were subsequently used to develop such integration. For example, reconnaissance units attempted to develop integration between themselves and other units by means of "sales pitches". On the other hand, they discovered that existing rules and procedures were not fitting the dynamic operations of TFU. As a result, reshaping such rules and procedures was attempted to fit operations, as was for example witnessed in the way FAC-ers were used as a radio relay station for deconfliction in the air. Subsequently, they experienced that integration issues and incompatibility of rules and procedures has safety consequences, as was witnessed in the problems FAC-ers experienced in their Restricted Operations Zone.

From the previous section, it may hence be inferred that the influences of TFU's interaction network on self-organizing strategies and the subsequent emergence of safety found while studying 107 ASBt were not unique for them. Other units within TFU too seemed to experience similar influences and consequences. Moreover, they seemed to use similar self-organizing strategies in shaping the interaction network in order to operate safely, which did not always succeed. As such, it seems to be possible to attempt verifying the hypotheses on the relation between TFU's design, self-organization and the emergence of safety developed in Chapter 3.

4.5.3 The Reduction Phase

The **first hypothesis** emphasized the relationship between "mixing and matching" as a design strategy and missing structural coupling between units in the expeditionary organization. It was found in this chapter that units, such as reconnaissance units and FAC-ers, too had to familiarize themselves extensively within TFU. It seemed to be the case more units had poorly integrated input and output relationships with other units within TFU's primary process. Also, it was shown that units experienced missing agreements between, for example, Air Force and Army units. This hints at missing structural coupling between units in TFU's control structure. Moreover, a Task Force commander highlighted that "an organization" had to be created from scratch out of the 49 units of which TFU was assembled. This highlights that missing structural coupling between units may be a more widely spread issue within the Task Force. Quite clearly, the quote of the Task Force commander links this finding to the "mixing and matching" process by which the Task Force was assembled. As such, it can be stated the first hypothesis, developed from the perspective of 107 ASBt, can be verified at the level of TFU.

The **second hypothesis** stated that: "A combination of missing structural coupling within TFU and TFU's enactment threatened safety of 107 ASBt and TFU during operations". In the results section, it is highlighted that the apparent absence of agreements between Army and Air Force units, resulted in "constant surprises". Also, a Forward Air Controller pointed to similar "surprises" within his restricted operations zone. This indicates that these units apparently too had to operate with underdeveloped integration for critical interdependencies and that this resulted in safety issues during operations. Combined with the statement from the Task Force commander highlighted above, this seems to give support at the level of TFU for the second hypothesis that was developed from the perspective of 107 ASBt. It seems to be the case that missing structural coupling was a more general problem within TFU, which combined with TFU's enactment in the Uruzgan operating environment, had safety consequences. In addition, this highlights the relevance of the arguments on IOR's "design parameters" put forward in the previous chapter. That is to say, at the level of TFU too, safety issues can be related to missing structural coupling, which is not accounted for by IOR's design parameters.

Concerning the **third hypothesis,** it was found that several units were attempting to develop input-output relationships between themselves and other units within TFU in order to contribute safely to TFU's operations. Forward Air Controllers, air traffic controllers and reconnaissance operators employed similar "sales pitch" strategies compared to the strategies 107 ASBt's used to contribute to TFU's operations. Also, it was shown that other units were engaging in efforts to develop and refine rules and procedures in order to operate safely. This was shown in the way Apaches and other units tried to use FAC-ers as a "radio relay station". As such, it can be argued that hypothesis three, which stated that: "Self-organization of 107 ASBt's operators was mainly aimed at self-designing 107 ASBt into TFU's organizational structure", can be verified at the level of TFU.

As to the **fourth hypothesis,** it was discovered by TFU how the ability to operate in Uruzgan could be improved by means of innovating with assets such as the Forward Air Controllers, Apaches and fire support. In terms of De Sitter (1994) such innovation within TFU can be defined as local product innovation because, while enacting the Uruzgan environment, TFU's units were constantly reinventing the way they could best tackle operational issues by changing configurations of units. At the same time, such innovation resulted in new configurations in which they had to operate with accompanying integration problems as was shown during operations of Apaches and Forward Air Controllers. Hence, it can be argued that hypothesis four, which stated that: "enactment of TFU in its environment and accompanying innovation of TFU's units with the Sperwer-UAV resulted in ongoing integration issues because of the changing configurations of units in which 107 ASBt operated", can be verified at the level of TFU.

Most units that were included in the study in this chapter somehow discovered along the way that procedures that they were using did not work for developing safety of their operations within TFU. As was shown by the difficulties Apaches had to receive and transmit information about deconfliction in the air, the problems FAC-ers had to deconflict 81-millimeter mortars and controlling their restricted piece of airspace. As a result, operators of these units attempted to change these rules and procedures in order to develop safety of their operations. These attempts, however, did not always result in safe and controllable operations within TFU, as was highlighted by a FAC-er who simply decided to accept that he could not always deconflict aircraft in his restricted operations zone. In this way, it can be argued that incompatibility of rules and procedures resulted in permanent safety threats for TFU. As a result of these findings, it can be pointed out that **hypothesis six**, which stated that: "due to incompatible rules and procedures, 107 ASBt and TFU were confronted with permanent safety threats during UAV operations" can be verified at the level of TFU. However, with regard to **hypothesis five**, that stressed to hindering effect of "rotation" of units within the Task Force, no evidence was found to verify this finding with other units within TFU.

It should be noted however that this chapter has included a limited number of TFU's units. Yet, a Task Force commander explained that within TFU, about 49 different units within the Task Force had to form "an organization" along the way. Therefore, it seems to be the case that more units within TFU may have had experiences similar to the experiences reported by the units studied in this chapter. Hence, it is plausible to propose that more units had to develop safety of operations within TFU by self-designing structural coupling, creating and reshaping control loops, local product innovation and experienced issues with regard to incompatible rules[7] and procedures while attempting to operate safely within TFU. This may subsequently stress the relevance of the hypotheses 1, 2, 3, 4 and 6 presented for TFU as a whole.

Next, it is pointed out that while self-designing, TFU's operators seemed to shape and reshape their interaction network in a particular way, by developing particular kinds of input and output relations and control loops. More specifically, it may be interpreted that they seem to search for specific kinds of interdependence and forms of coordination between themselves and other units within TFU. To gain more detailed understanding of this, the next section aims to unravel this by using Thompson's (1967) widely used concepts of interdependence and coordination.

4.5.3.1 Complexity and Searching for Interdependence and Coordination Within TFU

Thompson (1967) distinguishes between three different forms of interdependence: pooled, sequential and reciprocal interdependence. When two units have pooled interdependence, they are part of the primary process of an organization but perform separate functions and are not directly dependent on each other. Sequential interdependence refers to dependence in which the input of one unit depends on the output for another. The dependence between intelligence and operational activities within TFU seems to have such a sequential character. For example, a reconnaissance operator quoted previously did not want to start his operations without the input from the Sperwer. Reciprocal interdependence refers to units that rely on each other's input and output. This was the case between 107 ASBt, Apaches and Forward Air Controllers, for example. For carrying out work, in particular during ad-hoc operations, these units were reciprocally dependent on each other. According to Thompson, each of these types of interdependence requires a different form of coordination.[8] Standardizing input and output of units best coordinates pooled interdependence. Coordination by means of a predetermined central plan is best suited for units that are sequentially interdependent. Thompson (1967, p. 56) states that coordination by means of a central plan involves creating schedules for the interdependent units, which is less rigid than standardization. With regard to reciprocal interdependence, Thompson (ibid.) stresses that this form of interdependence is best governed by means of mutual adjustment.

From the way TFU's operators tried to develop input-output relationships and change rules and procedures, it can be inferred that they gradually discovered and created reciprocal interdependence during operations, for which mutual adjustment was needed for developing safe operations, instead of central coordination. The results in Chapter 3 and this chapter showed, however, that there was a tendency within TFU to coordinate movements "in the field" and in the air centrally from TFU's OPS-room. As was described in Chapter 3, all kinds of liaison officers from different units were involved in the process of deconflicting units in the field. For assets in the air such as Apaches and UAVs it was even attempted to deconflict movements through the Combined Air Operations Centre in Bahrain. Such centralized coordination attempts did not seem to fit the dynamic character of TFU's operations in Uruzgan. That is to say, operations in the field seemed to change quickly in reaction to environmental dynamics for which coordination by means of a central plan was too slow and too complicated. This, in combination with an organizational network in which some units needed to discover existing rules and procedures, led to difficulties and seemed to hinder the emergence of safety at the level of the task force.

These arguments are highlighted by Apaches that reported to have problems with connecting with TFU's OPS-room to get updated information on "friendly" movements in the air. Also, Forward Air Controllers reported to be surprised from assets that were centrally tasked from TFU's staff. Moreover, although 107 ASBt's liaison officer attempted to deconflict the Sperwer's movements from inside TFU's OPS-room, the Sperwer had serious local deconfliction issues due to its inability to participate in "see-and-avoid" and local radio contact. A Forward Air controller even reported that TFU's staff once launched a Sperwer to improve "situational awareness" in TFU's OPS-room, which hindered him in engaging hostile opponents in the field. What seems to be the case is that units "in the field" and TFU staff were trying to develop safety by means of different and sometimes conflicting coordination methods for particular, often self-designed, forms of interdependence.

It can be argued that these sometimes conflicting attempts to develop safety were originating from an organizational network in which units were still discovering and continuously changing relations with each other while applying and refining existing rules. Searching for interdependence and suitable coordination mechanisms is inevitably present in organizations, especially while operating in a dynamically complex environment. Weick (1974, p. 360), for example, points out that "in the everyday world there are probably connections that are both constant and variable, frameworks that are both rigid and variable (. . .) organizations have analogues of variable connection, flexible frameworks and sliding bonds". However, within TFU, conflicts between different coordination mechanisms, that surfaced in the quest for finding suitable coordination mechanisms for changing forms of interdependence, seemed to have created a "grey" uncontrolled area in which critical dependencies were not coordinated, or missed. This was shown by the dangerous interactions between 81-millimeter mortars and other flying assets, Dutch Apaches and the Sperwer, Artillery and fighter jets and the Sperwer and various helicopters. These interactions can be interpreted as *hidden interactions* (cf. Perrow, 1999, p. 79) because they were missed by coordinators and seemed to be appearing from out of nowhere from the perspective of operators such as FAC-ers.[9]

Next to the self-organizing attempts to coordinate particular forms of interdependence with incompatible coordination mechanisms, hidden interactions seem to be associated with an organizational interaction network that is hard to grasp for individual units and operators. It seems to be the case that within TFU, the search for forms of interdependence and coordination was complicated by complexity of TFU's interaction network in which 49 different units tried to find out with whom to work and how to coordinate that work. A simple formula ((n(n – 1))/2) (cf. Kuipers, Van Amelsvoort, & Kramer, 2010) shows that with 49 different and poorly integrated units (n = 49), 1,176 interactions are potentially possible. This, combined with inevitable searches for interdependence and coordination that are always be present in organizations makes it hard, or even impossible, for operators and TFU staff to develop insight into dependencies between units within TFU and develop suitable coordination mechanisms. Such complexity due to the sheer number of "building blocks" may also further explain the existence of "hidden interactions" and the problematic emergence of safety at the level of TFU.

Furthermore, by means of the concept of *structural complexity* (e.g., De Sitter, 1994; Kuipers et al., 2010) it is argued that, next to the number, the *nature* of building blocks may also have contributed to the complexity found in the network between TFU's units. The concept of structural complexity, which was also briefly highlighted in Chapter 3, points to the notion that high degrees of functional concentration, per definition, leads to an interaction network that is complex and incomprehensible for operators. It can be argued that within TFU, functional concentration was present. That is to say, Figure 3.8 shows that specific specialist activities, such as intelligence, the Battle Group, Air support, Provincial Reconstruction Teams and Engineers were all located at specialist departments. Hence, it can be argued that next to the sheer number of building blocks and missing integration, functional concentration within TFU too contributed to organizational complexity within TFU.

With regard to these issues with TFU's design, it is argued that several aspects of TFU's organizational structure can be related to the way military parent organizations in the Netherlands are designed. Firstly, as was highlighted in the first chapter of this book, the layout military parent organizations in the Netherlands do not match expeditionary demands. Therefore, the need to "mix and match" all kinds of different units from parent organizations into expeditionary organizations, which was regarded as the origin of missing integration, can be related to the layout of Dutch military parent organizations. Secondly, most rules and procedures seemed to be transplanted from parent organizations to the expeditionary context. For example, this was shown by the way FACers, 107 ASBt and Apaches tried to develop safety of their operations by means of standard "brigade" and NATO deconfliction procedures. Subsequently, the next section focuses in more detail on influences of the military parent organizations in the Netherlands.

4.5.3.2 The Influence From the Military Parent Organizations in The Netherlands

As was pointed out in Chapter 3 and section 4.3, TFU was mainly built from units from the Royal Netherlands Army parent organization. Also, it was shown that the Dutch Army is structured by means of so-called brigades. A brigade is a unit of about 3000 soldiers and is mainly designed for classical large-scale armed conflicts between nation states. Within the Dutch Army, the Brigade is regarded as an entity in which all functions necessary for military operations are grouped. This is often referred to as the level of "combined arms". As can be seen in Appendix One, the Dutch Army and its brigades are built from many specialized units that all perform a separate function or activity such as maneuver (infantry), fire support (artillery), logistical, medical, engineering and intelligence units. Following IOR's "design parameters" and based on the figure presented in Appendix One, the organizational structure of the Dutch Army's parent organization can be interpreted as highly functionally concentrated[10] because all kinds of performance, preparing, supporting and controlling activities are divided over many specialized units.

Yet, the Dutch defense doctrine states that the present Army organization with many specialized units has the ability to be flexible (ministry of Defense, 2013, p. 89). Indeed, an organization with many specialized units provides the opportunity to assemble many different expeditionary organizations. Kramer and De Waard (2007) define this type of apparent flexibility as "composition flexibility". However, Kramer and De Waard (2007)[11] also argue that assembling many different specialized units into an expeditionary organization decreases operational flexibility, the ability to function as a "well-oiled machine" and adapt to local circumstances. The case presented in this chapter highlights the latter. For TFU, "composition flexibility" of the Army parent organization by "mixing and matching" functionally concentrated units from the parent organization into an expeditionary organization clearly resulted in missing integration, which was associated with direct safety consequences due to TFU's necessity to act in its environment.

Furthermore, as was stated in Chapter 3, TFU was not only "mixed and matched" from units of the Royal Netherlands Army. The Air Force, Military Police and Navy too provided "building blocks" for TFU. These other parent organizations, and the Royal Netherlands Air Force in particular, are often regarded as being less functionally concentrated (see De Waard & Kramer, 2008). However, it can be argued that grouping all air support and transport aircraft into one separate organization (i.e. the Air Force) shows traces of functional concentration at the level of the military parent organization as a whole.[12] Similar signs of functional concentration can be found in the Military Police (MP) and the Marines of the Royal Netherlands Navy. That is to say, for comprehensive military expeditionary missions such as TFU, specialized MP building blocks are often added to the expeditionary organization. Also, during later missions, Marine units provided building blocks for TFU's Battle Group, Fire Support and Intelligence. As such, the Dutch military seems to be confronted with a *holographic composition problem* due to high levels of functional concentration throughout the organization. That is to say, due to high levels of functional concentration at various organizational levels a "mixing and matching" expeditionary organizing strategy has to be applied to come up with an expeditionary organization. This composition problem was present within units such as 107 ASBt, within TFU and both within and across parent organizations.

Also, it was shown that the way of designing military organizations seems to be (implicitly) transplanted from parent organizations to expeditionary organizations. Although the configuration in which units had to work in TFU differed substantially from the configuration in which they were used to work in their parent organization, the way in which they were grouped together in that new configuration shows a traditional, functionally concentrated, military organizational design. This is highlighted by dividing infantry, artillery, intelligence, logistics and engineers in different departments. This finding does not seem to be unique for the Dutch military organization. From an US military perspective, Snook (2000) highlighted that: "Task Forces are designed by taking basic unit building blocks and assembling them *along hierarchical lines consistent with the mission and time-honored military traditions*" (italics added). This means that it is likely that the US military too expeditionary Task Forces are designed along the way the military organization at home is designed.

Lastly, high degrees of functional concentration may explain the problems in applying rules and procedures that are developed for the traditional Army brigade. As was highlighted in Chapter 3, low levels of autonomy and process oversight at the operational level characterize highly functionally concentrated organizations. This results in the need for hierarchical and centralized control (e.g., Kuipers et al., 2010). Therefore, it comes as no surprise that many rules and procedures within TFU were characterized by a tendency to coordinate by means of standardization and centralized plans. This however, showed to be quite incompatible with, often self-designed, reciprocal interdependence between units during operations in Uruzgan's dynamically complex environment for which mutual local coordination was often needed.

As such, this section has highlighted that the rather problematic relationship between organizational design and the emergence of safety within TFU is intertwined with design issues at the level of the military organization as a whole. In the next section, it will be attempted to generalize the findings in the preceding sections to the level of expeditionary organizations in general.

4.5.4 Integration Phase

To generalize aspects of the findings presented in this chapter and formulate hypotheses on the relation between organizational design, self-organization and the emergence of safety for expeditionary organizations in general, this section will use analytical generalization (cf. Yin, 2003, pp. 30–32). This means that this section attempts to build analytical arguments by combining results from within TFU with existing literature to demonstrate the applicability of these results to expeditionary organizations in general. This also implicates that the new hypotheses that are developed are located at Van Strien's level B of knowledge generalization because analytic generalization should result in hypotheses that apply to the broader family of expeditionary organizations.

First of all, a main observation on the findings in this chapter is that the units studied attempted to self-organize safe operations by means of shaping the interaction network in a way that can be interpreted as self-design. They did so for two reasons, firstly to overcome missing structural coupling within the Task Force. Secondly, they tried to adapt to a dynamically complex operating environment by means of local product innovation, which entailed configuring the network of partners with whom to interact while enacting the operating environment. As such, it can be argued that TFU's operators were constantly building and re-building their organization to operate both meaningfully and safely. In particular, and along Thompson's (1967) concepts of interdependence and coordination, it was argued that units created (and discovered) reciprocal interdependence for which local, mutual, coordination was needed.

Following recent developments in organization science, the organization resulting from these efforts shows characteristics of a "network organization" (e.g., Kuipers et al., 2010) in which relationships with partners, or other units, has to be constantly reshaped in order to the match a turbulent variety of tasks, or "orders". However, it seems to be the case that attempts to build such ad-hoc networks were hindered by characteristics of design of both the expeditionary organization itself and military parent organizations, which provided the building blocks and coordination mechanisms for the expeditionary organization. This effect seemed to have such an impact that local self-designing efforts did often not result in the emergence of safety at the level of the task force.

To show how these findings and the findings in the preceding sections in this chapter can be generalized to hypotheses for expeditionary organizations in general, analytical arguments are constructed. In constructing these arguments, findings of this chapter are supported with theoretical insights. Firstly, it is argued that more expeditionary organizations may suffer from integration problems similar to those of TFU, due to a complex mixing and matching process. It was already highlighted in Chapter 1 that more organizations, especially those at the left end of Modig's (2007) continuum seem to use a "mixing and matching" design strategy similar to that of TFU and also operate under dynamically complex conditions. Due to a similar "mixing and matching" design strategy, it also is likely that such temporary organizations are characterized by limited structural coupling, or limited input and output relationships and accompanying agreements, between organizational elements. More in particular, and in line with the "holographic composition problem" of the Dutch military organization stressed in the preceding section, it can be argued that such limited structural coupling is particularly present when expeditionary organizations are mixed and matched from highly functionally concentrated parent organizations. That is to say, the more parent organizations are functionally concentrated, the more complex the "mixing and matching" process will become and the more expeditionary organizations will suffer from missing integration between their units. Subsequently, it is argued that the findings of this chapter hold relevance to *those* expeditionary organizations that are assembled out of "stationary", or "parent" at the "left-end" of Modig's continuum, and that are characterized by a high degree of functional concentration.

This seems very specific and may give the impression that the findings in this chapter have limited generalizability. However, high degrees of functional concentration are found in organizations with a standard bureaucratic design (De Sitter, 1994) and it is well known that bureaucratic organizational designs are still commonplace in the contemporary business environment (Kuipers et al., 2010; Laloux, 2014). So, it may well be that more expeditionary organizations are assembled out of functionally concentrated, static, parent organizations and hence are faced with a complex "mixing and matching" process similar to that of TFU, which has similar effects on structural coupling between units within the expeditionary organization. Therefore, the first hypothesis is formulated as follows:

Hypothesis 1: Functional concentration in parent organizations, leads to a complex "mixing and matching" design process that limits structural coupling in expeditionary organizations.

It was also stressed in Chapter 1 that all expeditionary organizations operate in a dynamically complex environment and that operating in such an environment places emphasis on enactment and the necessity to act (cf. Kramer, 2007; Weick, 1979). Hence, it can be hypothesized that operating in a complexly "mixed and matched" expeditionary organization with accompanying limited structural coupling, will result in safety issues similar to those found in the TFU case. That is to say, due to such limited structural coupling, units will have to operate with an underdeveloped interaction network within the expeditionary organization, which has consequences for the way safety can emerge within these organizations. Hence the second hypothesis can be developed:

Hypothesis 2: Limited structural coupling within the expeditionary organization, combined with enactment and the necessity to act, threatens the emergence of safety in expeditionary organizations.

Subsequently, to overcome integration issues, it is likely that self-design emerges to create structural coupling between units and develop an organization that can operate meaningfully and safely in its operating environment. Furthermore, enactment and the necessity to act will place emphasis on reciprocal interdependence between units and the need for mutual adjustment during operations. That is to say, the complex nature of tasks to be carried out combined with the need for constant adaptation makes activities and units more dependent on each other and emphasizes the need for constant local adjustment to adapt both meaningfully and safely.

Also, enacting a dynamically complex operating environment will likely result in a particular kind of product innovation (cf. De Sitter, 1994) at the operational level in expeditionary organizations. That is to say, it is likely that due to enactment and the necessity to act in a dynamic complex environment, organizational action results in bottom-up discovery of innovative new configurations of units that are able to deliver a "new product" in relation to their operating environment. It can therefore be argued that operators in expeditionary organizations in general have to develop safety by means of self-design that aims for building ad-hoc networks similar to those found within TFU. Hence the following hypothesis can be formulated.

Hypothesis 3: Because of limited structural coupling and product innovation at the operational level, safety in expeditionary organizations is developed by operators engaging in self-design of ad-hoc networks.

The ability to self-design within TFU was hindered by organizational complexity within the expeditionary organization. It was found that organizational complexity was associated with hidden interactions, which threatened the emergence of safety at the level of the expeditionary organization. For TFU these characteristics were related to high degree of functional concentration within both the expeditionary and parent organizations in the Netherlands. With regard to generalization of this finding to expeditionary organizations in general, Modig (2007, p. 812) states that within temporary organizations work processes are often organized along "dominant traditions" within parent organizations. As such, it can be hypothesized that it is likely that "mixing and matching" expeditionary organizations out of functionally concentrated parent organizations, will result in expeditionary organizations that too are characterized by a high degree of functional concentration. Moreover, previous sections already highlighted, by means of the work of De Sitter (1994) that functional concentration in any organization results in structural complexity, a complex web of interactions that hinders controllability of the organizations operations.

It can hence be argued that it is likely that for those expeditionary organization that are assembled out of functionally concentrated parent organizations, organizational design is also characterized by a high degree of functional concentration and that these expeditionary organizations suffer from organizational complexity that threatens the emergence of safety. That is to say, it is likely that in these expeditionary organizations, structural complexity arises that may hinder the ability of operators to develop safety by means of self-design and threatens safety at the level of the expeditionary organization. Hence the fourth hypothesis can be formulated.

Hypothesis 4: Mixing and matching expeditionary organizations out of functionally concentrated parent organizations leads to functional concentration in expeditionary organizations, which results in organizational complexity that complicates the process described in hypothesis three and threatens the emergence of safety at the level of the expeditionary organization.

The last hypothesis developed in this section relates to incompatible coordination mechanisms that hindered self-design within TFU. It was pointed out that coordination by means of central plan, did not fit the network character of the organization that was self-designed within TFU. This was associated with critical interdependencies that were "missed" by controllers such as the TFU operations room and operators in the field. For two reasons, it is likely that expeditionary organizations that are built from functionally concentrated building blocks and originate from functionally concentrated parent organizations, suffer from similar coordination and safety issues.

Firstly, coordination by means of a central plan is a frequently used and maybe an inevitable way of coordination within highly functionally concentrated organizations. Perrow (1999) highlighted that in case of tight coupling, centralization of control is the only way to ensure safe organizational output. Functional concentration within any organization's primary process results in tight coupling between workstations. The only way to coordinate such tightly coupled workstations, therefore, seems to provide a centralized plan for the operations of these workstations. Therefore, it comes as no surprise that centralizing tendencies were found in the TFU case. Also, this argument points to the presence of such coordination mechanisms within both functionally concentrated parent and expeditionary organizations. Secondly, by using the argument based on the work by Modig (2007), in which she stated that it is likely that "ways of organizing" are transplanted from stationary parent organizations to temporary organizations, it seems feasible to hypothesize that coordination instruments, with tendencies to coordinate by means of a central plan, are brought along from parent organizations to expeditionary organizations. Quite understandably, these coordination mechanisms are incompatible with the self-designed network character of expeditionary organizations. Hence, the following hypothesis can be formulated.

Hypothesis 5: Coordination by means of a central plan, which can be related to a high degree of functional concentration in parent and expeditionary organizations, hinders the processes described in hypothesis three, and threatens the emergence of safety at the level of the expeditionary organization.

4.6 Conclusion

This chapter has developed hypotheses on ways in which self-organization and the emergence of safety within expeditionary organizations is influenced by structural organizational design. To do so, firstly, hypotheses developed from the perspective of 107 ASBt were verified. This subsequently resulted in the verification of five out of the six hypotheses on the relation between organizational design, self-organization and safety within TFU. Subsequently, analytical generalization was used to translate these findings to expeditionary organizations in general. Hence, by studying 107 ASBt and other units within TFU and applying analytical generalization, the relationship between organizational design, self-organization and safety in expeditionary organizations is specified at Van Strien's level B. These hypotheses therefore form the basis of the "conceptual map", which is the foundation of the theory that this book aims to develop. The next chapter aims to verify these hypotheses to provide a validated conceptual map for the development of a theory on organizational design, self-organization and the emergence of safety in expeditionary organizations, which is presented in Chapter 6.

Notes

1. This section serves as an extension to the background information on Task Force Uruzgan that was presented earlier in this book, in Chapter 3.
2. The runway of Tarin Kowt airfield was referred to as the "dirt-strip" because it was unpaved.
3. De Sitter would refer to this problem as a problem of external control capacity of 107 ASBt, which was transmitted to the interaction network of which 107 ASBt was part.
4. TAC-P stands for Tactical Air Control Party, which consists of a FAC-er, a laser operator and a driver.
5. S1, S2 and S3 are NATO abbreviations used by the Dutch Army to refer to personnel, intelligence and operational functions, respectively.
6. A brigade is built from several battalions of about 500 soldiers that are divided into several companies of about 150 soldiers. Companies are subsequently divided into several platoons.
7. Note that there is a difference between rules for interaction with other units and task-based rules such as "skills and drills" that are essential for conducting a particular task. The arguments in this chapter with regard to rules and procedures of TFU's control structure refer to the first definition.
8. Although Thompson developed this argument to lower "coordination costs", the analysis in this chapter will show that the relationships between different forms of interdependence and ways of coordination are applicable in a more broader sense.
9. This highlights the relevance of Taylor's (1981) definition of an accident as being a "black hole" in the experiences of operators.
10. Also, the Army parent organization seems to score high on other parameters, as defined by IOR. For example, division between preparing, supporting and operational activities hints at a high "value" for parameter 2. This indicates that, although it was argued that IOR's parameters were not able to explain major design-related issues at the level of the Task Force, IOR's parameters are able to analyze division of labor within military parent organizations. More specifically, it can be argued that the aforementioned design challenge of many Western military organizations can be attributed to their high-parameter organizational structures. This issue will be addressed in Chapter 6 of this book.
11. See also De Waard and Kramer (2008) for an English article on this subject.

12. As functional concentration of an organization's production structure is defined in relation to its stream of orders (cf. De Sitter, 1994), this can only be defined as functional concentration in relation the stream of expeditionary "orders" at the level of the military parent organizations.

References

Boeije, H. R. (2005). *Analyseren in kwalitatief onderzoek: denken en doen*. Amsterdam: Boom bestuurskunde.

Dubois, A., & Gadde, L. E. (2002). Systematic combining: An abductive approach to case research. *Journal of Business Research*, *55*(7), 553–560.

Kramer, E. H., & de Waard, E. J. (2007). Componeren met componenten. *Carre*, *1*, 38–44.

Kramer, E. H., de Waard, E. J., & de Graaff, M. C. (2012). Task Force Uruzgan and experimentation with organization design. In R. Beeres, J. Van der Meulen, J. M. M. L. Soeters & A. L. W. Vogelaar (Eds.), *Mission Uruzgan*. Amsterdam: Amsterdam University Press.

Kuipers, H., van Amelsvoort, P., & Kramer, E. H. (2010). *Het Nieuwe Organiseren: alternatieven voor de bureaucratie*. The Hague: Acco.

Laloux, F. (2014). *Reinventing organizations: A guide to creating organizations inspired by the next stage of human consciousness*. Brussels: Nelson Parker.

Ministry of Defense. (2013). *Dutch defense doctrine*. The Hague: Ministry of Defense.

Modig, N. (2007). A continuum of organizations formed to carry out projects: Temporary and stationary organization forms. *International Journal of Project Management*, *25*(8), 807–814.

Perrow, C. (1999). *Normal accidents: Living with high-risk technologies*. Princeton: Princeton University Press.

Richardson, R., & Kramer, E. H. (2006). Abduction as the type of inference that characterizes the development of a grounded theory. *Qualitative Research*, *6*(4), 497–513.

Sitter, L. U. de. (1994). *Synergetisch produceren: Human Resources Mobilisation in de produktie een inleiding in structuurbouw*. Assen: Uitgeverij Van Gorcum.

Snook, S. A. (2000). *Friendly fire: The accidental shootdown of U.S. Blackhawks over Northern Iraq*. Princeton: Princeton University Press.

Strauss, A., & Corbin, J. M. (1990). *Basics of qualitative research: Grounded theory procedures and techniques*. Newbury Park, CA: Sage Publications, Inc.

Taylor, D. H. (1981). The hermeneutics of accidents and safety. *Ergonomics*, *24*(6), 487–495.

Thompson, J. D. (1967). *Organizations in action*. New York: McGraw-Hill.

Waard, E. J. de, & Kramer, E. H. (2008). Tailored task forces: Temporary organizations and modularity. *International Journal of Project Management*, *26*(5), 537–546.

Weick, K. E. (1974). Middle range theories of social systems. *Behavioral Science*, *19*(6), 357–367.

Weick, K. E. (1979). *The social psychology of organizing*. New York: McGraw-Hill.

Wester, F., & Peters, V. (2004). *Kwalitatieve analyse: uitgangspunten en procedures*. Bussum: Coutinho.

Yin, R. K. (2003). *Case study research: Design and methods* (Vol. 5). Thousand Oaks, CA: Sage.

5 Iraq and MH17

Were Operations in Afghanistan Unique?

5.1 Introduction

In the previous chapter, hypotheses were developed that specified the relation between organizational design, self-organization and the emergence of safety for expeditionary organizations in general. By means of analytical generalization it was attempted to generalize findings within TFU to other expeditionary contexts. It was stated in Chapter 1, however, that the conceptual map developed in this book has to meet specific requirements regarding generalizability in order to be useful for the development of a theory at Van Strien's level B of knowledge generalization.

According to Yin, analytic generalization is only one of two steps that have to be taken in order to ensure external validity of a substantive theory that is developed by means of a qualitative methodology (2003, p. 37). The second step Yin proposes to ensure external validity of such a theory is *replication*. This means that the hypotheses that form the backbone of the grounded theory developed in the previous chapter must be "tested" by means of a second or third case study to see whether the mechanisms that are expected to occur in comparable contexts, do occur. Thus, to establish whether the hypotheses developed in the previous chapter of this book are also relevant for other expeditionary organizations, it has to be established whether the hypotheses based on the case studies within Task Force Uruzgan can be replicated in other expeditionary contexts. As such, this chapter will focus on answering the fourth research question of this book:

> **Can hypotheses on the relation between organizational design, self-organization and the emergence of safety in expeditionary organizations be verified by studying other expeditionary organizations?**

To formulate an answer to this research question two additional, existing, expeditionary cases are studied: a Dutch military expeditionary organization in Iraq and the crisis response organization that was established after the crash of flight MH17. These cases are selected by using a *replication*

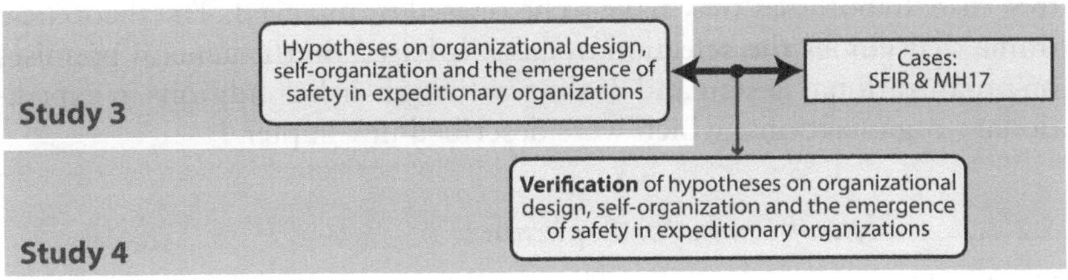

Figure 5.1 Research model of Study 4

SFIR = International Stabilization Force in Iraq; and MH17 = Malaysia Airlines Flight MH17

logic (cf. Yin, 2003, pp. 47–56). This means that these cases are selected by using specific criteria on the basis of which it can be expected that results similar to the results of the TFU case are found. Subsequently, a more deductive approach to qualitative research is taken to replicate the hypotheses developed in the previous chapter. The research steps of this chapter are visualized by means of the research model depicted in Figure 5.1.

This chapter proceeds as follows: firstly, the methodology that is used in this chapter to conduct the replication is explicated. Because existing case studies are analyzed in this chapter, the methodology section will—amongst other things—explicate how a "secondary analysis" will be used to analyze existing case study material. Also, the aforementioned "replication logic" is detailed. Secondly, the cases are introduced in separate sections. Thirdly, the analysis will be conducted. Lastly, a conclusion is presented.

5.2 Methodology

5.2.1 Replication Logic

According to Yin (2003, p. 47), selection of cases for replication in qualitative research should to be done by using a replication logic. Such a replication logic is the underlying rationale by means of which suitable cases can be selected. Following Yin, such a rationale firstly has to explicate whether the cases are selected to find *similar* or *contrasting* results. Secondly, a conceptual framework has to be constructed that states the conditions under which the particular phenomena of interest are likely to be found (Yin, 2003).[1]

For replication in this chapter, cases are selected for finding *similar* results. That is to say, cases are selected in order to confirm the hypotheses developed in the previous chapter. However, as Yin (ibid.) also stresses, it may turn out that hypotheses cannot, or can only be partly, confirmed. In that case, hypotheses may have to be revised or nuanced. The theoretical frame that guides the selection of cases is based on the general premises on organizational design and dealing with high-risk conditions in expeditionary organizations, which were described in Chapter 1.

5.2.1.1 Analytical Frame for Replication

Firstly, the concept "expeditionary organizations" can be used to select cases. This concept was introduced and defined in the first chapter of this book. Also, the previous chapter provided some more detail, by means of the work of Modig (2007) and De Waard and Kramer (2008). It was highlighted that expeditionary organizations are large collections of units or "building blocks" that were "mixed and matched" for a particular temporary task and that this temporary configuration differs significantly from the configuration of units in which they are located in their parent organization(s). Also, it was pointed out that parent organizations of the expeditionary cases that are selected were located in the "stationary" left end of Modig's continuum. More in particular, these parent organizations were characterized by a high degree of functional concentration. Secondly, the concept "dynamic complexity", which is highly relevant for the concept of expeditionary organizations, can be used for selecting cases. This concept was introduced in the first chapter by means of the works of Senge (1992) and Kramer (2004, 2007) and emphasizes that the temporary organizations that are selected have to operate under uncertain, ambiguous and reactive circumstances. By using these concepts two cases are selected: the Dutch military expeditionary organization that carried out operations in Iraq under the flag of SFIR and the crisis response organization that was established after the crash of flight MH17 in the eastern part of Ukraine.

The Dutch contribution to SFIR was a temporary organization assembled from different building blocks from the Dutch Army, Military Police and Air Force (see Delahay et al., 2009). In the case study report by Delahay et al. it is pointed out that the Dutch SFIR contribution did not resemble a "normal" military battalion, but that all kinds of "extra" units were added in order to assemble a task force. As such the "mixed and matched" configuration in which units were operating within the task force differed significantly when compared to the configuration in which they were located in their parent organizations. Furthermore, in the previous chapter, it was argued extensively that the parent organizations of the Dutch military are located at the left end of Modig's continuum and are characterized by a high degree of functional concentration, at different levels of the parent organizations.

The MH17 crisis response organization was temporarily assembled from different stationary government organizations such as the Dutch ministries of Security and Justice, Foreign Affairs, Defense and the Dutch Police. Also, several private parties can be interpreted as being part of the crisis response organization such as parts of Schiphol Airport, Malaysia Airlines and the Dutch Victim Support organization[2] (Torenvlied et al., 2015). This means that the configuration in which all these, both private and government, units had to work was significantly different when compared to their situation within the different parent organizations. Also, these parent organizations can be located in the left part of Modig's (2007) continuum because all these parent organizations have their own "primary process" during everyday operations to which units are returning after the crisis. With regard to the degree of functional concentration within these parent organizations, it cannot be stated that all these parent organizations have a high degree of functional concentration. However, it is well known that government organizations and ministries in particular are often characterized by bureaucratic organizational designs (see, for example, Boin, 2009) and therefore also are likely to possess a high degree of functional concentration.

Concerning the concept "dynamic complexity" both temporary organizations operated in an area that can be interpreted as uncertain, ambiguous and reactive. In Iraq, opposing parties were actively trying to undermine the operations of the Dutch SFIR mission. In the eastern part of Ukraine, pro-Russian separatists and the Ukrainian government army were, at the time of the MH17 crash, engaging in several battles, which resulted in an operating environment that was uncertain, ambiguous and reactive. Also, a large part of the crisis response organization did not operate in Ukraine but was operating in the Netherlands. In the Netherlands, no opposing parties were active. This means that this part of the crisis response organization was confronted with another kind of operating environment when compared to the part that was operating in East Ukraine. Although the crisis environment in the Netherlands could be described as uncertain and unpredictable, its reactiveness can be interpreted as being different. That is to say, although parties in the crisis environment did respond on the actions of the crisis organization, they did not try to actively undermine the operations of the crisis response organization. This made the crisis environment in the Netherlands, during the MH17 crisis, differently dynamically complex than the crisis environment in Ukraine. Still, the crisis environment in the Netherlands complies with the characteristics of dynamic complexity, as it can be argued that any crisis environment can be defined as uncertain, ambiguous and reactive (see also Moynihan, 2008).

After the selection of the cases and detailing a replication logic, it has to be explicated how existing data is analyzed to enable the analysis in this chapter to verify the hypotheses that were developed in the previous chapter. To do so, the next section elaborates on so-called secondary analysis of case study data.

5.2.2 Secondary Analysis of Case Study Data

Using existing case study material for analysis is referred to as *secondary analysis* (e.g., Heaton, 2008). Heaton (2008, p. 35) highlights that secondary analysis of existing qualitative data can be used to verify findings of previous research. However, to be able to replicate the hypotheses developed in Chapter 4, data used in this chapter has to possess certain characteristics. It was argued in Chapter 3, that a particular way of studying "normal work" enabled unraveling influences of organizational design on safety within expeditionary organizations. For replication of the hypotheses developed in the previous chapter such a normal work approach can be applied by using specific case study data. That is to say, to be able to replicate the hypotheses, the data has to be able create insight into whether the expeditionary organizational interaction network was also characterized by limited integration between operational units. Also, the data has to be able to create insight into whether operators attempted to create, shape and reshape interactions within the expeditionary organization. After that, this information can be interpreted using the "compass directions" presented in Chapter 3 to establish whether self-designing of ad-hoc networks, as defined in the previous section, took place. Secondly, it needs to provide information on the expeditionary organization and parent organizations in order to reconstruct whether similar effects of design of both the expeditionary organization and parent organization(s) on the expeditionary interaction network were present. In this section, it will be elaborated how data was collected in the cases selected for replication and why it is suitable for secondary analysis in this chapter.

With regard to the SFIR case, the case study report (see Delahay et al., 2009) argues that interview data was gathered by means of document analysis and interviews. A total of nine interviews were conducted with military personnel from different hierarchical layers of SFIR-4. The interviews were transcribed verbatim and content analysis was conducted from different theoretical perspectives. The interviews were conducted by means of the following topic list:[3]

1. How was SFIR-4 structured and organized?
2. What did normal operations within the Task Force look like?
3. How is safety of patrols organized during normal operations?
4. How does the unit deal with problems during patrols?
5. What procedures exist for emergency situations?
6. To what degree were these procedures trained, prior to the ambush?
7. What happened during the ambush?
8. What can be learned from the ambush?

As can be seen in the topic list, questions were directed towards "normal operations", problem-solving strategies, safety of patrols, organizational structure and the influence of procedures. From information on "normal operations" and problem-solving strategies it may be possible to infer how units interacted and whether they attempted to develop safe operations by shaping the nature of these interactions in such way that safety of operations at the level of the task force was improved. Also, information on the way SFIR-4 was structured and what procedures were used may enable linking characteristics of design of both the expeditionary organization and military parent organization to possible effects on interactions within the expeditionary organization. This seems to make the data gathered in the SFIR-4 study suitable for a secondary analysis that is in line with the goal of this chapter.

For an analysis of the MH17 crisis response organization, this chapter uses the data presented in an evaluation report that is publicly available (see Torenvlied et al., 2015).[4] The aim of the evaluation report was to get insight in the way the national crisis response organization functioned after the crash of flight MH17. This was done in three separate studies. Firstly, insight was created in the way the crisis response organization itself operated. Secondly, the perspective of the victims' families on the operations of the crisis response organization was taken. Thirdly, it was investigated how the crisis response organization communicated with media, society and Dutch parliament. This chapter will focus on the results of the first study because this study was aimed at reconstructing the way the crisis response organization dealt with the crisis in detail by means of 46 in-depth interviews[5] across hierarchical levels.[6] To reconstruct the activities of the crisis response organization, the MH17 evaluation report uses a distinction between five parallel[7] core activities: crisis response in The Hague, international diplomacy, crisis response at the crash site, crisis response to the victims' families and information provision to both the House of Representatives and to the media and society. The core activities were subsequently studied within three timeframes: the immediate crisis response on the 17th of July, the period from the 18th until the 24th of July and the period from the 25th of July until the 8th of September 2014.

A general premise of the first study was that, due to the dynamic crisis context, control of a crisis is developed gradually by means of activities at the operational level of the organization and that a main task of governing actors in the crisis organization is to facilitate these operational activities (Torenvlied et al., 2015, pp. 26–31). Hence, the interviews aimed to map problem-solving activities of employees across different hierarchical layers of the crisis response organization and reconstruct whether and in which ways controlling actors and fora within the crisis response organization operated facilitated operational activities. Also, substantial attention was directed to mapping the layout of the crisis response organization (see Torenvlied et al.,

2015, pp. 44, 184). This means that data collected within the first study of the MH17 study may provide information on the way operators within different units in the crisis response organization interacted and whether operators attempted to develop safe operations by shaping and reshaping the interaction network within the expeditionary organization. Also, due to the information that is present within the evaluation report on design aspects of the crisis response organization, it may be possible to relate effects on interactions to characteristics of the expeditionary organization. Furthermore, within the evaluation report, it is pointed out from what parent organizations different units and operators were originating. This may enable linking aspects of expeditionary organization to characteristics of parent organizations. Hence, the data from the evaluation report can be interpreted as being suitable for attaining the goal of this chapter.

5.2.3 Replication and the Role of Deduction

As becomes clear from the previous section, particular pieces of data are needed to verify, or replicate, the hypotheses developed in Chapter 4. This implies that this chapter uses a different analytical strategy as compared to Chapters 3 and 4. In the previous chapters, development of the hypotheses was done by means of using an abductive analytical approach. Abduction, as stated by Richardson and Kramer (2006) is a suitable approach to connect, or in terms of Dubois and Gadde (2002) systematically combine, theoretical constructs with empirical data to understand *new* situations. In this chapter, however, it is not attempted to understand new situations by means of theoretical constructs, this was done in Chapter 3 and partly done in Chapter 4 of this book. Instead, this chapter aims to determine whether the hypotheses that were developed in the previous chapters apply to other expeditionary contexts. As such, it attempts to investigate whether "general rules" apply to other specific cases, which can be interpreted as a deductive analytical strategy (cf. Richardson & Kramer, ibid.). Applying such a deductive analytical strategy means that the hypotheses developed in the previous chapter, are used as an analytical framework with which the cases are analyzed. However, because these hypotheses are about organizational design and its relation with a specific interpretation of the safety concept, parts of the conceptual compass described in Chapter 3 are still needed to relate case study data to concepts on organizational design in order to verify these hypotheses because, as was highlighted at several places in this book, characteristics of organizational design cannot be observed directly but have to be reconstructed analytically.

5.3 Description of the Cases

In this section, first the SFIR-4 case is described. After that, the MH17 case is detailed. Before reading this section, it should be noted that, for both the SFIR and the MH17 case, using the results of the previous chapter as an analytical framework for secondary analysis enables this chapter to be selective in describing the cases. As both cases are studied extensively, this chapter cannot describe both in every detail. This is, however, not regarded as problematic because the goal of this chapter is not to give an exhaustive overview of both cases but to deductively verify the hypotheses of the previous chapter. This section and the next section will present the cases in such a way that enables this chapter to do so.

5.3.1 Iraq, Dutch Troops Ambushed[8]

From December of 2003 until March of 2005 the Dutch military organization contributed substantially to the international Stabilization Force in Iraq (SFIR). The Dutch contribution to SFIR consisted of expeditionary organizations that were built around an infantry battalion[9] from the Dutch Army's Air Assault brigade (see Appendix 1 for a schematic layout of the Army) that was complemented by a helicopter detachment, logistical units, engineers and units from the Military Police (MP; Delahay et al., 2009, pp. 17–19). An officer of the Dutch SFIR mission explains this "mixing and matching" within the Dutch SFIR detachment:[10]

> *We were not sent as a battalion but as a Battle Group. This means that all kinds of assets are added that are normally not part of the battalion: logistics, transport, Military Police, intelligence . . . all kinds of things.*

An Army officer explains what it meant to cooperate with these "newly added" units:

> *That is what I would like to address as a problem. Units from outside our club were added at the last moment. They were motivated but came from an entirely different world.*

In the night between August 14 and 15, 2004, around 23:45 hours, opposing forces in the town of Ar Rumaythah ambushed Dutch military units of SFIR-4.[11] Delahay et al. (2009, p. 14) describe that: "During an investigation on an earlier shooting incident, a small unit from the Military Police was attacked by hostile opponents, which resulted in one fatality and one wounded military policeman". Kramer (in Delahay et al., 2009, p. 61) shows that a "misunderstanding" complicated the military response to the ambush. Procedures within the Army prescribed that units who leave the compound, should use a particular radio frequency to report to the Operations Room (OPS-room) of the Company responsible for that particular area, in this case "Bravo-Company". This procedure is aimed at ensuring that it is known which units are outside the compound. The MPs, however, did not report to the OPS-room because they did not seem to be aware of this particular procedure and hence, did not have the right radio frequency. A non-commissioned Army officer explains:

> *They* [MPs] *did not load the right radio frequencies for Ar Rumaythah. That is why they could not contact OPS. They were just driving around, while we did not know where they were. We cannot help them when they load their radio in the wrong way.*

As a result, the MPs could not contact the OPS-room of Bravo-Company after the attack. They tried to communicate their position to the battalion OPS-room by means of a satellite telephone. Although battalion-OPS did not receive their location, it was realized that the situation was serious. As a result, a Quick Reaction Force (QRF), medical evacuation (medevac) and Apache helicopters were put on stand-by. Meanwhile, a unit on patrol nearby overheard the attempts of the MPs to communicate their distress via radio and decided to assist, as a commander explains:

> *They* [the patrol] *were going north, to the border of their section and listened to radio traffic. At a certain moment, they reported themselves at the company communication network and said: Listen . . . I can be there in five minutes, what do you want? Ok, I am aborting the patrol and we are going there now!*

On arrival at the scene, the patrol assisted in securing the area and reported the details of the location of the ambush to the OPS-room of Bravo-company. Ten minutes later, the first QRF from Bravo-Company with two ambulances and a recovery vehicle arrive at the scene. At about the same time, two Dutch Apache helicopters and an American Black-Hawk medevac helicopter were ordered by battalion-OPS to go to the location of the ambush.

At the moment the first QRF left the compound of Bravo-Company a second QRF was formed. This second QRF was bigger than the first and consisted of armed vehicles, an ambulance, a salvage vehicle and a crane-vehicle. Also, a Forward Air Controller (FAC-er) is added to the QRF to help directing and landing of helicopters. The second QRF leaves the compound at about 00:30 hours. The moment the second QRF enters the city of Ar Rumaythah, it is attacked with heavy weapons. Standard procedure in such a situation is to go forward in high speed in an attempt to escape from the attack. After a while, the second QRF arrives at the scene where the MPs were ambushed. At this moment, it is discovered that one vehicle is missed in action. After this is reported to the OPS-room of Bravo-company, a third armored QRF is formed to search for the missing vehicle. At roughly the same time, the battalion OPS-room, which is informed about the escalating incident, decides to send their QRF to the city of Ar Rumaythah. A commander of Bravo-Company explains his vision about this decision:

> *At that moment, I could not use a unit from outside* [from outside Bravo-Company]. *As long as I can do it myself* (. . .) *I don't want them here. One: before they are up to date with what is going on . . . I don't have that time. Two: before I have them guided to the good location, because they do not know the terrain, I don't have that time . . . I recall that I shouted: Stop this show! If I need anything I can ask for it. Then they* [the battalion QRF] *decided to stop moving.*

The commander subsequently decides to put the battalion QRF into waiting position outside the city and receive the arriving helicopters. The same commander states:

> *The commander of the battalion QRF came to me. . . . Then he received the assignment to assume a "blocking position" and receive the helicopters. That is what they did.*

Upon arrival at the location of the ambush, the FAC-er consults with the two Apaches to discuss tasks of the helicopters. They decide to task one Apache to flying above the city to secure the third QRF from Bravo-Company, the other Apache is tasked to secure the Black-Hawk medevac helicopter. The FAC-er explains:

> *What I thought was important was that we lost a vehicle, and that helicopters are perfect for assisting to find them. They not only have weapons but also have a mega-view. I was thinking about using one helicopter for guiding us through the city and look for the missing vehicle. . . . And then I had to arrange it because they were originally tasked to protect the medevac.*

Tasking the Apache to securing the third QRF decreased the amount of gunfire from opposing forces that the QRF and other units was encountering. As a result, they and the other vehicles could enter and exit the city without much trouble. Eventually, all personnel, including deceased and wounded soldiers, returned to the base of Bravo-Company around 03:30 hours.

The fact that the MPs did not report themselves to the OPS-room of Bravo-Company seems to have complicated the response in the first minutes after the ambush. A non-commissioned officer, however, explains that these problems between Army units and the MP were not an incident but a more general problem between Army and MP units within the Dutch contribution to SFIR:

> *The MP's didn't know how to operate with radios and stuff like that. They were just driving around over there.*

A non-commissioned officer explains that this happened more than once with all kind of units that were "added" to the Battle Group.

> *Those people are going on a mission and sometimes have an office job at home, and then they think after one month: "I am going to look around here". And we received people at the compound that were not registered in the area. Often, they responded: "but we didn't load the radio for your area". When something would have happened in the city of Ar Rumaythah, they wouldn't be able to contact us. Sometimes they don't even know how radios work.* (. . .) *Especially the MPs and some higher non-commissioned officers and officers didn't know that.*

5.3.2 Crisis Response After the Crash With Flight MH17

Malaysia Airlines Flight MH17 was shot down above eastern Ukraine on the 17th of July in 2014. All 298 persons on board died in the crash of the airplane. The Dutch national crisis response organization was initiated to deal with the events following the crash. In the winter of 2014, Dutch parliament initiated an evaluation of the national crisis response organization. The evaluation was commissioned to the Scientific Research and Documentation Centre[12] of the Dutch ministry of Security and Justice[13] and carried out by a multidisciplinary research team of the University of Twente. This section is based on their report[14] and provides a description of the actors, organizations and fora involved. After that, a description of relevant findings is presented. In the descriptions below, claims are supported by references to the report. These references are numbered and placed between brackets [x]. In Appendix 2, detailed references to the report are listed.

5.3.2.1 The Dutch National Crisis Response Organization

For describing the Dutch national crisis response organization, a distinction can be made between actors, fora/committees in The Hague that are described in the national handbook for crisis management[15] (see Ministry of Security and Justice, 2013) and so-called "crisis partners". These crisis partners are mostly operational parties that differ per crisis. Regarding the actors and fora in The Hague that were activated, the national handbook states that, because every crisis is different, activation can be done flexibly [1]. As such, not all fora described in the handbook were activated. Also, in the course of the crisis, new (governing) fora were assembled to match the specific demands of the MH17 crisis [2].

After receiving news of the crash at the 17th of July 2014 at about 17:00 hours, in The Hague two interdepartmental fora were gradually activated [3]. These fora can be interpreted as the core of the governing part of the national crisis response organization: the interdepartmental crisis control team (in Dutch: ICCb[16]) and the ministerial crisis control team (in Dutch: MCCb[17]). In the ICCb, high-ranked civil servants of the ministry of Security and Justice, the ministry of Foreign Affairs, the ministry of Defense and the ministry of General Affairs took seat. In the MCCb the ministers of these ministries took seat and were accompanied by advisors on communication, Police and Defense. The ICCb and MCCb were coordinated by the Dutch National Coordinator on Counterterrorism and Security (in Dutch: NCTV[18]) and gathered in the building of the ministry of Security and Justice that facilitates the national crisis response organization by means of a National Crisis response Centre (NCC) [4]. Also, within the ministry of Security and Justice, the National Crisis Communication Team (in Dutch: NKC[19]) supports external communication activities and is assembled from communications advisors from the different ministries involved [5]. With regard to "flexible" crisis fora, after some time a "steering group MH17" was formed, in which operational activities of the repatriation mission in Ukraine were coordinated [6]. Also, due to the amount of questions from Dutch parliament an ad-hoc parliamentary accountability team was formed [7].

As for "crisis partners" multiple parties started their activities immediately after they heard from the crash of flight MH17. These were parties in the vicinity of Schiphol Airport such as the Airport's crisis management team, Malaysia Airlines' Europe/UK headquarters and the operational team of the safety region of Kennemerland[20] [8]. Also, several parties that are related to care of victims and victims' families started activities such as the National Team of Forensic Investigations (in Dutch: LTFO[21]), family liaison officers[22] of the Dutch Police and the Dutch Victim Support organization [9]. Furthermore, several municipalities started activities that related to caring for victims' families [10]. Besides these parties, the ministry of Defense and the ministry of Foreign Affairs started employing operational activities to send employees to Ukraine.

5.3.2.2 Description of Relevant Findings

Most activities in the first crisis response on the 17th of July 2014 were aimed at reconstructing a passenger list and list of next of kin,[23] taking care of the victims' families at Schiphol Airport, starting a national telephone number and initiating a party to travel to Ukraine and visit the crash site [11]. The evaluation report highlights that in the first crisis response a number of actors and organizations in the vicinity of Schiphol Airport attempted to assemble and validate a passenger list and start immediate help to family members of passengers [12]. To do so, Malaysia Airlines communicated a passenger list to the Military Police at Schiphol Airport [13] and initiated shelter for family members at the local Steigenberger Hotel [14]. Because the passenger list missed crucial information on the nationalities of the victims, employees worked through the night in order to verify that information [15]. At the same time, the Operational

Team of the safety region of Kennemerland, in which the airport of Schiphol is located, was activated and started investigating options to start a national emergency number [16]. They, however, pointed to the national impact of the MH17 crash and had the position that the national government should take care of such an emergency number [17]. The different actors and organizations in the vicinity of Schiphol Airport were organized in the Council of Consultation[24] (CoC), which was initiated an hour after the news of the crash of flight MH17 was known [18].

A main finding of the evaluation report on the first crisis response was problematic communication and coordination between the actors in The Hague and the actors and organizations in the vicinity of Schiphol Airport [19]. For example, it was unknown in The Hague that a passenger list was given to the Military Police two hours after the crash of flight MH17 [20]. Also, the report highlights that several attempts to reach the National Crisis Centre, both with regard to the passenger list and the initiation of a national emergency telephone number, failed [21]. Besides that, the following morning, the NCTV visited Schiphol Airport to inform the actors and organizations there that "they were taking over" [22]. This "governance strategy" did not facilitate the work that was still carried out by the various actors and organizations in the vicinity of Schiphol, that were still working on validating the passengers list [23].

Activities in the second period, between the 18th and the 24th of July 2014, centered on reaching the crash site, repatriating victims' remains, organizing the national day of mourning and assisting the families of victims [24]. The evaluation report highlights that a small party of forensic experts and Military Police personnel arrives in Ukraine and attempts to reach the crash site of flight MH17 [25]. It is pointed out in the report that the trip leads the team via Charkiv and Donetsk to the crash site, which is controlled by rebel forces in the eastern part of Ukraine [26]. The report describes that this trip is undertaken through an area that resembles a war zone, and that personnel of the team is not equipped with protective material such as helmets and bulletproof vests [27]. Upon their arrival at the crash site, the team discovered that Ukrainian State Emergency Service (SES) personnel were underway in recovering the remains of victims [28]. These remains are then transported to a train in Torez. The team subsequently boards the train, which after some time and discussion with rebel forces goes "en-route" to Charkiv via Donetsk where it arrives the 22nd of July [29].

Assistance to the victims' families in the first week started in an ad-hoc manner, as the report highlights, due to problems with validation of the passenger list and the creation of a list of next of kin [30]. Next to these issues, the evaluation report highlights that family liaison officers, who were praised by families on their work, were doing numerous tasks, which were outside the traditional scope of their role [31]. This was mainly due to the central role they developed from the beginning of crisis, which was also emphasized by members of the MCCb [32]. As such their tasks expanded from gathering material to facilitate identification of victims' remains to taking care of victims' families at various levels, including social assistance. Core activities in the third period, from the 25th of July until the 8th of September 2014 were focused on a repatriation mission at, and around, the crash site and assistance to victims' families [33].

The evaluation report describes that during the first week of the crisis response, several actors in The Hague were concerned about the progress of the repatriation of victims' remains to The Netherlands. To accelerate repatriation, several scenarios are developed to deploy a large repatriation mission to the crash site. After some time and discussion, this mission is defined as an unarmed policing mission, headed by a high-ranked police officer [34]. Personnel of the mission consisted of both military and police personnel [35]. After arrival of a large part of its personnel in the area, several attempts are undertaken to reach the crash site. In the first days of the mission these attempts are aborted due to military activity in the area that resulted in safety concerns for mission personnel [36]. The mission reached the area at the first of August and continues repatriation efforts until the 6th of August [37]. During the period of their deployment, both the Staff of Large and Special Missions (SGBO)[25] of the National Police and the Directorate of Operations (DOPS) of the ministry of Defense controlled the mission. According to the evaluation report, this resulted in coordination problems because the police was much more hesitant to operate in a hostile area then the ministry of Defense [38]. After some time, as is highlighted in the report, mission commanders stop feeding the police with information on mission activities [39].

Regarding the assistance of victims' families, the Dutch Victim Support organization and municipalities also aimed at providing assistance and care. In the first weeks however, the evaluation report highlights that the three organizations seemed to be working "uncoordinated" [40], which resulted in a lack of information sharing and families getting agitated because they were being visited by all kinds of parties asking the same questions [41]. After some time, and due to bottom-up improvisation [42], coordination between parties that assisted victims' families improved. Also, it is highlighted in the report that contact of family liaison officers with actors in The Hague was hindered by complicated coordination through several governing parties both within the Police and the national crisis organization [43].

5.4 Analysis

In this section, the analysis of the cases introduced above is presented. To do so, the hypotheses developed in the previous chapter, and accompanying arguments, are used as an analytical framework. These hypotheses are as follows:

Hypothesis 1: Functional concentration in parent organizations leads to a complex "mixing and matching" design process that limits structural coupling in expeditionary organizations.

Hypothesis 2: Limited structural coupling within the expeditionary organization, combined with enactment and the necessity to act, threatens the emergence of safety in expeditionary organizations.

Hypothesis 3: Because of limited structural coupling and product innovation at the operational level, safety in expeditionary organizations is developed by operators engaging in self-design of ad-hoc networks.

Hypothesis 4: Mixing and matching expeditionary organizations out of functionally concentrated parent organizations leads to functional concentration in expeditionary organizations, which results in organizational complexity that complicates the process described in hypothesis three and threatens the emergence of safety at the level of the expeditionary organization.

Hypothesis 5: Coordination by means of a central plan, which can be related to a high degree of functional concentration in parent and expeditionary organizations, hinders the processes described in hypothesis three, and threatens the emergence of safety at the level of the expeditionary organization.

Firstly, the SFIR case is analyzed. Secondly, the analysis on the MH17 case is explicated.

5.4.1 Analyzing the SFIR Case

The description of the SFIR case starts off with an ambush of Military Police personnel who aimed to investigate an earlier shooting incident. It becomes clear that, what was also witnessed within the TFU case, procedures between units of the SFIR Task Force were underdeveloped and organizational integration between the units within the Task Force that were studied seemed to be problematic. The MPs didn't know the specific Army procedures for leaving the compound. This hindered the response of the SFIR Task Force, and of Bravo-Company in particular. The company did not have information on the location of the MPs. As was also witnessed within the TFU case, subsequent actions that are aimed at controlling the event, and establish safety of the MP units that were under fire, were oriented toward creating ad-hoc relationships between units. In the case, it was described that another patrol overheard radio transmissions of the MPs, decided to take action and signaled the location of the ambush to the company OPS-room.

With regard to the **first hypothesis**, it can be argued that support can be found. The case description starts by highlighting that the Dutch SFIR organization consisted of a battalion to which all kinds of other units with specific functionalities were added. According to respondents, this complicated integration within the task force. They stated that units that were added "came from an entirely different world" and didn't know how to operate within a task force such as SFIR-4, which was highlighted by the unawareness of radio procedures. Hence, it seems to be the case that—at least to some extent—structural coupling was missing between the "core" of SFIR-4 and "added units". That is to say, at least between these two groups of units, input-output relations and accompanying coordination mechanisms did not seem to be entirely present. From the case description, it can also be inferred that these issues of coupling between units can be tied to the way the units were "mixed and matched" within the Task Force. Like TFU, SFIR-4 too was assembled out of many different, specialized units into a configuration that did not resemble the way the military parent organization is designed. Furthermore, the Dutch SFIR organization was largely assembled out of the Army parent organization in the Netherlands, which design was already defined as highly functionally concentrated. This implies that SFIR-4 too was assembled by means of a complex mixing and matching process that may explain the issues of structural coupling between Army units and MP.

Some might argue, however, that the Military Police has such a special position within a military organization, as the organization's police force, and that this may also account for their limited integration within the task force. At the end of the case description, however, more general integration problems between the units of the Dutch SFIR organization are highlighted, which may lead one to conclude that limited structural coupling between MPs and Army units within the Dutch SFIR organization can be interpreted as being symptomatic for of a broader problem within the organization. As such, it is argued that the SFIR case provides support for the first hypothesis.

As to the **second hypothesis**, the integration problems between Army units and the MPs clearly manifested in safety issues during operations as it delayed the response after the ambush had taken place. This highlights that the units described in the SFIR case, apparently, had to act with underdeveloped coupling, which had consequences for safety during operations. The second hypothesis therefore seems to be able to explain the relation between some aspects of SFIR-4's design and safety outcomes at the level of the task force.

The **third hypothesis** stressed that due to missing structural coupling and local product innovation, self-design emerges that is aimed at forming ad-hoc networks to develop safety of operations. It can be read in the case results that indeed ad-hoc reciprocal relationships were created to overcome issues of integration, as was witnessed between the patrol that overheard radio traffic and the MPs, which hints at the presence local self-design of a network that was aimed to improve safety of the ambushed units. Also, it was shown that a FAC-er tasked an Apache helicopter to guiding them through the city instead of protecting the medevac helicopter. The resulting new, and self-designed, network seems to have improved safety of personnel on the ground and accelerated the response and recovery of personnel and material from the ambush site.

Hypothesis four pointed to the relationship between design of parent and expeditionary organizations, organizational complexity within the expeditionary organization and safety outcomes at the level of the expeditionary organization. It is argued that only some minor traces can be found in the case that support parts of the hypothesis. That is to say, clear traces were already found that the Dutch SFIR organization and its parent organizations were/are characterized by high degrees of functional concentration of their organizational structure. Therefore, along the arguments on structural complexity by De Sitter, it seems logical to state that within the Dutch SFIR organization too organizational complexity was present. However, the information in the case provides very little information on organizational complexity to confirm that part of the fourth hypothesis. The only event that in some way may be interpreted as a symptom of organizational complexity is that after the ambush the battalion OPS-room decides to task the battalion QRF to the city, which seems to come out of thin air for the local commander on the ground. Although this did not help him in providing a solution for the incidents, no evidence is found that this hindered self-design or resulted in safety issues at the level of the expeditionary organization.

The **fifth hypothesis** was about the negative influence of "coordination by means of a central plan" on self-design and the emergence of safety. It is argued that some traces can be found in the SFIR case that support the hypothesis. After the battalion OPS-room had decided to task the battalion QRF to the city, the on-scene commander explains that this decision is not helpful because the battalion QRF is not acquainted with the area. The decision by the battalion OPS-room shows similarities to the top-down way personnel in TFU's operations room aimed to coordinate actions in the Uruzgan province. In the SFIR case, the local commander finds an ad-hoc solution to this problem and tasks the battalion QRF to a "waiting position". Nevertheless, the top-down way in which battalion-OPS sends their QRF to the location of the ambush shows traces of coordination by means of a central plan, which did not seem to help the local efforts of the on-scene commander. However, no clear evidence is found that relates this issue to either a hindering effect on self-design of ad-hoc networks or safety outcomes at the level of the task force.

Summing up, the SFIR-4 case provided confirming evidence for hypotheses 1, 2 and 3. Some evidence for parts of hypotheses 4 and 5 were found, but the case did not provide evidence that the particular design aspects addressed in these hypotheses influenced self-design in such a way that it had negative consequences for the emergence of safety at the level of the Task Force.

5.4.2 Analyzing the MH17 Case

At first glance, it seems questionable whether the MH17 case provides confirming evidence for the five hypotheses developed in the previous chapter. In the MH17 case, safety seems to be important, especially in the high-risk mission context in Ukraine, but safety issues do not seem to relate to aspects of design of the crisis organization. Neither during the Ukraine mission nor during crisis response efforts in the Netherlands. Yet, it is pointed out that aspects of design that were found within TFU and SFIR-4 seem to be present. It was highlighted in the results section that actors in the vicinity of Schiphol and family liaison officers experienced missing integration between themselves and other operational actors and between themselves and governing actors in The Hague. More specifically, aspects of organizational design, which were present in the other expeditionary cases, seem to relate to other issues at the level of the crisis organization than issues of safety. That is to say, it can be interpreted that they seemed to have some influence in delay of passenger list validation, initiating a national emergency number and miscommunication in the assistance to victims' families. Therefore, it seems worthwhile to investigate whether the hypotheses developed in the previous chapter also hold relevance for the relationship between organizational design and other outcomes at the level of the expeditionary organization. On the one hand, however, such an investigation goes beyond the "high-risk" scope of this book. On the other hand, it might open up the opportunity to contribute to literature on temporary organizations in a more general sense. Chapters 6 and 7 will direct attention to this in more detail.

The **first hypothesis** stated that high degrees of functional concentration in parent organizations results in a complex "mixing and matching" process that limited structural coupling within the expeditionary organization. In the MH17 case it can be found that indeed the crisis response organization seems to have suffered from missing structural coupling between units. This can be interpreted from the problematic interaction and communication between several actors in the vicinity of Schiphol, actors in The Hague and the police in relation to delay in validation of passenger lists, the national emergency number and the assistance to victims' families. The case description highlighted that between these actors "communication and coordination" were problematic at the beginning of the crisis. It seems to be the case that no developed linkages between these actors were present and that developed coordination mechanisms for these linkages were absent as well. Therefore, from an IOR perspective, it may be argued that, for these actors, developed input-output relationships and accompanying rules or agreements were not entirely present at the beginning of the crisis response.

However, it can be questioned whether this can be attributed to a complex mixing and matching process and functional concentration in parent organizations. Although the evaluation report explicated from what parent organizations the different units and operators were originating, the report does not provide information for analyzing structural design of parent organizations. Hence, it may be hard to confirm parts of the first hypothesis. However, it is argued that these aspects of the first hypothesis can be verified by means of using existing literature on crisis response operations. Boin (2009), for example, stresses the bureaucratic nature of government organizations taking part in crisis response efforts by referring to this issue as the "impossible job of crisis management". Within the MH17 crisis response organization, many government units from both local, regional and national levels took part. As such, it may well be that many parent organizations, and especially those related to government, are characterized by high degrees of functional concentration. Due to this, and the large size of the MH17 crisis response organization, it can be argued that a complex, and gradual, "mixing and matching" process took place in which many different units from varying, and often functionally concentrated, parent organizations were merged into the crisis response organization. This may, on its turn, have affected the degree of structural coupling present within the expeditionary crisis response organization.

With regard to the **second hypothesis**, it can be interpreted from the case description that limited structural coupling between units/actors had consequences. Similar to the necessity to act that was witnessed in the TFU and SFIR cases, units within the MH17 crisis response organization had to act, for example, to validate a passengers list, initiate a national crisis telephone number and care for victims' families. Also, they had to do this with underdeveloped structural coupling between organizational elements. This can, for example, be found in the observations that units worked "uncoordinated", which was associated with problems such as miscommunication and delay at the level of the crisis response organization. It seems to be the case that, uncoupled units/actors in, for example, the field of assistance to victims' families had to act, with the consequence that victims' families were visited by several parties, asking the same questions.

Also, it can be found that operators engaged in the process of self-design, which was emphasized in **hypothesis three**. For example, it was highlighted in the case description that family liaison officers and actors in the vicinity of Schiphol airport tried to create ad-hoc relationships and agreements with other actors to improve the operations of the crisis organization. Some actors went in lengths to (try to) establish linkages between themselves and other actors to improve the way victims' families were assisted. With regard to self-design, the results section highlighted that, along the way, family liaison officers and the other actors in this field, "improved their coordination". This seems to hint at a process in which the actors themselves engaged in actions to improve their local coordination, which implies the successful creation of an ad-hoc network. At the one hand, this form of self-design seems to be oriented towards overcoming the drawbacks of missing structural coupling. On the other hand, in the case of care for victims' families, the new network that seemed to be established, in which a new task for family liaison officers had a central place, improved the ability of the crisis organization to assist these families.

The **fourth hypothesis** stressed the relation between of characteristics of parent organizations, design of the expeditionary organization, organizational complexity and the process of self-design. It was already highlighted previously that the MH17 case provided ample information on design of parent organizations. Some observations can, however, be made about the design of the crisis response organization. It indeed seems that the MH17 crisis response organization was characterized by some degree of functional concentration. This can be inferred from the way in which different operational units, such as family liaison officers, the ministry of defense, municipalities, Malaysia Airlines and the Dutch foundation for victim support were operating. They all seem to have specialized and sometimes overlapping activities within the national crisis organization. What can be seen in the first period of the crisis response is that, apart from missing structural coupling, the overview that different units and actors had in this period, for example in relation to validation of passenger lists, was problematic. Such a lack of "process overview" may have hindered the way in which actors could "find" each other and establish local coordination for activities that seemed to be reciprocally dependent. A lack of process overview could in this case be interpreted as a symptom of organizational complexity. Along IOR's concept of structural complexity it can be argued that in an organization with many, often functionally concentrated, building blocks, between which coupling is underdeveloped, oversight that individual units have over an entire process is problematic. Some might argue that this complexity is inherently related to a first period of crisis response. However, due to functional concentration, and along the premises of the concept of structural complexity, it can be argued that this apparent design characteristic of the MH17 crisis response organization may have impeded the ability of actors to develop ad-hoc networks and hence contributed to delay in, for example, validation of passenger lists.

Also, some traces can be found in the MH17 case that seems to stress the relevance of the **fifth hypothesis** for the relation between organizational design other outcomes at the level of the expeditionary organizations. It can be argued that some coordination mechanisms used by governing actors within the national crisis organization can be interpreted as an attempt to coordinate by means of a central plan, which seemed to have hindered self-designing abilities of operational actors. This was, for example, witnessed in the difficulties family liaison officers had in getting information from different actors in The Hague, because they had to adhere to several hierarchical layers both within the police organization and the national crisis organization. This lack of information due to "long hierarchical lines" may have hindered family liaison officers in finding the right local actors in establishing an ad-hoc network with other actors for assisting victims' families. As such, these design aspects may explain some of the problems reported in caring for victims' families.

Another example can be found in the way the NCTV tried to coordinate activities of actors in the vicinity of Schiphol. The governing actions of the NCTV can be interpreted along the definition of coordination by means of a central plan, because the NCTV tried to take responsibility on, for example, validation of passenger away from crisis partners and allocate this responsibility centrally, in The Hague. The case description highlights that this strategy "did not facilitate" the work of several actors that was still ongoing on the verification of passenger lists. It hence, seems to be the case that in this way coordination by means of a central plan may have contributed to delay. However, the case description does not provide evidence of the effects of this coordination method on the self-designing abilities of operational actors.

With regard to the relation of these coordination mechanisms and design of parent organizations it, again, seems to be hard to trace this way of coordinating back to design of parent organizations, based on data present in the case description. Yet, based on the argument made by Boin (2009) on the influence of bureaucracy during crisis response, and because of the large amount of government actors taking part in the crisis response, it seems likely that coordination by means of a central plan found in the MH17 case can be traced back to the way government parent organizations are designed. That is to say, it is not surprising that mechanisms that try to coordinate by means of a central plan were present in the crisis organization as many actors were originating from large, and probably bureaucratic, government organizations.

Summing up, secondary analysis of the MH17 case provided some traces of confirming evidence for parts of the hypotheses developed in the previous chapter of this book. More in particular, the hypotheses seemed to be able to explain the relationship between aspects of organizational design, self-organization and other outcomes at the level of the crisis response organization than safety.

5.5 Discussion

Quite clearly, the goals and methodologies used in the two case studies presented in this chapter were different than the goal and methodology of the other empirical studies in this book. These case studies were not specifically focused on studying the relationship between organizational design, self-organization and the emergence of safety. As such, only some *traces* of support for the hypotheses could be found by deductively analyzing the cases with the hypotheses developed in Chapter 4. However, despite this inevitable shortcoming of a secondary analysis of existing case study data, this chapter has provided some support for the hypotheses developed in the previous chapter. Next to support, the verification in this chapter has also provided some *contrasting* elements. The MH17 case provided the opportunity to relate aspects of expeditionary organization design that, in the other cases were regarded as relevant to self-organization and the emergence of safety, to self-organization and other outcomes such as delay. Therefore, as Yin (2003) also stresses, hypotheses need to be refined. Before refinement of hypotheses can take place, however, some attention has to be directed to the relation between the concept of safety and the other outcome "variables" found in the MH17 case.

Apparently, it can be inferred that aspects of expeditionary organization design, present in the cases in this chapter, influence self-organization in such a way that both safety and other organizational outcomes are threatened. As such, these results seem to point to a particular, more general, mechanism between organization design, self-organization and outcomes at the organizational level in expeditionary organizations. It is argued that De Sitter's concept of *controllability* (1994, p. 207), which is based on Ashby's law of requisite variety (e.g., Ashby, 1957), is able to explicate this mechanism.

5.5.1 Discussing the Controllability Concept

Controllability, according to De Sitter (ibid.; De Sitter et al., 1997), refers to the ability of an organization to balance control demands and control options. Structural organization design, in his perspective, influences both through the ability of an organization's structure to increase regulatory capacity (control options) and decrease structural complexity (control demands). In the classic works of De Sitter and IOR, the properties of structural design that were thought to influence degrees of control capacity and structural complexity, and hence influence organizational controllability are described by means of the seven "design parameters" that were also introduced in Chapter 3. High "values" on these parameters, according to De Sitter, increases structural complexity and decreases control capacity, which subsequently results in poor controllability. Following De Sitter (1994, p. 42), such issues of controllability may manifest as issues on quality of work (e.g., poor motivation), quality of organization (poor flexibility and efficiency), and quality of working relations (poor communication pattern between employees). Hence the concept of controllability can be seen as proposing a mechanism between characteristics of structural design and outcomes at the level of the organization.

It was already stated in Chapter 3 that concepts developed in De Sitter's works, and therefore IOR too, are bound by a particular organizational context, to which De Sitter referred to as "Mainstream Holland Inc.". Therefore, the specific mechanism proposed by De Sitter's concept of controllability, which relies on his definition of the seven structural parameters, may be bound by such contexts as well. The more general foundations of the controllability concept however, are grounded in the works of Ashby. As such, the general nature of the concept as introduced in the beginning of this section may hence be applicable in a more general sense. Based on the results of this chapter, it is argued that for expeditionary contexts, the specific controllability mechanism between structural organization design characteristics and outcomes at the organizational level is different than the mechanism proposed by De Sitter. That is to say, for expeditionary contexts, the seven structural parameters seem to play a role in influencing outcome variables, which was highlighted by the use of the "functional concentration" concept, but in expeditionary contexts other design characteristics are also of relevance for outcomes at the organizational level.

Therefore, it seems worthwhile to investigate whether the hypotheses developed in the previous chapter can be used to shape a conceptualization for controllability in expeditionary contexts.

5.5.2 Refining the Hypotheses

The first hypothesis developed in Chapter 4 stressed the relation between functional concentration in parent organizations, complexity of the mixing and matching process, and consequences for structural coupling in the expeditionary organization. As argued in the earlier section, it can be stated that both the MH17 and the SFIR case provided support. Hence, the first hypothesis remains unchanged and can be formulated as follows:

Hypothesis 1: Functional concentration in parent organizations leads to a complex "mixing and matching" design process that limits structural coupling in expeditionary organizations.

As to the second hypothesis, that stressed the relationship between limited structural coupling and safety issues, it can be argued that both cases highlighted integration issues that could be interpreted as limited structural coupling. In combination with the necessity to act of the expeditionary organization in its environment, this manifested in problems. For the Dutch SFIR mission in Iraq, these problems were related to problematic emergence of safety, as Army units did not know the location of the ambushed MPs, which led to problems with initiated rescue efforts. For the MH17 case however, these problems were not related to safety outcomes. Instead the issues within the MH17 crisis response organization manifested as delays in validating passenger lists and delays in starting an emergency number. It can hence be argued that the hypothesized relationship between limited structural coupling and the emergence of safety, seems to point to a more general controllability mechanism for expeditionary organizations. That is to say, limited structural coupling seemed to decrease operators' control options and increase control demands in such a way that safety and other outcomes at the organizational level were directly hindered. Hence, the second hypothesis can be reformulated as follows:

Hypothesis 2: Limited structural coupling within the expeditionary organization, combined with enactment and the necessity to act, threatens controllability in expeditionary organizations

Subsequently, the third hypothesis highlighted that due to limited structural coupling and the inevitable dynamics of operating in a dynamic complex environment, self-design emerges that is aimed at creating ad-hoc network structures. In both cases presented in this chapter traces were found of such self-designing processes because operators in both the SFIR and MH17 case attempted to build ad-hoc networks, as a result from lacking coupling within the organization and as a result of a response to environmental dynamics. In the SFIR case, it was shown that operators seemed to do so to improve the ability of their organization to operate more safely. In the MH17 case operators seemed to develop ad-hoc networks to improve aspects of delay and miscommunication during crisis operations. Furthermore, both in the MH17 and the SFIR case, traces were found that such networks were also developed to increase the ability of the organization to operate under dynamically complex conditions. In the SFIR case this related to an innovative way of tasking Apaches together with other units, in the MH17 case such "local product innovation" was found in the way family liaison officers were shaping their network within the crisis organization. Hence it is argued that the third hypothesis developed in the previous chapter holds relevance not only with regard to safety but that it seems to point to a more general controllability mechanism for expeditionary organizations. That is to say, by engaging in the process of self-design, operators seem to increase their control options and decrease control demands by shaping and reshaping structural characteristics in the expeditionary organization, which influences safety and other outcomes in a positive way. Therefore, the third hypothesis is reformulated as follows:

Hypothesis 3: Because of limited structural coupling and product innovation at the operational level, controllability in expeditionary organizations is developed by operators engaging in the process of self-designing ad-hoc networks.

The fourth hypothesis stressed the relationship between design of parent organizations, design of expeditionary organizations, organizational complexity and consequences for emergence of safety in expeditionary organizations. For this hypothesis, analysis of the SFIR case provided some traces of evidence that such structural characteristics were indeed present but the analysis failed to provide evidence for an influence on self-designing efforts and safety outcomes. The analysis of the MH17 case, however, provided some traces of evidence that seemed to support the hypothesis for the relationship between these aspects of design and other outcomes than safety. Due to these inconsistent findings between the SFIR and MH17 case, however, the fourth hypothesis needs to be rejected.

With regard to the fifth hypothesis, it can be argued that both the SFIR and the MH17 case provided some traces of evidence for the presence of coordination by means of a central plan. Within the SFIR case, however, it could not be verified that this either hindered self-designing efforts or resulted in safety issues at the level of the expeditionary organization. For, the MH17 case, however, it was argued that some evidence suggested that coordination by means of a central plan may have hindered the formation of ad-hoc networks in such a way that it resulted in issues at the level of the crisis organization. This was highlighted by consequences for delay and miscommunication in the field of assistance to victims' families. Similar to rejection of hypothesis four, hypothesis five has to be rejected due to inconsistent findings between both cases.

Lastly, it can be argued that—based on the results of this chapter—some environmental characteristics seem to have influenced whether design characteristics of expeditionary organizations can be associated with either issues of problematic emergence of safety or other outcomes, such as delay, at the level of the organization. It was pointed out in section 5.2.1 that a difference between a military crisis context and the crisis context of the crisis response organization in the Netherlands was that the latter was characterized by a different kind of reactiveness. That is to say, in a military crisis context, reactiveness is characterized by opposing parties that deliberately try to undermine the expeditionary organizations, for example by means of the use of weapons. This was not the case in the crisis context in the Netherlands. Interestingly, organizational design characteristics that could be associated with safety issues in a military expeditionary context did not result in safety problems within the crisis organization but were associated with other outcomes such as delay. Therefore, it may be proposed that "extreme" reactiveness, as witnessed in the military cases, poses more stress on the expeditionary organization itself and makes aspects of design more safety critical. As such, it can be argued the more reactive a particular dynamically complex operating environment, the more organizational design characteristics will have controllability consequences that manifest themselves as safety issues within expeditionary organizations. Hence, the following hypothesis is proposed:

Hypothesis 4: The more reactive a dynamically complex environment, the more the design characteristics of expeditionary organizations can be associated with controllability consequences that manifest themselves as safety issues.

As a result of the analysis carried out in this chapter, and the possibility to elaborate on a more general controllability mechanisms for expeditionary organizations, the theory that will be developed in the next chapter, will be of a slightly larger scope than was initially intended by the research goal presented in Chapter 1. The next chapter will therefore use the findings of this chapter to develop a theory on the relationship between organizational design, self-organization and controllability for expeditionary organizations, which is located at Van Strien's level B of knowledge generalization.

Notes

1. Note here that the framework for detailing a replication logic is different from the analytical framework with which the cases in this chapter are analyzed. As stated in this section, the latter is based on the results from Chapter 4.
2. In Dutch: Slachtofferhulp Nederland.
3. The topic list is a literally translated version of the original topic list reported by Delahay et al. (2009). For the original Dutch version of the topic list, see their report.
4. Due to confidentiality of the original interview transcripts, this chapter uses the publicly available report for the analysis instead of the original interview transcripts.
5. The author of this book was part of the research team that evaluated the crisis response organization after the crash with flight MH17 and co-conducted 37 of the 46 interviews.
6. For the interview list, see Torenvlied et al. (2015, pp. 339–342)
7. The choice for parallel activities was made because crisis response activities at different locations and different hierarchical levels were initiated at the same time (Torenvlied et al., 2015).
8. The text in this section is based on the report by Delahay et al. (2009).
9. The battalion consisted of three infantry companies, a staff company and an anti-tank company.
10. The interview quotes in this section are originating from Kramer (in Delahay et al., 2009) and literally translated from Dutch to English.
11. SFIR-4 refers to the fourth "rotation" of the Dutch contribution to SFIR.
12. In Dutch: Wetenschappelijk Onderzoek en Documentatie Centrum.
13. Nowadays this ministry is called the Ministry of Justice and Security.
14. For the report, see Torenvlied et al. (2015).
15. In Dutch: Nationaal Handboek Crisisbesluitvorming.
16. ICCb: Interdepartementale Commissie Crisisbeheersing.
17. MCCb: Ministriële Commissie Crisisbeheersing.
18. NCTV: Nationaal Coordinator Terrorismebestrijding en Veiligheid.
19. NKC: Nationaal Kernteam Crisiscommunicatie.
20. For crisis response, the Netherlands is divided into 25 administrative safety regions, Kennemerland is one of these regions and responsible for crisis response activities in the vicinity of Schiphol Airport.
21. LTFO: Landelijk Team Forensische Opsporing (in Dutch).
22. In Dutch: Familierechercheurs.
23. In Dutch: Verwantenlijst.
24. In Dutch: Commissie van Overleg
25. In Dutch: Staf Grootschalig en Bijzonder Optreden.

References

Ashby, W. R. (1957). *An introduction to cybernetics*. London: Chapman & Hall.

Boin, A. (2009). The new world of crises and crisis management: Implications for policymaking and research. *Review of Policy Research*, *26*(4), 367–377.

Delahay, R., Kamphuis, W., van Bezooijen, B., Vogelaar, A. L. W., Kramer, E. H., & van Fenema, P. (2009). *Hinderlaag in Irak: een sociaal wetenschappelijke analyse*. Breda: Netherlands Defence Academy.

Dubois, A., & Gadde, L. E. (2002). Systematic combining: An abductive approach to case research. *Journal of Business Research*, *55*(7), 553–560.

Heaton, J. (2008). Secondary analysis of qualitative data: An overview. *Historical Social Research/ Historische Sozialforschung*, *33*(3), 33–45.

Kramer, E. H. (2004). *Organizing doubt: Self-organization and army units in crisis operations* (Doctoral dissertation). Eindhoven: Eindhoven University of Technology.

Kramer, E. H. (2007). *Organizing doubt: Grounded theory, army units and dealing with dynamic complexity*. Copenhagen: Copenhagen Business School Press.

Ministry of Security and Justice. (2013). *Nationaal handboek crisisbesluitvorming*. The Hague: Ministry of Security and Justice.

Modig, N. (2007). A continuum of organizations formed to carry out projects: Temporary and stationary organization forms. *International Journal of Project Management*, *25*(8), 807–814.

Moynihan, D. P. (2008). Learning under uncertainty: Networks in crisis management. *Public Administration Review*, *68*(2), 350–365.

Richardson, R., & Kramer, E. H. (2006). Abduction as the type of inference that characterizes the development of a grounded theory. *Qualitative Research*, *6*(4), 497.

Senge, P. (1992). *The fifth discipline*. London: Century Business.

Sitter, L. U. de. (1994). *Synergetisch produceren: Human Resources Mobilisation in de produktie een inleiding in structuurbouw*. Assen: Uitgeverij Van Gorcum.

Sitter, L. U. de, den Hertog, J. F., & Dankbaar, B. (1997). From complex organizations with simple jobs to simple organizations with complex jobs. *Human Relations*, *50*(5), 497.

Torenvlied, R., Wessel, R. A., Giebels, E., Gutteling, J. M., Moorkamp, M., & Broekema, W. G. (2015). *Rapport evaluatie nationale crisisbeersingsorganisatie vlucht MH17*. Enschede: University of Twente.

Waard, E. J. de, & Kramer, E. H. (2008). Tailored task forces: Temporary organizations and modularity. *International Journal of Project Management*, *26*(5), 537–546.

Yin, R. K. (2003). *Case study research: Design and methods* (Vol. 5). Thousand Oaks, CA: Sage.

6 Constructing a Theory on Temporary Organizational Design and Controllability in Dynamically Complex Conditions

6.1 Introduction

The results of the previous chapter resulted in both refining and rejecting some of the hypotheses that were formulated in Chapter 4. In this chapter, the remaining refined hypotheses will be used as the basis for constructing a theory. It was already highlighted in the previous chapter that the findings in the SFIR and MH17 case gave the opportunity to theorize on organization design and controllability in expeditionary contexts. Therefore, the fifth research question presented in Chapter 1 can be changed accordingly and is re-formulated as follows:

> **What theory on the relation between organizational design and controllability in expeditionary organizations can be constructed?**

In doing so, the theory developed in this chapter stretches the scope of this book. That is to say, the safety concept was chosen as a central concept because the aim of the book was to focus on particular temporary organizations operating under high-risk conditions. Now, after analyzing the results in the previous chapter, and by introducing the controllability concept, it turned out that design characteristics of these particular, expeditionary, temporary organizations did not only influence the ability to deal with a risky environment and risky interactions within expeditionary organizations, but also influenced other outcomes. In this way, the contents of the theory presented in this chapter may not only be relevant to expeditionary organizations that have to deal with high-risk conditions, but also for expeditionary organizations that have to deal with dynamic complexity in a more general sense. As such, the research model that guides the study in this chapter has to be changed accordingly. The amended research model is visualized in Figure 6.1.

Yet, the theory developed still needs to possess certain characteristics, as was also detailed in Chapter 1. Firstly, the theory needs to be located at Van Strien's (1986, 1997) level B of knowledge generalization, which

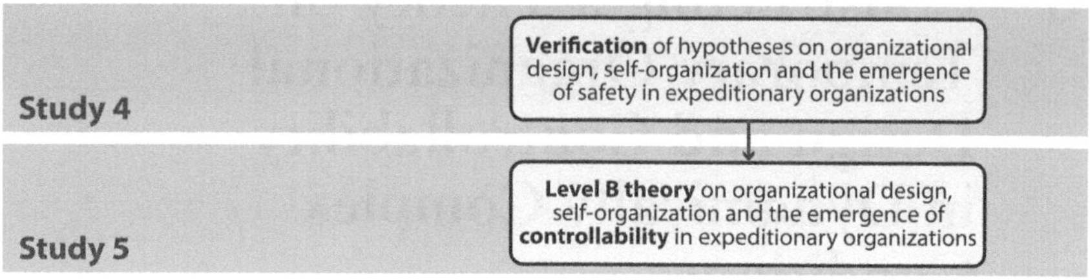

Figure 6.1 Research model of study 5

is the level of problem-oriented theory. Secondly, the theory has to possess a particular degree of explanatory power. Thirdly, the theory has to be of predictive value. Therefore, in this chapter firstly, based on the hypotheses developed in section five of the previous chapter, an elaboration of the contents of the theory will be given at Van Strien's level B. Also, a conceptual model is presented that visualizes the mechanisms of the theory. Furthermore, a section is devoted to explicating the "scope of explanatory and predictive claims" that are made by the theory. Secondly, although the theory developed in this book did not aim at developing a (normative) design theory, the third section in this chapter *explores* potential ways for finding solutions for the issues addressed in the theory. Thirdly, this chapter ends with a conclusion.

6.2 A Theory on Organizational Design and Controllability in Expeditionary Organizations

In this section first, the main results of the studies carried out in this book are presented. These results shape the main content of the theory at which the different studies in this book were aimed. As the hypotheses developed in the previous chapter are used as a foundation for the theory, it is argued that the statements presented in the section below are located at Van Strien's level B of knowledge generalization. The previous chapter was specifically aimed at verifying and refining hypotheses that were developed in Chapter 4, which were also located at Van Strien's level B because in Chapter 4, analytic generalization was used to "elevate" findings from within TFU to expeditionary organizations in general. Secondly, it is argued that the theory that this book aims to develop needs to be linked explicitly to assumptions from systems theory, at Van Strien's level A. As was highlighted in Chapter Two, implicit and inconsistent use of such assumptions may result in limited applicability of safety theory. Lastly, the scope of the theory is detailed, which elaborates on the scope of explanatory and predictive claims made in this chapter.

6.2.1 *The Relationship Between Organizational Design and Controllability in Expeditionary Organizations*

In this section mechanisms, or relationships, between concepts are explicated by using the refined hypotheses developed in the previous chapter. These mechanisms are visualized in a conceptual model, which is presented later on in this section. In this model, each proposed mechanism is given an alphabetical letter that refers to the italicized letter between parentheses in the statements presented.

First of all, as also stated previously, the findings in Chapter 5 resulted in the discovery that characteristics of organization design that influenced the emergence of safety could also be related to other outcomes at the level of the expeditionary organization. This opened up the road to theorizing on the relationship between organization design and controllability in expeditionary organizations.

A main finding was that structural organization design in expeditionary organizations was characterized by limited structural coupling between units that can be attributed to a complex "mixing and matching" process in which building blocks from parent organizations with high degrees of functional concentration are assembled into an expeditionary organization (*a*). Due to this design strategy, expeditionary organizations will enact a dynamically complex environment with an underdeveloped interaction network, which threatens controllability *(b)*. Controllability is subsequently developed by self-organizing activities of operators. These activities were characterized by the process of self-designing ad-hoc network structures *(c)*, which increases local control options and decreases local control demands and hence facilitates achieving controllability at the level of the expeditionary organization *(d)*.

Referring to the mechanisms between the concepts that are presented in the previous paragraph, it can be argued that shaping the organizational interaction network by means of self-designing ad-hoc networks is inevitably related to operating in a dynamically complex environment. That is to say, and along Weick's concept of enactment, in such an environment, organizations need to discover what needs to be done by acting. As the environment is characterized by variation and uncertainty, this means that organizational configurations that can deal with such an environment need to vary as well. Not surprisingly, therefore, in the cases presented in this book a particular kind of "product innovation" (cf. De Sitter, 1994, p. 360) at the operational level was found, which meant that operators developed new networks of units that were able to deliver an innovative "product" in relation to the operating environment. As such, the process of self-designing ad-hoc networks may be inevitably present during operations in a dynamically complex environment.

However, the first hypothesis developed in Chapter 5 also stressed that self-design was initiated due to limited structural coupling within the expeditionary organization that could be associated with an organizational design strategy that mixes and matches functionally concentrated building blocks into an expeditionary organization. This points to the notion that self-design within expeditionary organizations is apparently aimed at dealing with two different sources of uncertainty. At the one hand, it is aimed at dealing with the inevitable characteristics of a dynamically complex environment *(e)*. On the other hand, it is directed towards overcoming the drawbacks of creating expeditionary organizations out of functionally concentrated building blocks, which was associated with a complex "mixing and matching" process and the subsequent issues of integration. Hence, from a somewhat normative organizational design point of view, it may be argued that the former form of self-design is preferred over the latter. That is to say, it can be argued that burdening operators with a meta-level organization design issue, and the subsequent challenge to repair this through ad-hoc self-design, may be too much to ask in an environment in which all efforts should be directed towards dealing with a difficult and sometimes hostile high-risk environment.[1]

Furthermore, it was found in the TFU cases that organizational complexity and particular coordination mechanisms hindered the process of self-design substantially. Organizational complexity, which could be associated with functional concentration within both the expeditionary and parent organization, resulted in an incomprehensible organizational interaction network, which in some cases complicated self-designing efforts of operators. Also, it was found that some of the coordination mechanisms that were used, were characterized by bureaucratic influences that could be related to a high degree of functional concentration in parent organizations. These influences of organizational complexity and incompatible coordination mechanisms however could not be verified consistently in the SFIR and MH17 case. Hypotheses that stressed these relationships therefore had to be rejected, which also means that the mechanisms proposed in these hypotheses cannot be included in the conceptual model visualized below. The inability to confirm the hypotheses concerning these mechanisms may be attributed to the secondary case study methodology used in the previous chapter. Chapter 7 will direct more attention to this potential methodological limitation.

Lastly, with regard to controllability in expeditionary organizations, safety outcomes and other outcomes at the organizational level, it was argued that the more reactive a particular operating environment is, the more the aforementioned design characteristics of expeditionary organizations will result in controllability problems that manifest themselves as safety issues *(f)*.

The concepts and mechanisms that are central to the theory that this book aimed to develop are schematically visualized in the conceptual model presented in Figure 6.2. In the next section, a foundation based on systems theory will be given at Van Strien's level A, that relates to the level B statements presented previously.

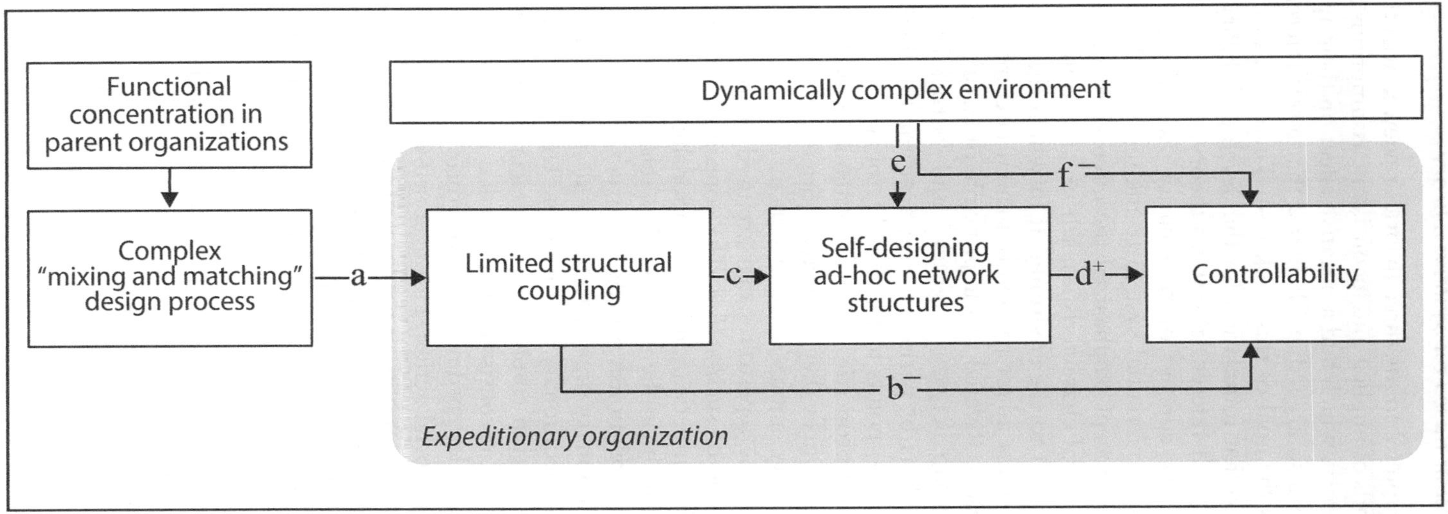

Figure 6.2 Proposed conceptual model

6.2.2 A Foundation Based on Systems Theory

A critique in Chapter 2 to the three theories reviewed was that some theories used all kinds of implicit and inconsistent assumptions and concepts from systems theory, which had a negative effect on their applicability in this book. It was also argued in Chapter 2 that a self-referential systems perspective suits the goal of this book best. Therefore, in this section, a consistent and explicit foundation for the developed theory will be constructed based on self-referential systems theory.

In Chapter 2, the concept of "circularity" was depicted as a main cornerstone of self-referential systems thinking (cf. Heylighen & Joslyn, 2001). This concept emphasized the circular relationship between the system's structural characteristics, self-organization and its adaptive capacities in relation to the environment in which the system operates. In this sense, systems adapt to environmental circumstances "in reference" to themselves. Related to the principle of circularity, it is argued that the relationship between "agency" and "structure" put forward by Giddens (1984) is of particular relevance for the theory developed here. Giddens (1984) points to the "duality of structure", which means that "the structural properties of social systems are both a medium and outcome of the practices they recursively organize" (in: Kramer, 2007, p. 61). Such a duality emphasizes that structures in social systems at the one hand provide the repertoires that are used in social action while it is also the outcome of such action. The concepts of duality and circularity hence enable understanding the relationship between social action and structures, which can be interpreted as relevant as a foundation for understanding the relationship between structural aspects of both the parent and expeditionary organization, self-design and controllability at the level of the expeditionary organization. That is to say, a large part of the preceding section emphasized that social action within an expeditionary organization consisted of self-design in an attempt to develop controllability. Self-designed network structures hence can be interpreted as the outcome of social action. However self-design was influenced by "system" characteristics both at the level of the expeditionary organization and the level of parent organizations. Hence, it can be interpreted that circularity and the duality of structure is witnessed in the interplay between the self-design process and the influence of structural characteristics of the expeditionary and parent organization(s) on this process. It was also shown that structural design properties at several organizational levels influence social action to such a degree that local self-organization, in the form of a self-designing process, was hindered, which jeopardized controllability outcomes at the systems level.

Within self-referential systems thinking, ways in which the structural inside of a system may facilitate or hinder self-organization and adaptation of the system are theorized frequently. Examples of such theorizing can be found in the works of Beer (1984) and Luhmann (1990). In his Viable Systems Model, Beer (ibid.), for example, theorizes about the specific functions a particular system should possess in order to attain viability in its environment. Luhmann, in short, theorizes on the constraining influences of a system's structure in its self-producing (or autopoetic) abilities of system elements. In this sense, it can be argued that the theory developed in this book may show what poor viability, due to characteristics of the "inside" of a system, may look like for a particular organizational form. Hence, self-referential system theories may be used to improve viability of expeditionary organizations by suggesting alternatives for the "inside" of the organizational system. However, this section deliberately omits suggestions that could be deduced from the works of Luhmann or Beer. Coming up with a perspective for formulating a design solution is not part of the theory developed in this chapter. Systematically translating level A systems theory insights to level B organization design premises is challenging and probably an entirely new study in itself (see, for example, Achterbergh & Vriens, 2010). Instead the theory developed in this book aims to possess explanatory and predictive characteristics, on which the next section deliberates.

Summing up, in this section, some cornerstones of a self-referential systems perspective at Van Strien's level A, such as circularity and Giddens's concept of duality of structure, were connected to the mechanisms of the theory described in the previous section. This is done to provide a background for understanding the relationship between organizational design and controllability in expeditionary organizations, as developed in this book.

6.2.3 The Scope of Explanatory and Predictive Claims

The mechanisms presented in the first section of this paragraph explained the relationship between organizational design characteristics and controllability in expeditionary organizations. Next, the limits of explanatory and predictive characteristics of the theory proposed have to be highlighted in order to stress that the model and accompanying mechanisms are applicable to only a family of particular organizations operating under particular environmental circumstances. This is done by emphasizing the concepts of expeditionary organizations and dynamic complexity once more.

By means of the work of Modig (2007), De Waard and Kramer (2008) and the cases studied, it was highlighted throughout this book that expeditionary organizations are temporary organizations that consist of large collections of units or "building blocks" that are "mixed and matched" out of functionally concentrated parent organizations that are located in the "stationary" left end of Modig's continuum. It was also pointed out in the course of this book that the concept of dynamic complexity is intertwined with dealing with high-risk conditions in expeditionary organizations. This was introduced in the first chapter by means of the work of Senge (1992) and Kramer (2004, 2007). These two concepts place specific boundaries on the mechanisms proposed in this chapter. That is to say, the mechanisms are only expected to explain and predict controllability issues (such as safety problems and delay) in expeditionary organizations that can be located within the boundaries placed by these concepts.

Lastly, by using the work of Weick (1979, p. 35) who employs Thorngate's (1976) principle of commensurate complexity, issues of generalizability, accuracy and simplicity can be addressed. Thorngate's principle boils down to the idea that no research can attain all three characteristics at the same time. Trying to attain two of the three characteristics results in sacrificing the third. This also seems to be the case with the theory presented in this chapter. It can be argued that the theory proposed is characterized by simplicity because it is constructed of four hypotheses and its mechanisms can be schematically presented in a figure that is comprehensible. However, with regard to the aspects of generalizability and accuracy some concessions were made in the course of this book. With regard to generalizability, it can be pointed out that, due to the aim of this book, the theory constructed had to be applicable to a wider range of expeditionary organizations. The theory presented previously was able to do so. However, in relation to this aim, the theory sacrifices some detail, or accuracy, of the proposed mechanisms. For example, the grounded theory and accompanying hypotheses developed in Chapter 3, possessed (far) more detail compared to the hypotheses developed in the previous chapter.

Lastly, as was pointed out before, the theory developed does not aim to possess prescriptive characteristics regarding a solution for organizational redesign or safety management. However, based on the preceding sections in this chapter, a possible way for finding solutions that facilitates the process of self-design in such a way that controllability in expeditionary organizations is promoted can be *explored*. This will be done in the next section.

6.3 A Possible Way for Finding Solutions: How to Design for Self-Design?

Based on the previous sections of this chapter it can be argued that facilitating controllability in expeditionary organizations points to 1) facilitating the process of self-designing ad-hoc networks and 2) minimizing high degrees of functional concentration within both the expeditionary organization and parent organizations. A possible way for finding solutions may therefore be found in literature that elaborates on design of so-called network organizations.

Literature on different forms of network organizations is abundant and growing (e.g., Alberts, Gartska, & Stein, 2000; Chisholm, 1998; Fjelstad, Snow, Miles, & Lettl, 2012; Miles & Snow, 1992; Volberda, 1996). However, Kuipers et al. (2010, p. 433) argue that such literature and theories quite often propose design strategies that do not address or attempt to change underlying organizational structures. Trying to "design" network organizations while leaving underlying, often bureaucratic, organizational structures intact, therefore, may result in what Kuipers et al. (2010) refer to as a "pseudo network organization". A similar critique to theorizing on "fluid" organizations, such as network organizations, can be found in the works of Schreyögg and Sydow (2010). They argue that too often theories on such fluid organizational forms neglect the role "structure" may play in such organizations.

Hence according to Kuipers et al., redesign of organizational structures is eminent for creating a network organization in which the process of self-design and emergence are facilitated. Accordingly, they developed a step-by-step redesign approach,[2] which consists of five steps that explicitly aim to change the underlying structural framework to facilitate self-design and adaptability at the organizational level.

The next section will therefore explicate the step-by-step approach developed by Kuipers et al. (2010). In this section, it will also be pointed out whether and how their approach can be used to formulate first and explorative steps to redesign both parent and expeditionary organizations to improve controllability in expeditionary organizations. This attempt in integrating aspects of the theory proposed in the previous paragraph of this chapter and the step-by-step approach of Kuipers et al. is, however, not to be understood as an attempt to develop redesign theory for expeditionary organizations. Relating aspects of the step-by-step approach to the theory developed in this chapter is to be interpreted as an explorative first step in this direction. In doing so, it has to be noted that the text in the following sub-sections are largely based on, and adapted from, Kuipers et al. (2010, pp. 428–460).

6.3.1 A Step-By-Step Approach for Designing Network Organizations

For designing network organizations, Kuipers et al. (2010) propose an approach that enables designing network organization by means of five steps (2010, p. 435). These steps are as follows:

1. Determining the object of redesign.
2. Determining the mission and the accompanying goals and strategy of the organization.
3. Determining design specifications. These are specifications that have to be kept in mind wile redesigning and are derived from three

characteristics of the organization's primary process: characteristics of the "flow of orders", the pattern of activities that is needed to perform these orders and the functional demands that have to be met while performing these activities.
4. Designing the new structural layout of the organization in which firstly the production structure is designed and secondly a matching control structure has to be developed.
5. Designing technical systems, starting with technical systems for the organization's primary process, after that technical systems for the supporting the control structure and lastly, technical organizational information systems.

In the next sections, the relevance of the steps is explicated for finding solutions for the hindering influences of functional concentration within both parent and expeditionary organizations on safety and controllability within expeditionary organizations.

6.3.1.1 Step 1: The Object of Redesign

Kuipers et al. (2010, p. 436) state that, for network organizations, the object of redesign is less clear compared with traditional organizations. Borders between network organizations and between network organizations and their environment may be less obvious than is the case in, for example, static bureaucratic organizations. In relation to improving controllability in expeditionary organizations, determining the object of redesign can, at first sight, be seen as unproblematic. That is to say, aspects of organizational design that hindered controllability within expeditionary organizations were to a large extent related to parent organizations with a high degree of functional concentration. For improving controllability in expeditionary organizations, the object of redesign therefore shifts, for a large part, from the expeditionary organization to parent organizations. This implies that for applying organizational redesign to expeditionary organizations, redesign of parent organizations seems eminent. However, the nature of some parent organizations complicates the application of some steps, and step three and four in particular, of the step-by-step approach developed by Kuipers et al. These complications are explicated below.

6.3.1.2 Step 2: Strategy

With regard to strategy, mission and goals, Kuipers et al. (2010, p. 437) point out that creating a fine grained and detailed strategy is hard, if not impossible, for network organizations. This is due to a dynamically complex operating environment in which network organizations operate, which means that tasks and goals vary quickly and are never the same.

Processes of network organizations are therefore not known beforehand. The chapters of this book have shown that the tasks and goals of expeditionary organization are mostly developed along the way by means of *enacting* (cf. Weick, 1979) a dynamically complex environment. These notions for formulating a strategy are, however, in conflict with the way strategy is often formulated within bureaucratic organizations. That is to say, bureaucratic organizations are mostly characterized by a predetermined strategy that is implemented in a top-down way (see also Mintzberg, 2000). Hence, a first step in limiting the hindering influence of bureaucratic parent organizations in expeditionary organizations may start with implementing a more bottom-up approach to organizational strategy in parent organizations.

6.3.1.3 Step 3: Design Specifications

Design specifications, as defined by Kuipers et al. (2010, p. 435), are characteristics of the primary process that have to be taken into account when (re)designing network organizations. According to Kuipers et al. so-called nonlinear processes characterize primary processes in network organizations. This means that, in contrast to stable processes that are characterized by repetitiveness, the processes of network organizations change continuously. The non-linear nature of tasks also means that processes in network organizations are characterized by a never-ending sequence of problem-solving cycles that guide enactment of the network organization in its environment.

With regard to the topic of this book, it seems to be straightforward that the character of (non-linear) processes in expeditionary organization seems to be in contrast with the nature of processes in parent organizations. Being located at the left end of Modig's continuum, static parent organizations with high degrees of functional concentration may well be characterized by stable and repetitive processes that cannot be changed easily. It is therefore rather obvious that static processes have to be changed to fit expeditionary demands. However, this may be impossible for some parent organizations. That is to say, for some parent organizations, such as the police in the case of the MH17 crisis response organization, contribution to the expeditionary organization is not part of the "regular" primary processes. This is different compared to, for example, the Dutch military organization for which expeditionary tasks form a major part of its primary process. Hence, some parent organizations cannot simply change the nature of their processes to fit expeditionary demands. This implies that operators who originate from these stable parent organizations and are transplanted to an expeditionary organization will always be confronted with the (rather large) difference between linear and non-linear processes.

6.3.1.4 Step 4: Criteria for Redesigning the Structural Layout of Organizations

For designing network organizations, balancing between what to make "fixed" and what to keep "loose" within the network organization is the central problem in defining criteria for the structural layout. This challenge centers on the question: "which structural conditions facilitate useful emergence?" (Kuipers et al., 2010, p. 445). That is to say, which structural conditions facilitate emergence that improves the ability to deal controllably with a dynamically complex expeditionary environment? Finding structural conditions that enable such forms of self-organization and emergence also implies that network organizations without any structure do not exist and that some form of structure and hierarchy is still needed.[3] In developing structural criteria, the so-called P-C-I sequence (P-B-I in Dutch, cf. De Sitter, 1994) is followed. This sequence means that, firstly, criteria for the production structure are developed, starting with the macro level and working the way down to meso and micro levels of the organization. An important aspect of (socio-technically designed) network organizations is that they are structured along flows of orders at the macro level. This means that, instead of dividing activities per specialism, activities are grouped together along a division in the orders an organization has to conduct. Kuipers et al. stress, however, that for network organizations borders between these macro level units have to be permeable because orders will always cross borders at the macro level, due to the ever-changing turbulent nature of order flows. With regard to the meso (department) and micro (team) level, network organizations depend largely on self-design, which is facilitated by some form of control that keeps track of partnerships within the network.

As to the applicability of these design premises to improve controllability in expeditionary organizations, and in line with the earlier sections, application of this step applies to a large extent to parent organizations. Tackling bureaucratic structures in parent organizations and applying the macro, meso and micro level design "rules" for network organizations as stated previously results in less functional concentration and therefore decrease its hindering effects on the operations of expeditionary organizations. However, it was already stated that some parent organizations, such as the Dutch police organization, have their "own" distinct primary processes. Applying the network design premises to these parent organizations may result into too much "looseness" and internal turmoil within parent organizations. It can however be argued that when redesign of some parent organizations is impossible, applying network design concepts to the level of the expeditionary organizations may provide some grip in overcoming integration issues and decrease functional concentration at the level of the expeditionary organization.

For designing a control structure, Kuipers et al. (2010) do not mention any detailed criteria. A reason for this may be that the term "control structure" and the premises of network organizations, which rely heavily on self-organization, seem to be contradictory. That is to say, rules and procedures may be interpreted as hindering any form of self-organization, including self-design. However, according to De Sitter (1994) design of control structures is, in a general sense, about grouping controlling activities such as "measuring", "evaluating", "adjusting" and operational, tactic and strategic regulation.[4] A main sociotechnical premise, of course, is that in network organizations these controlling activities should be grouped as "low" as possible, to facilitate the process of self-design. This might imply, as is also often suggested by sociotechnical redesign theory, that the controlling activities "measuring", "evaluating" and "adjusting" should not be split to give operators maximum insight and autonomy over their work. Also, this may mean that in a network organization operational regulation, which is about autonomy on day-to-day operations, and tactic regulation, which is about the ability to change the way the work is designed, should be grouped as low as possible. It may be even argued that, in a network organization, operators should have substantial influence in changing and developing organizational goals, which implies that strategic regulation should also be grouped as low as possible. However, as Thompson (1967) also highlighted, in "complex organizations" some form of hierarchy, is still needed to reduce complexity of the organizational network. This might, at least, mean that next to redesigning production structures to create a form of hierarchy suitable for network organizations, some of the aforementioned controlling activities may be grouped in some sort of controlling entity within the network organization. This may be required because of critical interdependence between (macro level) sections within the network organization.

Following De Sitter's P-C-I sequence, which was highlighted previously, it should be emphasized here that applying these proposed principles of designing a control structure to parent organizations cannot be done without firstly addressing production structure design. When, for example, high degrees of functional concentration are not addressed and remain to exist, it is questionable whether any of these premises of designing a control structure can be implemented. Yet, again, for some parent organizations, the redesign of parent organizations along the premises of network organizations seems to be problematic. For these parent organizations, which were also addressed earlier, the aspects of control structure design addressed in this section may be applied to redesign at the level of expeditionary organizations to facilitate controllability during expeditionary operations. Nevertheless, also in such cases, substantial attention first has to be directed to redesign of the expeditionary production structure for which the premises of network design can be used.

Next, criteria are developed for the "information structure", such as the need for supportive technical information systems. This will be addressed in the next sub-section on design-step 5.

6.3.1.5 Step 5: Designing Technical (Information) Systems

Kuipers et al. (2010) argue that technical (information) systems have to facilitate the self-designing nature of network organizations. They point out that it is eminent that such systems should facilitate searching and discovering contact with other members of the network organization in order to find suitable partners for carrying out operations. However, De Sitter (1994, p. 101) points out that in organizational practice, technical information systems are often implemented in ways in which the design of the organization's production structure is treated as a given. In relation to this, Van Bezooijen and Kramer (2015) point to limitations of the concept of "network centric operations" (NCO; see also Alberts et al., 2000), which is used frequently in Western armed forces. In short, the concept of network centric operations aims to share information between all units of an organization by connecting all units by means of Information Technology (IT). Such increased information sharing is thought to result in increased situational awareness and an improved ability of military task forces to operate under dynamic circumstances. Van Bezooijen and Kramer (2015) stress that connecting all kinds of units with each other without addressing the underlying structural organizational framework may result in "tight coupling" (cf. Perrow, 1999) between units that, on its turn, may influence controllability negatively. Examples of this phenomenon might be found in Chapters 3 and 4, in which it was highlighted that Sperwer-UAV images were shared with all kinds of units within the TFU operations room. On the one hand, sharing these images resulted in innovative Sperwer assignments. At the other hand, sharing these images led to assignments with increased, and sometimes hidden, dependencies at the level of TFU between the Sperwer-UAV and other flying units that compromised safety within TFU. Therefore, it can be regarded as eminent that production structure and control structure design of parent organizations are addressed before technical information systems are implemented in expeditionary organizations. When this is not possible, due to the nature of particular parent organizations as was outlined previously, applying the principles of designing network organizations to expeditionary organizations may provide solutions.

6.4 Conclusion

This chapter aimed to construct a theory on organizational design and controllability in expeditionary organizations. To do so, the remaining, refined, hypotheses of the previous chapter were used to explicate mechanisms between concepts. It was firstly argued that the hypotheses developed in Chapter 5 broadened the scope of this book, which instead of confining findings to "dealing with high risk conditions", made findings more broadly applicable. Also, the mechanisms between concepts that were proposed seemed to comply with the theoretical criteria presented in Chapter 1. In addition to that, it was explored how the theory developed relates to prescriptive sociotechnical theory on organizational redesign, which was argued to have relevance for improving controllability in expeditionary organizations. However, during this exploration, it became clear that applying a step-by-step approach to design network organizations to the design problem of expeditionary organizations has both possibilities and limitations. Developing re-design theory for this particular form of temporary organizations may hence be a potential fruitful avenue for further research on temporary organizations. The next chapter will reflect on the research presented and the theory developed in this book and it will also address potential avenues for further research in more detail.

Notes

1. A similar point is stressed by Kuipers et al. (2010) on self-organization in bureaucratic organizations. They point to the observation that in these organizations quite often employees are supposed to "network". Kuipers et al however argue that this often results in employees that try to make a structurally complex organization workable while their efforts could be better directed at dealing with issues originating from the environment (e.g. customers' demands).
2. In Dutch: herontwerpketen
3. See Schreyögg and Sydow (2010) for a similar argument.
4. See Achterbergh and Vriens (2010) for an in-depth discussion and overview of these controlling activities.

References

Achterbergh, J., & Vriens, D. (2010). *Organizations: Social systems conducting experiments*. Berlin: Springer Verlag.

Alberts, D. S., Gartska, J. J., & Stein, F. P. (2000). *Network centric warfare; Developing and leveraging information superiority*. Washington D.C.: CCRP Publication Series.

Beer, S. (1984). The viable system model: Its provenance, development, methodology and pathology. *Journal of the Operational Research Society*, *35*(1), 7–25.

Chisholm, R. F. (1998). *Developing network organizations: Learning from practice and theory*. Boston, MA: Addison-Wesley Longman.

Fjeldstad, Ø. D., Snow, C. C., Miles, R. E., & Lettl, C. (2012). The architecture of collaboration. *Strategic Management Journal*, *33*(6), 734–750.

Giddens, A. (1984). *The constitution of society*. Berkeley, CA: University of California Press.

Heylighen, F., & Joslyn, C. (2001). Cybernetics and second order cybernetics. *Encyclopedia of Physical Science & Technology*, *4*, 155–170.

Kramer, E. H. (2004). *Organizing doubt: Self-organization and army units in crisis operations* (Doctoral dissertation). Eindhoven: Eindhoven University of Technology.

Kramer, E. H. (2007). *Organizing doubt: Grounded theory, army units and dealing with dynamic complexity*. Copenhagen: Copenhagen Business School Press.

Kuipers, H., van Amelsvoort, P., & Kramer, E. H. (2010). *Het Nieuwe Organiseren: alternatieven voor de bureaucratie*. The Hague: Acco.

Luhmann, N. (1990). *Essays on self-reference*. New York: Columbia University Press.

Miles, R. E., & Snow, C. C. (1992). Causes of failure in networko. *California Management Review*, *34*(4).

Mintzberg, H. (2000). *The rise and fall of strategic planning*. Harlow: Pearson Education.

Modig, N. (2007). A continuum of organizations formed to carry out projects: Temporary and stationary organization forms. *International Journal of Project Management*, *25*(8), 807–814.

Perrow, C. (1999). *Normal accidents: Living with high-risk technologies*. Princeton: Princeton University Press.

Schreyögg, G., & Sydow, J. (2010). Crossroads—organizing for fluidity? Dilemmas of new organizational forms. *Organization Science*, *21*(6), 1251–1262.

Senge, P. (1992). *The fifth discipline*. London: Century Business.

Sitter, L. U. de. (1994). *Synergetisch produceren: Human Resources Mobilisation in de produktie een inleiding in structuurbouw*. Assen: Uitgeverij Van Gorcum.

Thompson, J. D. (1967). *Organizations in action*. New York: McGraw-Hill.

Thorngate, W. (1976). "In General" vs. "It Depends": Some comments of the Gergen-Schlenker debate. *Personality and Social Psychology Bulletin*, *2*(4), 404–410.

van Bezooijen, B., & Kramer, E. (2015). Mission command in the information age: A normal accidents perspective on networked military operations. *Journal of Strategic Studies*, *38*(4), 445–466.

van Strien, P. J. (1986). *Praktijk als wetenschap: methodologie van het sociaalwetenschappelijk handelen*. Assen: Uitgeverij Van Gorcum.

van Strien, P. J. (1997). Towards a methodology of psychological practice: The regulative cycle. *Theory & Psychology*, *7*(5), 683–700.

Volberda, H. W. (1996). Toward the flexible form: How to remain vital in hypercompetitive environments. *Organization Science*, *7*(4), 359–374.

Waard, E. J. de, & Kramer, E. H. (2008). Tailored task forces: Temporary organizations and modularity. *International Journal of Project Management*, *26*(5), 537–546.

Weick, K. E. (1979). *The social psychology of organizing*. New York: McGraw-Hill.

7 Discussion and Reflection

7.1 Introduction

This final chapter will present five sections that reflect on the theory that was developed in the previous chapter. In reflecting, the findings presented in Chapter 6 are placed in wider scientific and methodological contexts, which enables this chapter to address both pros and cons of the theory developed. Firstly, a reflection will be detailed at Van Strien's level C. This means that the results of this book are placed in the wider context of studies on expeditionary organizations. Secondly, a reflection is provided at Van Strien's level B that aims to place the results of this book in the context of theory on safety during high-risk operations and theory on organization design and temporary organizations. Thirdly, a methodological reflection is presented that aims to discuss the methods that were used in this book. Finally, the last section addresses suggestions for future research.

7.2 A Reflection at Van Strien's Level C

It was highlighted throughout this book that the theory developed is located at Van Strien's level B of knowledge generalization. This meant that the mechanisms presented in the previous chapter are thought to have explanatory and predictive power in a broader category of organizational, level C, contexts. As such, the theory developed can be used to reflect on existing research in such expeditionary contexts. This section will therefore place the theory in the context of recent studies on military expeditionary organizations, crisis response organizations and other forms of expeditionary organizations such as temporary construction organizations. The section concludes with some limitations regarding applicability of the theory developed to Van Strien's level C.

7.2.1 Relevance for Studying Military Expeditionary Operations

This book is not the only study into problems of organizational design within military task forces. Kramer (2004, 2007) conducted much research on the influence of organizational design on flexibility and adaptability of military task forces. Also, Snook (2000) already addressed lack of integration and the role of military parent organizations' design in explaining a friendly fire incident in 1994. However, it can be argued that a study on the relation between organizational design, safety and other controllability outcomes in expeditionary organizations is of added value to this existing work. Firstly, although Kramer highlighted the relevance of organizational design for adaptability and flexibility, he did not explicitly address the relation between organizational design and the emergence of safety in military task forces, which has shown to be a rather relevant subject for military expeditionary organizations in the different studies presented in this book. Secondly, in relation to the work of Snook, it can be pointed out that the different studies in this book did not only attempt to explain problems in one particular incident but attempted to unravel mechanisms present in expeditionary organizations in general. In this sense, Snook's analysis, which was already introduced in Chapter 1, may be interpreted as supporting at least parts of the theory developed in this book.

Also, from more organization-psychological perspectives, researchers addressed the role of leadership (e.g., Vogelaar & Dalenberg, 2012) trust (e.g., Van der Kloet, 2005; Soeters, Bijlsma, & Van den Heuvel, 2012) and (organizational) culture (e.g., Soeters, Winslow, & Weibul, 2006) in relation to expeditionary military operations. It can be argued that this book provides a theory that can be of added value to this line existing research because it uses a perspective that is taken rarely within organization-psychological research projects cited previously. That is to say, this book has developed a perspective that is able to relate organizational design to safety and other controllability issues present in expeditionary organizations, whereas more psychologically oriented perspectives seem to be mostly insensitive to influences of organizational design on organizational outcomes.[1]

Lastly, the theory developed may hold relevance for literature on civil-military cooperation in military expeditionary contexts. Rietjens and Bollen (2008, p. 2), for example, highlight the temporary ad-hoc nature of civil-military cooperation in military expeditionary contexts and stress that absence of coordination mechanisms hinders viable cooperation in such expeditionary configurations. By means of the theory developed in this book, an explanation may be proposed that furthers understanding of civil-military interaction. That is to say, such problems may be related to the way both the expeditionary organization and parent organizations are designed.

7.2.2 Relevance for Studying Crisis Response Organizations

Literature on crisis response organizations seems to frequently acknowledge issues of integration and coordination during multidisciplinary operations (e.g., Steigenberger, 2016). For example, Smith and Dowell (2000) point out that crisis response organizations suffer from a "lack of coordination between various agencies". Also, Ansell, Boin, and Keller (2010) address problems of integration during "transboundary" crises, which are crises that span over multiple government agencies and/ or national borders. Explanations of the origins of these issues, however, often seem to disregard the influence of organizational design on controllability of crisis response operations. Explanations and solutions are mostly attributed to management practices and decision-making (e.g., Drabek, 1985), information sharing (e.g., Bharosa, Lee, & Janssen, 2010), communication (e.g., Kapucu, 2006), and aspects of (organizational) culture (e.g., 't Hart, 1993). Van Duin and Wijkhuijs (2015, p. 202) argue that crises are inevitably associated with chaos, researchers should therefore temper their criticism in evaluating government authorities. This surprising comment by Van Duin and Wijkhuis seems to advise moving science away from critically studying crisis response actions in the first phases of crisis response. By taking an organizational design perspective, the results of this book may hence contribute to this line of research in providing alternative explanations for issues of integration and coordination in crisis response organizations, that seem to be particularly relevant in the first phases of crisis response.

In relation to the relevance of "network organizations" for crisis response, some crisis management studies acknowledge the importance of studying crisis organizations as network organizations. For example, Boin (2009) points out that managing large networks is inevitably related to managing crisis response organizations. Related to this, Moynihan (2008, 2009), stresses the learning aspect of crisis networks and the influence of a "hierarchical structure" of an Incident Command System. With regard to the results of this book it can indeed be stressed that learning and (self-) designing network organizations is inevitably related to operating in crisis organization. However, although Moynihan seems to address organizational structure, his conceptualization of structure mainly focuses on a particular (rather top-down) centralizing control system for facilitating coordination and providing grip for rules and procedures during crisis response. It may be questionable whether such an interpretation of structure is helpful in overcoming the issues sketched in the studies in this book. Firstly, such a conceptualization of structure seems to follow Thompson's definition of coordination by means of a central plan, which sometimes hindered operational crisis response efforts. Second, such a conceptualization of structure does not address underlying choices in division of labor and the way in which activities are grouped and coupled in both the crisis response organization and parent organizations, which seems to be rather relevant for crisis response as the previous chapters tried to show. Boin (2009), however, seems to address some aspects of a bureaucratic division of labor in government organizations and its influence of crisis management operations. Yet, it was already pointed out in the previous chapter that he refers to dealing with such influences as the "impossible job" of crisis management. Based on the theory developed and the potential way for solutions that was put forward in the previous chapter, the results of this book may provide a potential way out.

A recent study into crisis response operations that also explicitly addresses aspects of organizational design influencing operations is conducted by Wolbers (2016). Wolbers studied aspects of coordination and integration of recent crisis response cases such as the response after the Turkish Airlines crash at Schiphol in 2009. Quite interestingly, Wolbers points to the positive role "fragmentation", or missing integration within the crisis response organization, may play in continuously shaping and reshaping crisis response networks. He stresses that instead of seeing fragmentation as something "negative", lacking integration between crisis response units spawns innovative ways of working. These results of Wolbers' study may be interpreted as being partly in line with the results of this book. That is to say, it was pointed out throughout this book that limited integration, interpreted as the absence of structural coupling between units, indeed leads to a self-designing process that shapes new and innovative networks of units during expeditionary operations. However, this book explicitly highlighted that limited integration, or fragmentation in Wolbers' terminology, was also associated with controllability issues within crisis response organization. Such effects of missing integration on controllability manifested in issues such as miscommunication and delay that substantially impacted how the crisis organization was functioning. This hindering effect seems to be neglected by Wolbers. Hence, the results of this book may shed some new light on Wolbers' concept of fragmentation.

7.2.3 Relevance for Other Expeditionary Organizations

In line with military expeditionary organizations and crisis response organizations, research on project organizations in construction frequently elaborates on problems of coordination, integration and performance. For example, Flyvbjerg, Bruzelius, and Rothengatter (2003) refer to the "megaproject paradox", by which they mean that more and more large temporary project organizations are assembled that perform poorly with regard to outcomes such as costs and time delay. Explanations for these controllability issues are sought by Flyvbjerg et al. in a lack of accountability and risk sharing between partners in such a temporary project organization. The results of this book may provide alternative starting points for an explanation for temporary building projects' poor performance. More in particular, it seems to be the case that many of these organizations can be defined as expeditionary organizations because they are quite often "mixed and matched" from large, probably static, building corporations. Also, temporary building projects are confronted with an environment that can be called dynamically complex, due to competition forces, financial pressure and public and political forces. As such, the aspects of organizational design put forward in this book may also influence controllability in these temporary building projects.

Next to the more financial controllability issues addressed by Flyvbjerg et al. safety literature frequently elaborates on safety issues in construction projects. For example, Swuste, Frijters, and Guldenmund (2012) provide a review on safety issues and possibilities for improvement in construction organizations. Swuste et al. point out that organizational aspects for improving safety in organizations are underdeveloped and that a much-heard reason for this is that "construction is different" (ibid., p. 1341). This "difference" relates, according to Swuste et al., to the nature of the construction process and the dynamic and fluid character of many construction organizations. Related to the work of Flyvbjerg et al., and along the arguments provided earlier, it can be argued that many temporary construction organizations may be characterized as expeditionary organizations and that the temporary nature and dynamics of the construction environment indeed makes these organizations "different". Hence, the results of this book may provide some alternative explanations for the difficulties in implementing organizational safety measures and may also provide an alternative perspective on safety issues in temporary construction organizations. That is to say, the "mixed and matched" character of organizational designs in expeditionary organizations may make it hard to integrate safety procedures of the different organizational units and actors taking part in the construction project. Also, an explanation for safety incidents from the perspective of organizational design may contribute to literature on safety issues in construction projects.

7.2.4 Limitations at Level C

In this section, some limitations are put forward with regard to the relevance of the theory developed in this book for research at Van Strien's level C of knowledge generalization. A first limitation is that, although the theory possesses explanatory and predictive characteristics, it does not have a prescriptive character. This can be interpreted as a limitation because in literature on safety during high-risk operations and organization design literature much effort is directed to providing prescriptive solutions. A counterargument to this limitation may however be that a first step in developing measures for improvement is a systematically developed explanatory foundation. The theory developed in this book may provide such a foundation.

A second limitation of the theory developed in this book at Van Strien's level C may be the nature of explanatory statements proposed in the theory. That is to say, this book has provided insight into the relation between organizational design safety and controllability in expeditionary organizations. Although this influence was found to be relevant for operations of expeditionary organizations, safety and other controllability effects may also come into existence due to other influences than design influences. Hence, the results of this book are not to be interpreted as an all-explaining theory of *all* controllability effects in expeditionary organizations. In the next section, the theory developed will be placed into the context of research at Van Strien's level B of knowledge generalization.

7.3 A Reflection at Van Strien's Level B

A review of theory on safety during high-risk operations was already conducted in Chapter 2. This review concluded that the three theories reviewed were not suitable for getting an understanding of the relation between organizational design, self-organization and the emergence of safety in expeditionary organizations. This already emphasizes the relevance of the results of this book in relation to theory on safety during high-risk operations. In this section, therefore, the results of this book are placed in the broader context of safety theory. Secondly, literature on temporary organizations and organizational design theory is used to reflect on the results of this book.

7.3.1 Relevance for Safety Theory

In a more general sense, Grote (2009) stresses a "sociotechnical systems design approach" in studying safety in organizations. Also, Guldenmund (2007) addresses aspects of an organization's "structure" in studying safety in organizations. In relation to these works, this book has used a particular definition of organizational design, based on the Integral Organizational Renewal approach. This (IOR) interpretation of organizational design, which can neither be found in the sociotechnical works of Grote nor in the works of Guldenmund, has shown to be of explanatory value with regard to safety and other controllability issues in expeditionary organizations.

In relation to the nature of claims stressed in the preceding chapter, it has to be noted that the results of this book do not imply that more psychological or technical approaches to safety are irrelevant. Instead, the results of this book are to be interpreted as complementary to such approaches. Such complementarity is also argued in relation to the "normal work" approach taken in this book. It was pointed out, for example in Chapters 3 and 4, that studying normal work of operators gave insight into the dynamics of working on the crossroads between environmental challenges and influences from the organizational context. This approach was adopted from Dekker (2005) who stresses a similar point in relation to normal work of operators. However, although Dekker recognizes the crossroads at which operators find themselves, he does not give a "design" interpretation to organizational influences that operators experience. Instead, Dekker points to the influence of procedures and regulations. Based on Integral Organizational Renewal premises and the theory developed in this book, it can however be stated that procedures and regulations are part of an organization's control structure and that these can never be addressed without going into the details of the system being controlled. As such, the interpretation this book has given to the normal work can be regarded to have added value to the approach put forward by Dekker.

7.3.2 Relevance for Literature on Temporary Organizations and Organizational Design Theory

From an organization science perspective, the result of this book can be placed in the wider context of theory on temporary organizations. Chapter 1 already highlighted the works of De Waard and Kramer (2008) and Modig (2007). De Waard and Kramer (2008) argue that theory on temporary organizations seems to disregard the relationship between temporary and parent organizations. Modig (ibid.), however, explicitly highlighted this relationship and pointed out that static parent organizations may hinder work in temporary organizations due to the repetitive nature of routines and vertical coordination mechanisms. A result of this book is that indeed aspects of parent organizations hinder work in temporary organizations in such a way that outcomes at the level of the temporary organization are compromised. In particular, the theory developed in this book has shown that an organizational design perspective provides explanations for such hindering influences that go beyond the mere observation of conflicting routines and coordination mechanisms. A such, the studies presented in this book can be interpreted as building on the work in this particular avenue of research on temporary organizations by theorizing on the relationship between temporary and parent organization in a more detailed manner.

A second organizational science tradition in which the results of this book can be located is, quite obviously, that of the Sociotechnical Systems Design and the Integral Organizational Renewal approach in particular. As pointed out in Chapter 1, IOR, and especially the works of De Sitter (1994) is developed for a particular kind of organizations, standard bureaucratic organizations that De Sitter referred to as "Mainstream Holland Inc.". As such, the object of study of this book was different than the object of study within "classic" IOR theory. Nevertheless, it was argued that IOR concepts could be used as a heuristic analytical compass in guiding empirical studies. This approach proved to be useful and enabled the unraveling relationship between organizational design, safety and other controllability outcomes in expeditionary organizations.

In this sense, this book contributes to IOR by applying it heuristically as an analytical perspective. Moreover, it was found in the course of this book that safety and other controllability problems that related to organizational design within expeditionary organizations could not solely be explained by using IOR's "design parameters", of which functional concentration is the first and foremost. Apparently, these design parameters are developed based on organization with existing and already developed structural coupling between organizational elements. In this book, it was found that safety and other controllability problems could be associated with the absence of structural coupling between units. This was at the one hand certainly related to functional concentration within parent organizations, and therefore relates to the first design parameter of De Sitter (1994). However, De Sitter's parameters could not account for the relationship between missing structural coupling and controllability outcomes within the expeditionary organization itself. An explanation for this finding may be that De Sitter's works are aimed at, and probably limited to, "Mainstream Holland Inc.". Although expeditionary organizations are built from bureaucratic parent organizations, they themselves are not comparable to "Mainstream Holland Inc.", due to the underdeveloped nature of its organizational design. As such, the findings in this book draw some boundaries for application of some concepts developed in classic IOR and hence may provide an opportunity to develop IOR into a theory that can also be applied to organizations with more contemporary structural shapes. As a first start for such endeavors, the previous chapter aimed to propose mechanisms between structural design and outcomes at the organizational level that may serve as an operationalization of a sociotechnical controllability mechanism for expeditionary organizations. Furthermore, as an advance to such future contributions, the previous chapter explored the applicability of "hyper flexible network design" from Kuipers et al. (2010) to the context of expeditionary organizations. This application gave some starting points to improve controllability in expeditionary organizations but also ran into some difficulties regarding the nature of some parent organizations, which complicate the application of the "step-by-step" approach put forward by Kuipers et al. Hence, the results of this book can, at the one hand, be interpreted as building on the still young "network" tradition within IOR. On the other hand, it seems to be the case that substantial work remains to be done in order to come up with a suitable sociotechnical redesign solution for facilitating self-design in expeditionary organizations.

7.3.3 Limitations at Level B

As discussed before in this book, the theory developed was not built for having prescriptive properties. This provides a first limitation at the problem-oriented level of knowledge generalization that Van Strien referred to as level B. A second limitation at Van Strien's level B may be found in the use of IOR concepts throughout this book. By choosing this perspective from the start, this book may have become insensitive to other theoretical perspectives that may enable studying organizational design and controllability in expeditionary organizations. Although this may pose some limitations to the results presented, the choice for IOR concepts as a heuristic analytical perspective was motivated and resulted in relevant findings. Also, the use of IOR concepts as a conceptual compass led to the inclusion of other relevant theoretical concepts, such as Thompson's concepts of interdependence and coordination and Perrow's concept of hidden interactions in the construction of the theory. Nevertheless, and this was also pointed out previously, alternative explanations for safety and other controllability outcomes in expeditionary organizations should not be regarded as irrelevant. Instead, applying different level B perspectives for studying issues in expeditionary organizations, and organizations in general, can be regarded as a scientific strategy that provides reflective and valid results.

7.4 A Methodological Reflection

In this section, the methods used in this book will be reflected upon. This seems necessary as this book did not have one particular methodological perspective but combined different methodologies to answer the different research questions. In Chapters 3 and 4 of this book, a grounded theory methodology was used in a slightly different way than was proposed by Wester and Peters (2004) as such, the next section will reflect on the use of grounded theory methods in this book. After that, the different analytical strategies that were followed throughout this book are subject of reflection.

7.4.1 A Reflection on Grounded Theory Methodology

In Chapters 3 and 4 the different phases described by Wester and Peters (2004) were used to construct a grounded theory both within 107 Aerial Systems battery and Task Force Uruzgan by using a particular "normal work" approach in order to detect influences of organizational design on self-organization and the emergence of safety. These phases were, respectively, the exploration, specification, reduction and integration phase. In Chapter 3 these analytical phases were used to explore the relationship between organizational design, self-organization and the emergence of safety within an expeditionary organization. In Chapter 4, the phases were used to verify the hypotheses derived within 107 ASBt by studying other units within Task Force Uruzgan and to come up with hypotheses at van Strien's Level B. In both cases, the methodology proposed by Wester and Peters was used to combine case study data with theoretical premises in an abductive fashion. Wester and Peters however, do not explicitly elaborate on such use of theoretical insights. This means that a contribution of this book may be that their phases can be used to develop grounded theory by means of using theory throughout the research process of constructing a grounded theory. Similar developments of Wester and Peters's phases have been suggested by Richardson and Kramer (2006). However, they proposed the use of theory as being part of the reduction and integration phase, whereas in this study theoretical concepts, mainly originating from IOR, were used in all phases. This was done deliberately because the main interest of this book did not lie in all aspects of the experiences of operators but at a particular aspect of their experiences, related to design and safety. A main issue in reconstructing organizational design influences was that these could not be witnessed as such and had to be constructed analytically during the four analytical phases. As such, the way this book used theoretical insights in Wester and Peters's analytical phase may be suitable for qualitative research aimed a similar subject. That is to say, it may be suitable for qualitative research aimed at a particular part of operators' experiences while being confronted with (latent) constructs of interest that can only be "seen" by analytically combining experiences of operators with existing theoretical insights.

7.4.2. A Reflection on Systematic Combining

To develop a theory, different analytical techniques were used in this book. In Chapter 3 and 4, analytical abduction was used to study case study data by means of a theoretical compass. In Chapter 5 deduction was used to verify hypotheses in two other expeditionary cases. As such the method of "systematic combining", as developed by Dubois and Gadde (2002, 2014), was used in a specific way. Although Dubois and Gadde elaborate on the abductive use of existing theory in developing theory from qualitative analyses, they do not refer to combining different analytical strategies. Also, the different studies presented in this book crossed different levels of knowledge generalization. A categorization developed by Van Strien was used to keep claims and theories at different levels apart. For example, abductive analytical strategies in Chapter 4 resulted in hypotheses at Van Strien's level B, whereas in Chapter 5 deduction was used to verify level B claims at level C in order to strengthen these claims. As such, this book is characterized by alternating analytical strategies at different levels of knowledge generalization. It can therefore be argued that explicating the different analytical strategies and different levels of knowledge generalization used in case study research is of added value to the method of systematic combining as developed by Dubois and Gadde. In Figure 7.1, the different analytical strategies and different levels of knowledge generalization used in the different research stages of this book are presented.

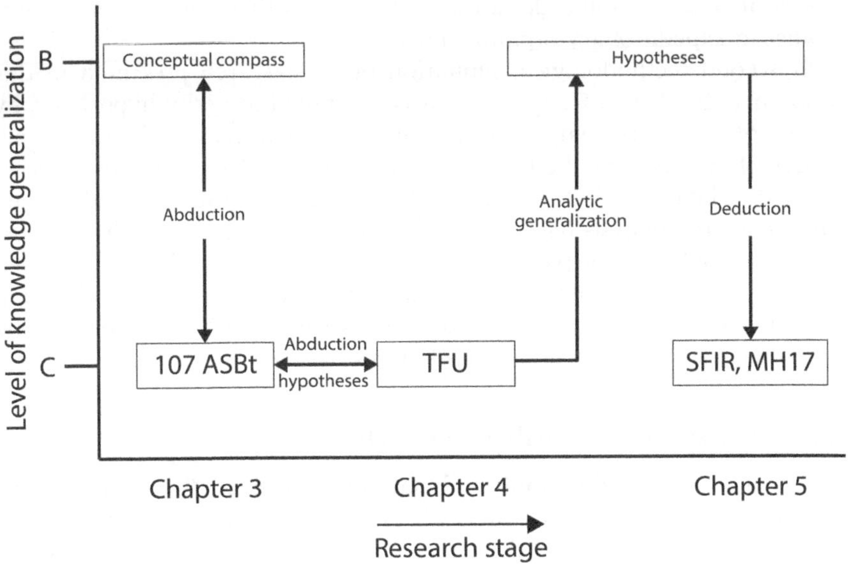

Figure 7.1 Analytical strategies, levels of knowledge generalization and research stage

7.4.3 Some Methodological Limitations

The Army's 107 Aerial Systems battery has been useful starting point for the studies in this book. However, attempting to generalize results from this unit to other units and organizations may at the same time provide a limitation. That is to say, although hypotheses developed by studying 107 ASBt were generalized to TFU, it may well be that other units experienced all kinds of design influences that were not included in this book. This was also highlighted in Chapter 4 by stating that 107 ASBt had some specific characteristics that were unique to them. Also, 107 ASBt was part of the intelligence unit within TFU, which made them part of a particular section of TFU's primary process. Counterarguments to this limitation can be found in the notion that the problems of other units resembled those of 107 ASBt and were hence regarded as key design influences on self-organization and the emergence of safety. Also, analytic generalization was used to generalize hypotheses from TFU to other expeditionary organizations. This made sure that, by combining the findings within TFU with existing organizational theory, relevant hypotheses for expeditionary organizations in a more general sense were formulated. Furthermore, this strategy has resulted in findings that could at least partly be verified in the Iraq and MH17 cases. Nevertheless, in replicating the theory, researchers should remain sensitive to other influences of organizational design on safety and other controllability outcomes in expeditionary organizations.

A second methodological limitation of the research presented in this book may be that in Chapter 5 it was attempted to verify hypotheses by means of secondary analysis of case study data. This may explain why only traces of evidence for the hypotheses were found. Also, some hypotheses needed to be rejected. A reason for this may be that the case studies used for secondary analysis had a research goal and used methods that yielded data that could only be partly used. As such, and this will also be addressed in the next section, future research may use to the hypotheses developed in Chapter 4 and attempt to verify these in other expeditionary contexts by using methods similar to those used in this book.

7.5 Suggestions for Further Research

The last section of this book will elaborate on some directions for further research. Firstly, some suggestions will be given for research at Van Strien's level C. Secondly, directions for further research at level B will be presented.

7.5.1 Suggestions for Further Research at Level C

As highlighted in the previous section, replication of the theory developed in this book in other expeditionary contexts is recommended. This might include studying other military missions and crisis response organizations. For example, the present military mission of the Dutch Armed Forces in Mali consists of a task force that is assembled out of different building blocks from the Army and Air Force and hence may provide an interesting case for replication. With regard to crisis response organizations, replication might also be possible employing secondary analysis of existing evaluations. For example, the evaluation report on the crash of the Turkish Airlines airplane at Schiphol in 2009 points out that, over and over again, similar problems of integration and coordination are found by the Dutch Safety Board (2010). Juffermans and Bierens (2010) who conducted a review on operations of medical services found similar issues after recent crises in the Netherlands. As such, using the theory developed in this book may provide an alternative, organizational design, perspective to "learning after crises" which may have added value compared to the more traditional political, communication, information sharing and psychological explanations sought in crisis management literature.

With regard to replication in other expeditionary contexts, literature on temporary organizations is abundant and growing (e.g., Bakker, 2010; Bakker & DeFillippi, Schwab & Sydow, 2016). Some examples of temporary organizations that may fall under the category of expeditionary organizations are construction projects (e.g., Bryman, Brensen, Beardsworth, Ford & Keil, 1987), shipbuilding project organizations (e.g., Levering, Ligthart, Noorderhaven, & Oerlemans, 2013), offshore organizations (e.g., Gaisford, 1986) and architecture projects (e.g., Lieftink, Smits & Lauche, *in press*). Hence, future research may attempt to replicate the theory developed in this book within these temporary organizations.

7.5.2 Suggestions for Further Research at Level B

It was highlighted in Chapter 1 that literature on temporary organizations, and the role of organization design in such organizational contexts was mainly based on "contingency theory", which is a particular and critiqued avenue in organizational design literature. The studies in this book have shown that a sociotechnical approach to design in temporary organizations has added value. As such, future studies on organization design in temporary organizations may adopt a sociotechnical perspective as well. With regard to organizational redesign theory at level B, it was highlighted previously that developing a redesign theory that fits expeditionary organizations and their "parents", seems necessary. It was shown in the previous chapter that the kind of organization Kuipers et al. (2010) defined as a network organization differs from the expeditionary organization, as defined in this book. This difference was particularly salient in relation to the role that parent organizations play in problems within expeditionary organizations. It was emphasized that "the object of redesign" referred to both the expeditionary organization and parent organizations, which complicated the applicability of the step-by-step approach developed by Kuipers et al. This implies that their step-by-step approach should be redeveloped in order to fit the design problem of expeditionary organizations. Also, using the results to reflect on IOR's "design parameters" and its concept of controllability, as was also stressed in Chapter 5 of this book, could further develop IOR and Sociotechnical Systems Design into an organizational design perspective that is applicable to more contemporary organizational forms.

Note

1. For a similar argument, related to psychological stress within organizations, see Christis (1998).

References

Ansell, C., Boin, A., & Keller, A. (2010). Managing transboundary crises: Identifying the building blocks of an effective response system. *Journal of Contingencies and Crisis Management*, *18*(4), 195–207.

Bakker, R. M. (2010). Taking stock of temporary organizational forms: A systematic review and research agenda. *International Journal of Management Reviews*, *12*(4), 466–486.

Bakker, R. M., DeFillippi, R. J., Schwab, A., & Sydow, J. (2016). Temporary organizing: promises, processes, problems. *Organization Studies*, *37*(12), 1703–1719.

Bharosa, N., Lee, J., & Janssen, M. (2010). Challenges and obstacles in sharing and coordinating information during multi-agency disaster response: Propositions from field exercises. *Information Systems Frontiers*, *12*(1), 49–65.

Boin, A. (2009). The new world of crises and crisis management: Implications for policymaking and research. *Review of Policy Research*, *26*(4), 367–377.

Bryman, A., Bresnen, M., Beardsworth, A. D., Ford, J., & Keil, E. T. (1987). The concept of the temporary system: the case of the construction project. *Research in the Sociology of Organizations*, 5, 253–283.

Cherns, A. (1976). The principles of sociotechnical design. *Human Relations*, *29*(8), 783–792.

Christis, J. (1998). *Arbeid, Organisatie en Stress. Een visie vanuit de sociotechnische arbeids-en organisatiekunde*. Amsterdam: Het Spinhuis.

Dekker, S. W. A. (2005). *Ten questions about human error*. New York: Lawrence Erlbaum.

Drabek, T. E. (1985). Managing the emergency response. *Public Administration Review*, *45*, 85.

Dubois, A., & Gadde, L. E. (2002). Systematic combining: An abductive approach to case research. *Journal of Business Research*, *55*(7), 553–560.

Dubois, A., & Gadde, L. E. (2014). "Systematic combining"—a decade later. *Journal of Business Research*, *67*(6), 1277–1284.

Dutch Safety Board (Onderzoeksraad voor Veiligheid). (2010). Crashed during approach, Boeing 737-800, near Amsterdam Schiphol Airport 25 February 2009.

Flyvbjerg, B., Bruzelius, N., & Rothengatter, W. (2003). *Megaprojects and risk: An anatomy of ambition*. Cambridge: Cambridge University Press.

Gaisford, R. W. (1986). Project management in the North sea. *International Journal of Project Management*, *4*(1), 5–12.

Grote, G. (2009). *Management of uncertainty: Theory and application in the design of systems and organizations*. London: Springer Verlag.

Guldenmund, F. W. (2007). The use of questionnaires in safety culture research – an evaluation. *Safety Science*, *45*(6), 723–743.

Hart, P. 't. (1993). Symbols, rituals and power: The lost dimensions of crisis management. *Journal of Contingencies and Crisis Management*, *1*(1), 36–50.

Juffermans, J., & Bierens, J. J. L. M. (2010). Recurrent medical response problems during five recent disasters in the Netherlands. *Prehospital and Disaster Medicine*, *25*(2), 127–136.

Kapucu, N. (2006). Interagency communication networks during emergencies: Boundary spanners in multiagency coordination. *The American Review of Public Administration*, *36*(2), 207–225.

Kramer, E. H. (2004). *Organizing doubt: Self-organization and army units in crisis operations* (Doctoral dissertation). Eindhoven: Eindhoven University of Technology.

Kramer, E. H. (2007). *Organizing doubt: Grounded theory, army units and dealing with dynamic complexity*. Copenhagen: Copenhagen Business School Press.

Kuipers, H., van Amelsvoort, P., & Kramer, E. H. (2010). *Het Nieuwe Organiseren: alternatieven voor de bureaucratie*. The Hague: Acco.

Levering, R., Ligthart, R., Noorderhaven, N., & Oerlemans, L. (2013). Continuity and change in interorganizational project practices: The Dutch shipbuilding industry, 1950–2010. *International Journal of Project Management*, *31*(5), 735–747.

Lieftink, B., Smits, A., & Lauche, K. (in press). Dual dynamics: Project-based institutional work and subfield differences in the Dutch construction industry. *International Journal of Project Management*.

Modig, N. (2007). A continuum of organizations formed to carry out projects: Temporary and stationary organization forms. *International Journal of Project Management*, *25*(8), 807–814.

Moynihan, D. P. (2008). Learning under uncertainty: Networks in crisis management. *Public Administration Review*, *68*(2), 350–365.

Moynihan, D. P. (2009). The network governance of crisis response: Case studies of incident command systems. *Journal of Public Administration Research and Theory*, *19*(4), 895–915.

Rietjens, S. J. H., & Bollen, M. T. I. B. (2008). *Managing civil-military cooperation: A 24/7 joint effort for stability*. Hampshire: Ashgate Publishing.

Sitter, L. U. de. (1994). *Synergetisch produceren: Human Resources Mobilisation in de produktie een inleiding in structuurbouw*. Assen: Uitgeverij Van Gorcum.

Smith, W., & Dowell, J. (2000). A case study of coordinative decision-making in crisis management. *Ergonomics*, *43*(8), 1153–1166.

Snook, S. A. (2000). *Friendly fire: The accidental shootdown of U.S. Blackhawks over Northern Iraq*. Princeton: Princeton University Press.

Soeters, J., Bijlsma, T., & Van den Heuvel, G. (2012). Multinational military cooperation in Uruzgan. In R. Beeres, J. Van der Meulen, J. Soeters, & A. L. W. Vogelaar (Eds.), *Mission Uruzgan* (pp. 161–178). Amsterdam: Pallas, Amsterdam University Press.

Soeters, J. L., Winslow, D. J., & Weibull, A. (2006). Military culture. In *Handbook of the sociology of the military* (pp. 237–254). Boston, MA: Springer Verlag.

Steigenberger, N. (2016). Organizing for the big one: A review of case studies and a research agenda for multi-agency disaster response. *Journal of Contingencies and Crisis Management*, *24*(2), 60–72.

Swuste, P., Frijters, A., & Guldenmund, F. (2012). Is it possible to influence safety in the building sector? A literature review extending from 1980 until the present. *Safety Science*, *50*(5), 1333–1343.

Van der Kloet, I. (2005). *A soldiery perspective on trust* (Doctoral dissertation). Tilburg: Tilburg University.

Van Duin, M., & Wijkhuijs, V. (2015). Vliegramp MH17. In M. Van Duin & V. Wijkhuis (Eds.), *Lessen uit crises and mini-crises 2014* (pp. 167–204). The Hague: Boom bestuurskunde.

Vogelaar, A. L. W., & Dalenberg, S. (2012). On your own in the desert: The dynamics of self-steering leadership. In R. Beeres, J. Van der Meulen, J. Soeters, & A. L. W. Vogelaar (Eds.), *Mission Uruzgan* (pp. 93–106). Amsterdam: Pallas, Amsterdam University Press.

Waard, E. J. de, & Kramer, E. H. (2008). Tailored task forces: Temporary organizations and modularity. *International Journal of Project Management*, *26*(5), 537–546.

Wester, F., & Peters, V. (2004). *Kwalitatieve analyse: uitgangspunten en procedures*. Bussum: Coutinho.

Wolbers, J. J. (2016). *Drawing the line: Cross-boundary coordination processes in emergency management* (Doctoral dissertation). Amsterdam: Ridderprint.

Appendix 1

Organizational Layout of the Royal Netherlands Army Until Reorganization in 2012[1]

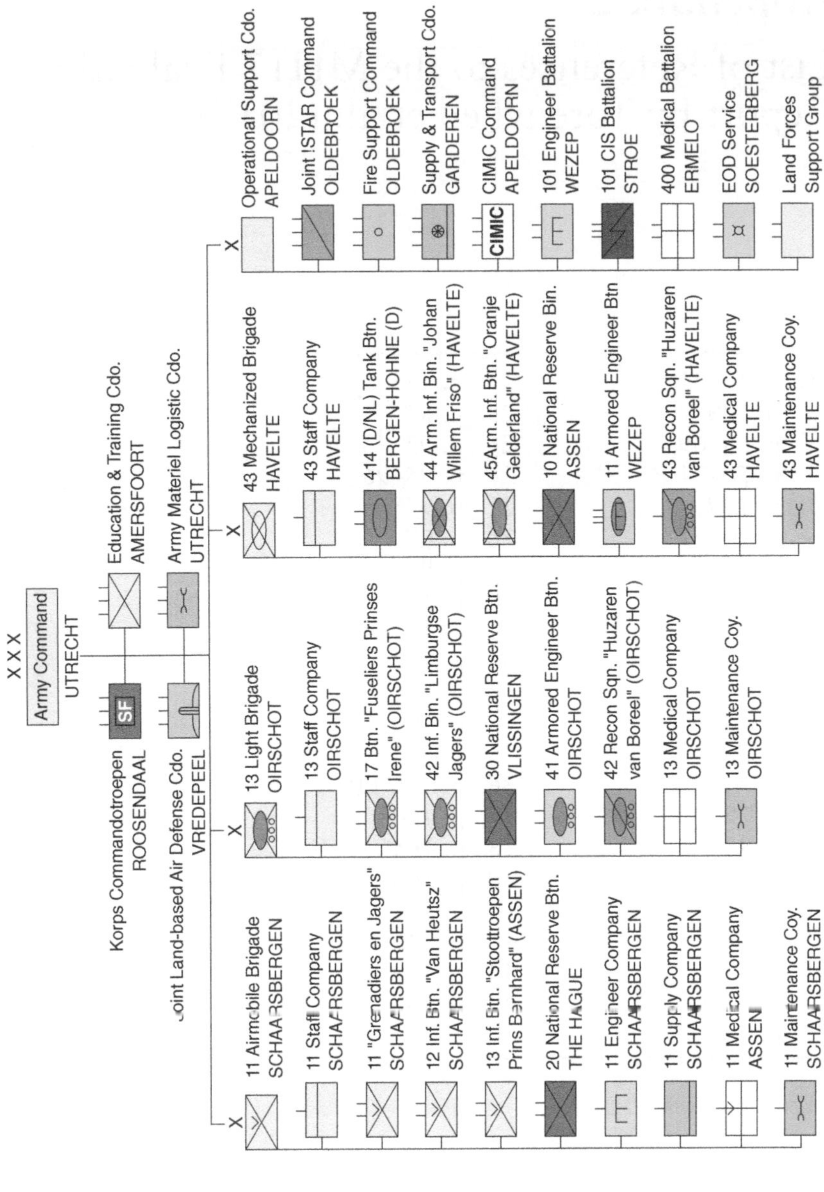

Note

1. "Royal Netherlands Army Structure from 2008 to 2011" by I, Noclador is licensed by CC BY 3.0.

Appendix 2

List of References to the MH17 Evaluation Report by Torenvlied et al. (2015)

1. p. 30–31
2. p. 109
3. p. 68–69
4. p. 70–71
5. p. 109
6. p. 70–71
7. p. 67
8. p. 76
9. p. 81
10. p. 84
11. p. 76–87
12. p. 76–84
13. p. 76
14. p. 84
15. p. 79
16. p. 82–83
17. p. 83
18. p. 76
19. p. 157
20. p. 156
21. p. 83; p. 155
22. p. 79
23. p. 155
24. p. 87
25. p. 92–93
26. p. 95–96
27. p. 95
28. p. 97
29. p. 96–98
30. p. 101
31. p. 101
32. p. 122
33. p. 105
34. p. 106
35. p. 105
36. p.118–119
37. p. 120
38. p. 165
39. p. 166
40. p. 122
41. p. 122
42. p. 166
43. p. 167

Subject Index

Note: Page numbers in *italics* indicate a figure and page numbers in **bold** indicate a table on the corresponding page.

For Product Safety Concerns and Information please contact our EU representative GPSR@taylorandfrancis.com Taylor & Francis Verlag GmbH, Kaufingerstraße 24, 80331 München, Germany